FOUR
★ ★ AGAINST ★ ★
THE WEST

ALSO BY JOE PAPPALARDO

Red Sky Morning: The Epic True Story of Texas Ranger Company F

Inferno: The True Story of a B-17 Gunner's Heroism and the Bloodiest Military Campaign in Aviation History

Spaceport Earth: The Reinvention of Spaceflight

Sunflowers: The Secret History: The Unauthorized Biography of the World's Most Beloved Weed

FOUR
★ ★ AGAINST ★ ★
THE WEST

The True Saga of a Frontier Family That Reshaped the Nation—and Created a Legend

JOE PAPPALARDO

ST. MARTIN'S PRESS
NEW YORK

First published in the United States by St. Martin's Press, an imprint of St. Martin's Publishing Group

 For information, address St. Martin's Publishing Group, 120 Broadway, New York, NY 10271.

www.stmartins.com

Designed by Omar Chapa

The Library of Congress Cataloging-in-Publication Data is available upon request.
ISBN 978-1-250-28754-0 (hardcover)
ISBN 978-1-250-28755-7 (ebook)

First Edition: 2024

10 9 8 7 6 5 4 3 2

For Bill and Mike, and those others who call me "brother"

Everything that you have told me I found to be true, and I am led to believe that—if there is such a noble and high virtue in the art of guessing—three other men like you cannot be found in the world.

—EMPEROR BERAMO IN *THE PEREGRINATION OF THE YOUNG SONS OF THE KING OF SERENDIB*, CRISTOFORO ARMENO (RELATING A PERSIAN FOLKTALE), 1557

The family weakens
By the length we travel

—"THREE DAYS," JANE'S ADDICTION, 1990

CONTENTS

INTRODUCTION

There's a simple formula for biographies that has existed since John Boswell finished *The Life of Samuel Johnson* in 1791: pick an inspirational subject and spend hundreds of pages describing why that person's life was pivotal to history. It's a good formula, and this book ignores it entirely.

Instead of an individual, this tome traces four lives in parallel—those of the famous Judge Roy Bean and his brothers, James, Samuel, and Joshua. And instead of providing inspiration, each is at some point during his saga bound to rub folks the wrong way. They did so while alive; why should readers feel any differently?

However, these questionable men are also fascinating. Each was immersed in the formative history of the US Southwest, making appearances on the Santa Fe Trail, in the Mexican-American and Civil Wars, on the California coast during the Gold Rush, in wild west Texas train-construction camps, and prowling the deserts and mountains of prestate New Mexico and Arizona. That's an alluring amount of epic American frontier history to cover with a single litter of brothers.

The strange phenomenon of siblings is that their similarities make it easier to compare differences. The Bean brothers aspired for comparable things but set about achieving them in very different ways. They crossed and shared paths, often dramatically, but each eventually carved his own way through the evolving American landscape.

Each brother experienced the frantic spread of the United States during the era of "Manifest Destiny." This remains a loaded term in the twenty-first century as much as when it was coined in the mid-1800s. It today generates a lot of emotion: anger, nostalgia, guilt, and regional pride. Those less steeped in the era may be surprised at how a disparate mix of greed, ambition, brute force, and civic responsibility (sometimes embodied in the same person) created the contemporary United States.

The emergence of coast-to-coast America empowered a generation to believe they could influence the development of an entire continent—and they proved they could. They routinely did terrible and amazing things, to paraphrase W. E. B. Du Bois, that expanded the edge of their style of civilization.

But who were the *people* who rode the wave of Manifest Destiny? They weren't cardboard cutouts of heroes and villains, as easy as that would be to process. The truth is more nuanced, and therefore interesting. Seeing Manifest Destiny from the point of view of the humans swept up in it transforms the national experience into a story of personal choices, circumstances, and consequences.

This is where profiling four brothers comes in handy. When one takes a fork in the road, historically, it opens up more than just a new setting. It represents a choice—to join the army, to settle in Mexico, to run for office, to support the Confederacy—that another brother faced.

Four Against the West tells the brothers' true stories but doesn't dissect them in academic dissertations or with overt moralizing. We don't have to judge them by modern standards or explain away their behavior as being "of their time." We can measure each brother against the other, just by following the adventurous narratives of their lives. They are mirrors to each other, even at a distance. And I think from page one you'll find that the brothers don't deserve an equal amount of deference.

But don't feel obligated to like or dislike Roy, Sam, Josh, and James. You don't have to root for them to enjoy this book, but you *do* have to be willing to travel with these brothers over many long miles to understand them. Do that and you'll witness four stunning examples of the raw human drive that ushered in the rise of modern America.

Joe Pappalardo, Texas, 2023

PART ONE

Empire plants itself upon the trails.

—WILLIAM GILPIN, *MISSION OF THE NORTH AMERICAN PEOPLE*, 1874

ROY

Louisville, Kentucky

March 1841

Phantley Roy Bean Jr. eyes the flatboat with excitement and trepidation. This floating wooden shack, scarcely fifty feet long and made of scrap wood, will be the sixteen-year-old's home for the next two months. It has no keel—that'd cost too much time and money—and therefore will depend on the crew, of which he's now one, to steer it with long poles.

It's more than eight hundred miles from the banks of the Ohio River to the skiff's destination of New Orleans. That's a long way to be dodging sandbars, steamboats, and river pirates, but Roy—the name he now uses—is too eager to leave to feel many nerves. When he does, there's bourbon.

These commercial boats require at least four crew and a pilot, who are contracted per trip. Roy's a strapping youth, good with horses and familiar with rifles from a lifetime of hunting. He can read and is learning to gamble. And coming from a family of southern landowners, he's comfortable manhandling slaves. That's an important quality, given the cargo the flatboat is carrying—a dozen people, destined for sale in the slave markets of New Orleans.[1]

---

1 Direct records of this job are impossible to come by, but Roy Bean spoke of it, according to several sources. Two examples: "Bean told his friends in San Antonio . . . he was

It's been illegal to import slaves from outside the United States since 1808, but Congress's action did nothing to stem the internal market. The population of rural Kentucky is in steep decline, and as people leave they sell their slaves. The prices in New Orleans, the premier market for the human trade, are much higher than in Kentucky; at $600 to $1,200 a person, even a handful of slaves will pay for the trip and cover the crew's pay.

Thousands every year make the trip after being "sold down the river," and the unsavory business leaves slave-driving bargemen eager to find crew. Even an untested teenager, if they show enough pluck. And Roy has pluck to spare.

Running away from home is the best example of this. It's a bold move, but Roy sees it as an obvious one. There's little to keep him in Kentucky besides his family, and the Bean family is on a downward trajectory. In fact, the entire country seems to be faltering.

When Roy was a child in Mason County, his family owned a sizable parcel of land and plenty of people to work it. An 1820 census listed a homestead of thirty-two people. Only six of them were Bean family members—father Phantley, mother Anna, and their four children. James was the eldest, born in 1814. Joshua was next, born in 1818, followed the next year by Samuel. Keeping pace, Sarah provided some household gender balance in 1820. Their parents must have exhausted themselves, Roy figured, because he didn't arrive until 1825.

The Bean children grew up in an entitled existence of household servants, field slaves, and obedient hired hands. There were eight slaves in the family's holdings, five of whom were females under twenty-four years old.

---

engaged in driving slaves of another party from Kentucky to New Orleans." R. Franklin Hall, "Forgotten Beanville," *San Antonio Express*, December 31, 1933. "When he was 'about sixteen,' Roy sometimes hinted, he made the trip to New Orleans himself. He went with a party taking a batch of slaves to market." C. L. Sonnichsen, *Judge Roy Bean: Law West of the Pecos* (Boerne, TX: Mockingbird Books, 1942): 14, relating discussions he had in Langtry, Texas.

The homestead also had a workforce of sixteen hired laborers, all living on-site.[2] Phantley Sr., who went by "Francis," was a skilled surveyor who took work establishing new post roads and racetracks. He also diversified; for example, he and his brother Benjamin in 1818 jointly backed a man named William Connett (from Mayslick) in opening a tavern. It was the first saloon in which the Bean family is known to have been involved, but it was far from the last.

Roy's father was a charismatic and energetic man, a larger-than-life figure to his sons. He was given to delivering speeches in his lingering Irish brogue.[3] Phantley Sr. consistently demonstrated how a man sizes up opportunities and uses confidence to claim them. His boys each shared a belief that they were men of action who deserved to capitalize on circumstances, no matter where in the world they found them. Nature and other, lesser men needed to yield before their ambitions. Even James, the eldest and most responsibly minded brother, inherited an aggressive pride.

These traits were not unique to the Bean family; they were hallmarks of American culture, particularly in the South. These attitudes migrated with settlers going into the western frontier and, in time, became the tenets of what's called Manifest Destiny.

Kentucky dashed the proud aspirations of the Bean family. In March

---

2 "United States Census, 1830," microfilm publication M19, National Archives and Records Administration, Washington, DC.

3 Maude McFie Bloom, "Shadows in Sam's Valley," n.d. Maude McFie Bloom Manuscripts, Box 36, New Mexico State University Library Archives and Special Collections, Las Cruces, NM. Held within this box are the worn pages of several unpublished book chapters written by author Maude Bloom, born in 1880 in Illinois and a 1903 graduate of New Mexico A&M. She wrote a thesis turned book titled *A History of Mesilla Valley*. One of the manuscripts in the NMSU collection, "Shadows in Sam's Valley," is focused on Sam Bean, whom she interviewed, thereby preserving vital details of the Bean family. The collection also contains the summary of her unfinished book about Sam and Roy Bean, "Los Dos Frijoles," which is cited later in this book.

1825 they sold a fifty-four-acre tract of land to neighbor Thomas Wells and moved from Mason into a humbler homestead in Shelby County. The 1830 census showed a household of just seventeen people—the family and eight slaves. By then, the Beans were already in a financial retreat, and things were about to get much worse.

In 1833, a cholera epidemic scythed through Kentucky, killing tens of thousands. The extended Bean family was swept into the carnage—a family slave named Harry Nichols offered a window on their suffering when he later recalled helping family members bury "three of old man Bean's children," among many others.[4] It's the first of several sporadic outbreaks, the disease sadistically taking long breaks between lethal waves.

In October 1835, Phantley Bean Sr. was struck down by a runaway team of horses, which killed him instantly.[5] Any hope to hold the family together in Shelby County fell to James, at twenty-one years old, and Joshua, at twenty. Sarah was fifteen, Sam fourteen, and Roy just ten.[6]

After their father's death, Kentucky's cholera-ravaged economy only grew worse. In 1837, the banks in the state all failed. It had something to do with the Bank of England overextending itself with loans, leading to a cut of all credit issuance to Americans, which halved the price of cotton

---

4 *Oskaloosa (KS) Independent*, February 23, 1884. Nichols would remain with the Bean family (through marriage, to the Asbury family) until the end of the Civil War.

5 Bloom, "Shadows in Sam's Valley." She described Sam's memory of the man and his end: "It had been a sad day when that merry-hearted husband had had his brains dashed out by a runaway team." Later, Sam will quote Roy recalling their father's penchant for lecturing.

6 Many biographies of Roy Bean ignore James Bean entirely, but all the children are listed by name in Phantley Sr.'s October 12, 1835, will, filed in Shelby County that December. On the other end of the timeline, Roy himself discusses his brother James in an interview in the *Pittsburgh (PA) Press,* September 25, 1893. There are discrepancies on official forms over Roy's birth, but 1825 agrees with early records and is listed on his tombstone.

that year. This in turn shuttered cotton companies and banks in New Orleans, and the infection reached New York, causing the Josephs Banking Co. to close and precipitating the panic of 1837, which crashed the dollar and tanked the entire US economy.

There was blame to go around—the loose credit in England, Andrew Jackson dissolving the Bank of the United States, bad weather—and the depression proved deep and lasting. Southern states suffered worse. The entire nation spoke of a malaise, but Kentuckians dubbed the era between 1834 and 1844 the "crisis decade."

Given the resurgent cholera and sputtering economy, this generation of Beans never had much of a chance in Kentucky. Roy has watched his community, state, and nation cracking apart. Who could blame him for cutting out?[7]

Hell, Uncle Ben didn't stick around to watch the world collapse around him any further. He left Kentucky in 1837, leaving an imploded economy and family graves behind for the promise of a place called Missouri. Benjamin Bean, from all reports, has settled on his own land near a lake outside the town of Independence, when it was just an obscure fur-trade village on the edge of the settled United States.[8] Since then, the hamlet has become the premier jumping-off point for settlers, traders, and explorers heading to the foreign lands of New Mexico, Oregon, and California.

Roy is natural at justifying actions he clearly wants to take for his own gratification, and he applies this skill to abandoning his family in Kentucky. With him gone, his brothers will have one less thing to worry about. Strapping horseman Joshua is ready to head off on his own, not to start a family per se but to escape the laborious monotony of homesteading.

---

7 Sam Bean regards his brother Roy as "a runaway" at age sixteen in his interview with Maude Bloom.

8 "Benjamin Bean—Bean Lake," *Annals of Platte County, Missouri*, 1897 NYPL Research Libraries, Digitized by the Internet Archive, https://archive.org/stream/annalsofplatteco00paxt/annalsofplatteco00paxt_djvu.txt.

Everyone knows that community-minded James will snare a wife as soon as he's able, but if Roy knows his brother at all, he expects him to go to Missouri. The eldest Bean tends to pander to and emulate his elders, and he'll float to his uncle in Missouri like a leaf pulled behind the wake of a barge. If Uncle Ben continues to find success out there, Roy bets James'll make the leap, whether he's married or not.

If the family doesn't move west, Sam might just go renegade, like Roy is now doing. The pair are in many ways opposites—Sam with blond hair, Roy with dark; Sam slow-spoken and Roy quick-tongued; Sam largely abstaining from drink, Roy happily indulging—but they share a streak of adventurism. The two indulged this trait as young squires roaming the hills and fields of Kentucky. Roy hopes his departure will ignite Sam's spirit of adventure, even if running off to New Orleans is too extreme an act. In any case, his brother is far too soft on slaves to consider working on a flatboat to New Orleans.[9]

Roy has grown wilder than his elder siblings, having lived without a father for more of his childhood than the others. He's clever and observant, but frustrated and rootless. And there's no reason to stay put. Not while there's a sprawling trade network running along the nation's great rivers. So as soon as he's old enough to be hired, Roy heads to nearby Louisville to find a flatboat. From there, on a rudderless barge carrying forlorn slaves, he can take the Ohio River to where it meets the Mississippi and head straight south for New Orleans and whatever the future holds.

Mississippi River
April 1841

Nights on the flatboat are both quiet and tense for the man on watch. Tonight it's Roy, who puffs on a cigar to stay alert. His ears strain for any noise in the darkness: telltale splashes of incoming pirate boats, clicks of

---

9 Maude McFie Bloom, in "Shadows in Sam's Valley," interviewed Sam Bean and unearthed the brothers' opposing attitudes toward slavery. If you get the tingling feeling of foreshadowing, there's a reason.

firearms being readied, the scrape of metal blades being pulled from scabbards. Amid the din of frogs, birds, and other riverside animals, anyone could be mustering for an attack.

But the rifles, knives, and pistols the crew carry are not just meant to repel river pirates. Roy considers their cargo, chained together under the glare of a lantern, as the real threat. He's not just a boat crewman; he's also a prison guard.

Even by the standards of a Kentucky slave's miserable condition, being shipped to New Orleans is a nightmare of cruel uncertainty. Being separated from all friends and family and sent away for resale creates a dangerous desperation. Slave rebellions have occurred during trips down the river, with flatboat crews killed during the bids for freedom.

Roy sees lights downstream, and they're getting larger—it must be a steamboat churning toward them. In daylight, he'd see the telltale smudge of stack smoke on the horizon. As the vessel gets closer, he can hear music on board and spies dark figures silhouetted in lamplit windows. To the steamboat's crew, Roy's slave skiff is a dot of light away from the river's center, but to the teenager, the steamboat is a reminder of the wider community on the Ohio and Mississippi Rivers. Both are plied by watercraft of all sizes and are serviced by a network of forts, trading stations, and taverns on the banks. These built-from-scratch outposts are hubs for news, political machinations, and commercial negotiations. In the world's empty places, a saloon can become a beacon of civilization.

Each stop has been an education for Roy. Drinking, gambling, and fighting are a way of life for these rough, working rivermen, and the teenager proves to be a quick student. Best of all, he's not alone in the world while he's at a saloon. Or at least he's alone with everybody else.

New Orleans, Louisiana
May 1841

Roy stands among the back of the crowd at the trader's yard, having shown up late to the auction's ten a.m. start. Attending the slave auction is not part of his job as a flatboat crewman, which ended on arrival. But he's never seen one before, and it seems like he should watch the end of his first trip.

New Orleans is slavery's unparalleled hub in the United States. Other cities confine their slave pens to one district, but this yard is just one of more than fifty sprinkled across New Orleans.[10] Some are under rotunda domes; others, like this one, are conducted in open-air markets. Humans are bought and sold every Saturday and Sunday.

Taking in the place's high brick walls and armed staff, Roy can see that the facility is an auction house only part of the time; it's really a full-time prison for slaves awaiting sale. The enslaved are assembled to one side. Roy scans the glum faces for those he shipped here, but it's not easy among the throngs. The men, women, and children on sale are of varying ages, each freshly washed, with hair combed and wearing clean clothes. They seem a far cry from the huddled, moaning cargo lying on the hard deck of the flatboat.

"When spectators would come in the yard, the slaves were ordered out to form a line," an escaped slave Henry Bibb, will describe in his memoirs. "They were made to stand up straight and look as sprightly as they could; and when they were asked a question, they had to answer it as promptly as they could, and try to induce the spectators to buy them. If they failed to do this, they were severely paddled after the spectators were gone. And the object for flogging under such circumstances, is to make the slaves anxious to be sold."[11]

When he and the flatboat crew dropped off their cargo at the yard,

---

10 There were auction houses across the city, but trading was pronounced at Esplanade Avenue at Moreau (now Chartres) Street, St. Louis Street between Royal Street and the levee, and New Orleans's banking district around Common, Carondelet, and Union Streets. "Purchased Lives: New Orleans, Slave Market of the South," Historic New Orleans Collection, accessed October 21, 2023, www.hnoc.org/virtual/purchased-lives/new-orleans-slave-market-south.

11 Henry Bibb, *Narrative of the Life and Adventures of Henry Bibb, An American Slave, Written by Himself*, 1849 (electronic edition, 2000): pages 273–86.

Roy was able to see the staff using their equipment to punish uncooperative slaves. Several had been pushed over, elbows touching knees, with a stick forced between the bends of their limbs. Hands tied and helpless, they endure beatings by the auctioneers, who use wooden paddles, the flat sides pitted with auger holes that form dark blisters on the skin. Roy notices that the blows only land where prospective buyers won't be able to see the damage.[12]

He spots a throng of slaves, their faces unemotional, dancing in a courtyard under the watchful eyes of the trade pen overseers. The idea, he's told, is to increase their health with some light exercise. To this end, the slaves here are also scrutinized by doctors and given healthy portions of food. It's not humane; it's just good for sales.

There are slaves exposed for bidding (i.e., displayed on the auction block), but most of the action happens on the sidelines, where savvy buyers can get a good look at the humans they're considering for purchase. Prospects are often taken into rooms and stripped, then examined for indications of disease or scars from neck chains or beatings, signs of unwanted defiance. Once in a while a man or woman will act out, usually when a family is being split apart. There's begging and crying, but such outbursts are rare and quickly tamped with brute intimidation. "I would have cried, if I dared to," writes Solomon Northup, who that same year experiences an auction from the perspective of those being sold, after seeing a mother and child forcibly separated in a trade yard.[13]

The final step is a trip to the notary tables. Under Louisiana law, all

---

12 Bibb, *Narrative of the Life.*

13 Solomon Northup, *Twelve Years a Slave,* 1853. Electronic version via the University of North Carolina at Chapel Hill Library, https://docsouth.unc.edu/fpn/northup/northup.html. He was enslaved after being tricked into taking a trip to Washington, DC. Roy's first trip to a New Orleans slave market would look similar to Abraham Lincoln's a few years prior.

slave sales must be recorded by notaries in the city, who deliver this bureaucracy from several desks on-site.

After the novelty wears off, Roy finds slave sales a morose and dull process. He quickly gets bored and leaves. On the street, it's impossible to forget that he's unemployed. Flatboats can't navigate upstream, so he knew it would be a one-way trip. He idly wonders if the skiff's owner got even a third of its seventy-five-dollar construction cost when he sold it.

With his pay, he could take a steamboat north toward home. But with some money in pocket and New Orleans to explore, what's the rush? Roy turns his back on the slave market's tall brick wall and the miseries inside, strides down cobblestone streets toward the Garden District, and the city of New Orleans swallows him.

JAMES

Independence, Missouri
October 1844

The sound of rifle fire brings the town of Independence to attention. Dozens of dirty, weary men in a wagon train are heralding the end of their journey from Independence to Santa Fe and back again. Just as a seaside port town turns out when its residents hear the celebratory cannon fire of returning ships, many in Independence hear gunshots and reflexively go to the downtown square to watch caravans arrive.

James Bean heads specifically to the Owens & Aull store on the square. This is not only a logical and popular place to gawk—the establishment has been the premier local outfitter of wagon trains for years—but while he's there James can mix with the Santa Fe Trail merchants, learn their trade, and gather some market intelligence about the trip and the destination. And hopefully demonstrate his diligent interest to Samuel C. Owens, who not only owns the store but funds start-up traders with their first wagons for a cut of the profit.

There's nothing quite like a Missouri freighter. A dozen are parked in the square, their white canvas covers still eye-catching despite the months of dust and grime smeared across their surfaces. They're each handcrafted,

Conestoga-style wagons, with telltale curved bodies and outward-canted endgates. But they're larger than wagons used elsewhere: engineers saved the Santa Fe trade by designing these heavier haulers after New Mexico governor Manuel Armijo imposed a new customs duty of $500 per wagon in 1839. In 1844 alone, dozens of these supersize vehicles, bearing five thousand pounds each and pulled by teams of oxen or mules, cross the Great Plains each season, heading for Mexico. (An estimated ninety-two wagons traveled down the Santa Fe Trail that year; most but not all were freighters.[14])

Independence has come a long way, and it's all because of migration and commerce. The village, the westernmost port on the Missouri River, was founded in 1827 as the jumping-off point for the western frontier fur trade. That geographic distinction means more now than ever as throngs of pioneers stock their wagons with supplies here before heading out to Oregon or California. The fur business has all but given way to a thriving trade with the northern Mexican cities of El Paso del Norte and Chihuahua.

During the winter months, Missouri traders purchase goods in the East and bring them to the trailheads in Independence. Departures begin in early May. Caravans expect to accomplish between ten and eighteen miles a day and can reach their destinations within a month and a half. The return trips start in September—the wagon train arriving today is the first of this season.

James spots the stout frame and blond hair of his younger brother Sam, who's milling around the storefront and chatting up the hired men. The returned traders are enjoying the attention of the throng of friends, family, and interested strangers. The traders seem to be oblivious to their stink. One of Independence's earliest residents, John McCoy, will later describe the strange ability of the men to ignore their own accumulated filth:

---

14 *Independence Journal*, September 19, 1844, as quoted in *Merchants' Magazine and Commercial Review*, November 1844.

"A greasy, dirty set of men they were. Water surely was a rare commodity with them. They little cared for it except to slake their thirst."[15]

The stories are already in the air: Comanches and Arapaho charging from hilltops, false-ponds[16] shimmering in the air to tempt thirsty travelers, desert trails empty of everything but the ruins of failed wagons and animals, and buffalo herds that stretch to the horizon. The men will camp outside the small town, engaging in all-night revelries that attract Sam Bean and other eager local youths.

"The hardships of the voyage and what they had suffered they knew would not be so interesting to the boys, and that phase of the trip was purposely kept in the background," Sam will later realize. "To cap the climax, they would wind up with a graphic description of the dark-eyed señoritas in the land of the Montezumas. That was a clincher. . . . Nothing thrilled my nerves so much as the stories the teamsters would tell us in Independence where a large number were congregated."[17]

James watches Sam fall under the spell of the Santa Fe traders and feels the same tug of romanticism despite his mercantile interests. But he has responsibilities that don't burden Sam, chiefly a wife and two young children. James Bean married Mary Ann Carson in Kentucky, and in 1843 his boy Aubrey was born there. His second son, Phantley Roy Bean (named after James's father and sharing the name with James's brother and a cousin), made the trip to Missouri in 1844 as an infant with his mother and older brother.

As a patriarch, James has done a poor job of keeping his immediate family together. Only Samuel came with him to Missouri, and his brothers

---

15 Quoted in Robert Luther Duffus, *The Santa Fe Trail* (Albuquerque: University of New Mexico Press, 1972): 103.

16 Mirages.

17 *Rio Grande Republican* (Las Cruces, NM, 1904), quoted in Sonnichsen, *Judge Roy Bean*, 17–23.

doubt he intended anything more than to position himself for a leap into the frontier. Sarah Bean Williams understandably remained in Shelby County with her husband (whom she married in 1837, when she was seventeen) and children, but Joshua has stubbornly stayed behind to see if Kentucky still holds anything for an ambitious young man.

Roy is still essentially missing, likely somewhere on the Mississippi, dead or alive is anyone's guess. He can always write to Sarah to learn where to find James, if he wants to get into the trading business here.

Wife and children notwithstanding, James knows there may be no avoiding time on the Santa Fe Trail if he wishes to realize his ambitions. In Independence, stature belongs to those who set out and survive the grassy ocean of the Great Plains. All the biggest merchants in the town make their own trips out west, overseeing the movement of merchandise as captains of wagon trains staffed by hired hands. It all sounds good until James looks closely at the dirty teamsters, seeing their stout but thin frames, their weathered cheeks, and the way their eyes sometimes lose focus, adrift in traumatic memories.

There is a lot of bluster from these battered men—boasting is a good way for teamsters to audition for the next job—but James can also learn valuable information. He's keen to know the attitude of Mexican officials and how much was spent bribing them. Of equal importance is information about what the Mexican merchants in Santa Fe are purchasing, and at what prices. There's an array of merchandise to choose from, including cloth, hardware, glass, guns, and books, most of it destined to be shipped south into central Mexico. Knowing the profit margins is vital, especially to a small, independent trader with limited wagon space and no ability to warehouse excess goods in Mexico.

The Santa Fe traders typically bring buffalo hides, Mexican blankets, and mules back to the United States for resale. More importantly, they bring payment for the goods they sold, in gold and silver Mexican dollars, silver bullion, and gold dust. The precious metal is sewed into green rawhide bags, hard as boulders, "that being found to be the safest way of transporting the money from Mexico," Sam notes.

This influx of silver and gold from Mexico has created a bubble of stable currency around Independence and Kansas City. As the rest of the nation wrestles with steadily devaluing currency, still reeling from the depression sparked by the bank crisis in 1837, the gateways to the west are flush with hard specie. Here in Missouri, it's become the currency of choice.

Economics can't kill the Santa Fe trade, but international politics may get a chance to, so talk at the store naturally fixates on Texas. President John Tyler is handing a fine mess to his successor with his support of annexing Texas as a state after its having so freshly and violently departed from Mexico. Everyone has on opinion, and divisions fracture political parties, Democrat and Whig alike. Absorbing Texas would mean expanding slavery, an ever-simmering issue that is gaining a scary intensity in the United States. Internationally, the US's adoption of a new state could spook the United Kingdom, with which Washington, DC, is negotiating possession of a swatch of land on the Pacific called Oregon.

The Texans are asserting that their southern boundary is the Rio Grande, while Mexico demands that the historical boundary remain in place: the Nueces River. On top of this contentious issue, Mexico has warned Washington, against annexing Texas, and despite being riven by internal struggles and Native American unrest, Mexico can still field large armies to defend its territory. The issue seems to have Whig stalwart Henry Clay over a barrel, whereas James K. Polk—yes, they tell the incredulous traders, that dark horse secured the Democratic nomination—is unwavering in his support of Texas annexation. If he wins November's election, war with Mexico could be inevitable.

However uncertain these dynamics may make the business environment, many people in Independence—and wealthy Mexicans in Santa Fe—would welcome a change, imagining trade booming without tariffs, politicians, and brigands getting in the way. They're also pretty sure that Americans can liquidate, bribe, or bully aggressive Indian tribes in the Great Plains, California, and New Mexico, something the Mexican government has entirely failed to address militarily or diplomatically.

All this international tension has a direct bearing on James Bean's future in the Santa Fe trade. He needs to parlay the meager remains of his family's money into a stable enterprise, and trade with Mexico is the way to do it. In short, James aims to pattern himself after the most successful man in Independence, Sam Owens.

Owens is an imposing man to be around. He can fix you with an intense gaze, his pinched face somehow resembling that of a bird of prey despite his prominent jowls and wide forehead. His hands are large and rough as sandpaper—this wealthy man earned his fortune.

After moving to Independence in 1837, Owens quickly established a store with Robert Aull, expanded to capture the wagon train market, and started to run his own wagons in and out of Santa Fe. He also bought and opened the landing to the west of Independence, which, until the flood the preceding year, had been the preferred place to load and unload goods. (By 1844 the river sports an inconvenient sandbar that is pushing this business to Kansas City, but the landing at Blue Mills remains busy and profitable, if more congested.) Owens also served in some of the city's prominent civic roles, including as the first Jackson County treasurer, increasing his stature.

Blue Mills is one of two steamboat landings in Jackson County. The other is called Wayne City, named for Lieutenant Anthony Wayne, who was memorialized for keeping the Kaw Indians at bay from the nearby bluffs in 1825. It's not a city at all, or even a town, but a supply port hamlet of stores, restaurants, and stables, and the closest landing to Independence. The thoroughfare that connects to it, Liberty Street, is becoming a narrow district of wagon and blacksmith shops.

Another boy joins them in the bustling crowd outside Owens & Aull. It's Ambrose Owens, the fifteen-year-old son of the businessman. Because Ambrose is close to James's brother's age, James and the boy have become friends. The pair scamper off to hear the first blood-curdling tales from the trail.

Luckily, it was easy for James Bean to meet the Owenses. His uncle Benjamin and Samuel Owens arrived in Missouri at the same time, forming a bond that tied settlers more closely in 1837, when the population was sparse, than it would now. Ben Bean's scheme involved buying land in neighboring Platte County, just across the Jackson County line, next to a lake that now bears his name. But developing Bean Lake may not be working out as planned—James's uncle has carved it up with conflicting deeds, a legal mess that compounds its deficiencies in location, being far from Kansas City, Independence, and the Santa Fe Trail.[18]

Uncle Ben is no financial role model, but he did make the Bean name recognizable among the pioneering class of Independence. Instead of being just another ambitious seeker, here James is a man with a real if unearned founder's pedigree. He has a chance to follow Sam Owens's playbook and provide a stable haven for his wife, children, and brothers, if they ever want one.

You can tell by the look in Sam's eyes that he'll be on a wagon train soon to explore the west. But for James Bean, Independence *is* the frontier. It's where he'll make his stand.

Independence, Missouri
May 1845

It's the season for wagons heading west. This is the first year James Bean has been here to see the scope of the action. By now there should be enough grass on the prairie to sustain the mules and oxen, and so the rush to leave is on, for everyone, all at once. The entirety of Jackson County seems infested with camps, where hundreds of wagons are being loaded with boxes of food supplies, leather goods, hardware, and ammunition, plus barrels of flour and whiskey. Settlers and traders alike purchase these goods.

It's easy to tell some of the cargo that's heading to Mexico; it's inside the sealed boxes stamped by US customs officials back east. There's a vibrant

---

18 W. M. Paxton, *Annals of Platte County, Missouri* (Kansas City: Hudson-Kimberly Publishing Co.). Digitized by the Internet Archive, http://www.archive.org/details/annalsofplattecoOOpaxt.

re-export market for cottons and calicoes from England and France, linens from Germany, and handkerchiefs and stockings from India.

James hasn't yet become immune to the sight of wagon trains leaving town, the lines of white canvas rolling to uncertain destinies. Today's departure is particularly emotional for him—one of the receding wagons contains teamster Samuel Bean, hired to drive a wagon of goods to Santa Fe.

The loss of his younger brother is keen but unexpected. If anything, it burnishes the family name in town. James can run things in Independence as his brother establishes himself on the trail. It could work out for both of them, assuming Sam survives. Once he's gone, information will trickle back from eastbound travelers on how the convoy is doing. Aside from that, all James can do is hope and carry on his work in Missouri.

James Bean's campaign to become a public man in Independence is going well so far. He started with property purchases, made in late 1844 and filed in January 1845.[19] He bought two plots downtown, close to the town square and mere blocks away from Owens & Aull. With that, the Bean family has a foothold in the true gateway to the west.

Bean has also found a financial partner, none other than newly elected state senator Joseph Reynolds. He's a grocer by trade, but he's better known as the former Jackson County sheriff. He just left law enforcement to start his first term in the statehouse and James Bean will run his grocery business while the senator's away on political business.

Reynolds's four-year tenure as a lawman was marked by an attempt to arrest Mormon founder Joseph Smith in a scheme orchestrated, in part, by Samuel Owens. The tale is an instructive example of the kind of men with whom James Bean went into business.[20] The Mormons had a footprint

19 Jackson County, Missouri, Recorder of Deeds, Real Estate Index, Books 11 and 12, 121–22, 357, 369, 385.

20 And of interest to the world's current membership of nearly seventeen million Mormons, presumably.

in early Jackson County history, operating two downtown stores and a newspaper. Owens's trouble with them began when a man named Sydney Gilbert arrived to operate "the bishop's store" in Independence. Aside from the religious mistrust between the county's established residents and the newcomers, Gilbert operated under a new Mormon creed called the law of consecration, which meant they gave stuff away for free to church members. To Owens, this was only a way to undercut competition. Their supply networks depressed the price of goods, angering the merchants of Missouri. When the Latter-day Saints were forced out of Jackson County in 1834, mobs trashed Gilbert's store.

Owens's war on the Mormons did not abate after that. In 1843, he sent a letter pleading for officials in Missouri and Illinois to act on a charge of treason filed against Smith six years earlier. The plan was to dispatch Jackson County sheriff Reynolds (an active if lesser member of this plot) to fetch the prophet for trial and probable execution. "I am in hopes that so soon as the propper [*sic*] papers come to hand you will take that course that will secure this imposter and have him delivered over to Mr. Reynolds," Owens wrote to Illinois governor Thomas Ford. "I only wish of the people of this State is that this man Joseph Smith may be brought to that Justice which the magnitude of his crime merits."[21]

Why would Owens care about Smith's fate after the Latter-day Saints were gone from Independence? Aside from his predilection for personal grudges and his revulsion for the budding religion, as the leading Independence merchant he was also concerned about Smith's recently filed

---

21 "Letter, Samuel Owens to Thomas Ford, 10 June 1843," Joseph Smith Papers, accessed October 22, 2023, www.josephsmithpapers.org/paper-summary/letter-samuel-owens-to-thomas-ford-10-june-1843/1#full-transcript. In September 1843, Joseph Smith was shown a copy of the letter from Owens and wrote in his journal, "To show the wickedness and rascality of John C. Bennett and the corrupt conspiracy formed against me in Missouri and Illinois, I insert the following under date of the letter. (June 10, 1843)." Joseph Smith, *History of the Church*, vol. 5 (Salt Lake City: Deseret Book Company, 1978): 422.

petitions to Congress, one of which was "applying to Congress for redress for sufferings in Missouri." Bad publicity from the Mormons' rough expulsion from Jackson County wouldn't be welcome, but the risk of well-organized Mormons returning to the Santa Fe trade could threaten Independence's dominance. Better to nip the threat in the bud.

Reynolds arrested Smith in Illinois in June 1843, but the plan to deliver him to Davies County failed when Smith was placed under temporary arrest by Sheriff James Campbell of Lee County, who clearly saw chicanery afoot that could again inflame members of the sect. (There's a long history of tumult surrounding the Latter-day Saints movement, and this was just one of Smith's forty-four arrests.) The sheriff conveyed the whole bunch to the municipal court of Nauvoo, Illinois, throngs of Smith's followers gathering to join them along the way in an impromptu pilgrimage. On July 1, the court tossed the warrant and freed Smith, the conspiracy to snare him thwarted.

It's hard to understand the Santa Fe traders without accounting for their paranoia about losing their good thing. The Mexico trade was a once-in-a-lifetime score, and the extreme steps they took to preserve and protect it stemmed from more than just greed, or even ambition. There was a desperation at play, born of fear, that prompted aggressive action and risk-taking.

That approach paid off in an influx of Mexican gold and silver, and any newcomer to Independence could only hope to be a cog in the wheel of the Santa Fe mercantile machine. This was exactly the enviable position that James Bean found himself in within a year of arriving. He ingratiated himself with Owens's circle, established himself as a property owner, and entered business with a respected, high-profile political figure.

There was more to James Bean than his familiar uncle. His surname may have got James in the door, but his quick advancement spoke for his qualities. Having a young family made him reliable, an eagerness for status made him pliant, and his business acumen made him useful. This combination got him inside the Owenses' orbit of Independence Santa Fe traders.

The last piece of James Bean's remake was public service. He wasn't idle on this front either, having been appointed as a county justice of the peace in late 1844.[22] You didn't need to be a judge or lawyer, or even win an election, to become a JP in Missouri. Basically, it was a position that was appointed by prominent citizens of the jurisdiction who made up the county commission, another governmental organ of local control.

For qualifications, good judgment and an awareness of local attitudes were most required. Indeed, a JP of the era was supposed to be the face of community justice. "Where a high court judge sought the precise meaning of a statute before making a ruling, the justice of the peace did not depend so heavily upon positive law that he failed to take into account common notions of what was right and fair," writes historian Bonnie Aileen Speck.[23]

So the real job of a justice of the peace was not just to execute but to interpret local law, mostly in small claims court cases. They were low-rung public servants, and people liked it that way. There were no precedents being set by adjudicating a disputed sale of a handful of hogs; in fact, locals expected JP rulings to reflect their norms. James Bean quickly proved himself to be reliable enough to perform this community service, mostly by being literate, adaptable, and even-keeled.

JPs also had more serious functions that brought locally flavored law and order to small communities. They heard petty criminal cases, for which fines and other, creative sentences often applied (a drunk paying

---

22 James Bean starts to appear as the officiant that year in "The Marriage Records of Jackson County, Vol. 1, 1827–1850," compiled by "Mrs. John Vineyard" in 1967. The author's name is probably Dorothy Vineyard. Accessed October 22, 2023, at http://usgenealogyresearch.atwebpages.com/Missouri/Jackson/marriages_records_1827–1850.pdf.

23 Bonnie Speck, "Minor Courts and Communities at the Frontier" (PhD diss., Wayne State University, 2010): 3.

for a broken window, for example, instead of doing time). In cases of more serious violence, JPs often launched investigations to determine if the crimes warranted being passed along to the nearest established criminal justice system. In this, a JP could see the worst of their communities.

James Bean has found a niche in the role that is much more pleasant: marrying folks. His first is recorded in October 1844, and plenty follow in early 1845. He doesn't corner the market, but he's a reliable fixture for matrimony in Independence.

On May 29, 1845, trouble strikes when he least expects it.

He's on horseback outside Independence when on the road ahead he sees a carriage. Who should be inside but Maria "Fannie" Owens, the young, free-spirited daughter of Samuel Owens. She's known to be a flirt and a sass, and the men of town love her for it, even if her gruff father does not. With her is John Harper, a lawyer from Georgia. He's set up an office downtown, but trust in him has been hard to come by. Especially for Sam Owens, who disapproves of the budding relationship between the attorney and his daughter. This is not general knowledge—it's really no one's business.

So James Bean only smiles when the couple tells him that they're heading to his Blue Springs office to be married. Here's an opportunity to create a romantic moment for the family, a love story with true western flair. "No reason we can't just perform the service here," James says.

The couple is delighted. They stand on the carriage's step as James Bean intones pleasantries from horseback. "With the power vested in me as the justice of the peace of Jackson County, I pronounce you man and wife," he finishes. He'll file the paperwork when he gets back to Independence, and it'll be official. (No licenses needed.)

It takes more than a day before the full story trickles out: Fannie Owens has married over her father's stringent objections. Samuel Owens considers Harper a scoundrel and had forbade their relationship. Fannie responded by hiring a carriage, proposing to the lawyer in his office, and heading immediately for Blue Springs to find the JP. Now Independence's biggest and proudest businessman has been left humiliated.[24]

The Owens family lawyers and advisers stop by to visit a horrified James Bean. The family is desperate for a loophole to annul the union and drive Harper from the family. But the judge's hands are tied—the county has recorded the marriage and his role is finished. Sam Owens gives up, and his daughter and unwanted son-in-law make their home in his large house. The family drama has just begun.

After all James Bean's work to become a trusted member of the Owens regime, he's put his foot in a cow pie. He's somehow found a way to become dependent on the most powerful man in town—and then has hurt him. At least young Ambrose Owens acknowledges it as an honest mistake.

The county, importantly, doesn't hold anything against the impetuous justice of the peace. If anything, the escapade earns him some name recognition and opens a niche: James Bean is the one in Jackson County to see for an easy marriage. It's a reputation that will stick.

---

24 John Taylor Hughes and William Elsey Connelley, *Doniphan's Expedition and the Conquest of New Mexico and California* (Topeka, KS: Heritage Books, 1907; 2009): 26–27. *Columbia (MO) Herald-Statesman*, November 26, 1847.

SAM

Council Grove, eastern Kansas
May 1845

As bustling as the caravan business is in Independence, Samuel Bean has never seen anything like the congregation of wagons he sees here at the Neosho River.

Just as two forks of this tributary of the Arkansas merge here, caravans are doing the same. Wagons are parked in every direction on the grass, each stuffed with merchandise, settler families, dreamers, adventurers, and trappers. The caravan captains are meeting, coordinating a time of departure, as the animals graze and teamsters sprawl around campfires.

Council Grove got its name in 1825, being the place where negotiations between US commissioners and Osage Indian chiefs ended with a treaty guaranteeing free passage. Now it's a rallying point for covered wagons. Beyond the Grove, as the experienced teamsters are too eager to tell a greenhorn like Sam, you can expect the Indians to want to murder you. Wagon trains cluster here, forming convoys that provide safety in numbers.

There's a natural spring here too. The seasoned men seem fixated on water—how much is stored, where the next refill is coming from, how quickly the men and beasts consume it. Attacks from Native Americans might be the topic of most campfire tales, but Sam feels more afraid of the deserts that he'll soon be facing. He can't shoot at thirst.

It's been two weeks of walking alongside a team of six yoked oxen pulling a wagon along the Santa Fe Trail. He's got a whip, but he's been instructed by the wagon owners not to use it too much. Beating animals into a frenzy is sneered at as a Mexican "bull-cracker" approach; the oxen respond to instruction and some coaxing at the yoke just as well. And nothing gets their attention better than the sound-barrier-breaking snap of a whip overhead. However, Sam finds that the teamsters' patience for the beasts—and his own—often crumbles when the wagons struggle up steep banks of the endless river crossings stretched in rows across Kansas.

A good day's trip means dry weather. Sam's already seen what happens at creeks and rivers swollen by rain: frustrating pile-ups as wagons get stuck and all available teamsters get in the water to coax the animals, to jam boards under jammed wheels, and if needed to push stalled wagons up slick banks. "Think of the poor drivers who had to pick out the mates and yoke them up every morning for the day's journey over swollen creeks and small rivers, that came up to the armpits and left the water sloshing in the shoes," he says. "Often have I slept of a night with wet feet and body wet up to my arms, but never took cold."[25]

The landscape is alien. For the past week Sam's been virtually swimming through the tall bluestem grasses, higher than his waist. When the wind gusts, the plains around him seem to undulate like water. But he's told that from Council Grove onward, these grasses will give way to shorter stuff that somehow clings to life in the arid environment. This is also the last hardwood they'll see for a long while.

Despite Sam's hardy constitution, the respite at Council Grove is a welcome one. He enjoys mingling with the teamsters he's admired in downtown Independence, fascinated by their addiction to adventure. "There

---

25 Sam Bean's remembrances in this chapter come from an 1904 article in the *Rio Grande Republican* included in its entirety in Sonnichsen, *Judge Roy Bean,* 17–23.

was a very strange infatuation about these men," he observes. "They would go trip after trip across the plains, and the oftener they went and the more hardships they suffered the more intense was the desire to go again."

Sam's body aches in ways he thought impossible, but he's nearly used to it. He's a well-built young man already packing on new, lean muscle. He also has a constitution that he's finding can be pushed to new limits. The grind of the teamster life is unlike anything he's experienced: regimented, laborious, exhausting, and somehow rewarding.

Each morning on the road begins with a quick breakfast of flour cakes, bacon, and coffee, before the teamsters tend to the animals. They fetch the oxen from where they've been grazing, paying close attention to their infamously delicate hooves, wrapped in leather moccasins for protection. Then they'll yoke the animals, form up at the captain's orders, and start to roll. Anything less than ten miles a day is considered subpar and more than eighteen miles unobtainable.

When Sam's group is ready to leave Council Grove, he counts two hundred wagons in the combined train. Whether this serves as an impediment to Comanche and Arapaho raids or an enticement to attack remains to be seen. Every man in the convoy has a rifle, knife, and pistol—certainly every teamster does—and the caravan can circle into a fortress if needed, the animals stowed inside a protective ring.

Every hour on the road poses additional risk. From now on, they stay in motion during the nights when the moon allows it. During these spooky marches, Sam takes heart in hearing his indomitable teamsters sing, keeping popular tunes fresh by adding crude new lyrics: "In the stillness of the night they would ring the changes on their old Missouri songs."

Santa Fe Trail (modern Oklahoma–New Mexico border)
July 1845

"They don't look very much like a rabbit ears," says Sam Bean, eyeing the two distant humps on the horizon and knowing there will be a story from the teamsters that'll take his mind off his thirst. It's day two of an expected three without fresh water; he's surrounded by a hard plain studded with stick-figure cactus, sprouts of sharp yucca, and clumps of haggard weeds.

He's told that the two peaks, the only features on the southern horizon, aren't meant to look like rabbit ears, but the frostbitten ears of an Indian. Up top of one of 'em, the Cheyenne buried Chief Rabbit Ears after he died in battle with the Spanish, who called him "Orejas de Conejo," by the way. That was in 1717, and since then the Cheyenne, Mexicans, and everyone else have adopted the name. Those jagged edges look like the chief's ears after the cold chewed 'em up when he was just a brave.

Sam is satisfied; every big formation on the Santa Fe Trail seems to have a legendary and tragic backstory. The tales make him feel small, not in size but in permanence. Stories here are like animal bones—they stay in place, bleached by the sun and weather, until they become part of the permanent landscape. That Cheyenne died 129 years ago, and folks out here are *still* talking about his ears.

Seeing Rabbit Ears, the six-thousand-foot-tall ruins of ancient volcanos, is an important milestone since it's the only water source for thirty miles in any direction. Such scarcity on the trail necessitated the Council Grove megacaravan being split into its original parts, each traveling staggered and separate. But the landmarks also represent a milestone for Samuel Bean—it's the first time he's seen New Mexico, the state he'll one day call home.

The wagon train steers toward Corrumpa Creek and follows its sandy banks to a rock shelf called McNees Crossing. For years the site has been a vital link to the Santa Fe Trail's Cimarron Cutoff route, named for a trader killed by Indians there in 1828. Season after season of wagon traffic has beaten a dirt ramp down to the rocky crossing, a cut that's already more than five feet deep and twenty feet wide.

Past the crossing, Sam sees creases of wagon tracks departing the road and cutting across the dry grass. Sam's wagon train does the same, rattling northeast along the riverbank in search of a patch of good pasture for the animals.

Three days of rejuvenation follow. Sam hunts, checks on the grazing oxen, and patches his freshly washed clothes. The teamsters fill all available vessels with water from a nearby waterfall, running steady with the winter's melted runoff. The cold nights are warmed by mesquite stick fires and whiskey bottles. Banjos, harmonicas, fiddles, and stargazing provide entertainment.

The Santa Fe Trail has been an assault on Sam's senses: the sight of buffalo herds clustered in impossible numbers in the waist-high grass of the Cimarron River bottoms, the sound of wolves howling in the night, the acrid smell of burning buffalo crap, the taste of bitter coffee in metal cups that somehow always gather campfire ash.

Sam's got hundreds of miles to go before they reach their destination, including a ninety-mile waterless stretch called the Jornada del Muerto. They'll also soon be deep into territory where the Apache have, for hundreds of years, waited to attack travelers. But so far, he wouldn't trade this experience for all the safe nights in Independence.

Outside Santa Fe, Mexico
July 1845

As soon as the wagon train crests a hilltop, its teamsters spy the rectangular homes in the valley below, and the firearms come out. Sam Bean aims his pistol at the empty horizon and fires, flush with pride that he's survived his first trip without any mishaps. But as great a sight as the town is, the architecture of Santa Fe underwhelms. It looks more like a collection of scattered bricks than a city. There are patches of corn and wheat fields between the adobe homes. Three streams run through town, providing irrigation for these urban plots.

The gunshots must have alerted every customs official in Santa Fe to get ready to fleece the new arrivals. On the surface, the Mexican government soaks the traders' profits with a customs duty on dry goods that's officially 25 percent of their worth, plus the $500 per wagon charge. The problem here is the arbitrary value placed on the goods by the officials at the customs house. Paying a steep bribe for a low estimate could increase a profit margin, but falling afoul of a truly corrupt official could lead to a staggering loss.

The lament of the Missouri merchants is that they suffer double taxation on the same goods, once upon importation from Europe and again when shipped to Mexico. This led the US Congress to pass the Drawback Act in March. Now traders can be reimbursed for all but 2.5 percent of the US duties of foreign merchandise, provided advance notice is given to re-export the goods to Mexico. (They're shipped to Mexico in original packages, and with certified invoices.) The reach of the Santa Fe traders is long enough to shake money from the federal government in Washington—and in exchange, the merchants are emboldened to continue their soft invasion of northern Mexico.

The wealthy people in Santa Fe hold no love for the government in Mexico City either, and it's been the epicenter of rebellions before. In political fights, local merchants tend to side with the American traders. In August 1843, provisional president Antonio López de Santa Anna passed a decree closing the customs houses in Chihuahua and Santa Fe. The outcry from monied interests in northern Mexico forced him to back down a few months later.

For all the struggle to get there, most of the traders scorn what they see of what will one day be called New Mexico. There is a shocking level of neglect of buildings, animals, and citizens. "The people were nearly all in extreme poverty, and there were absolutely none who could be classed as wealthy except by comparison," noted one American visitor, trader James Josiah Webb, the year before. "The houses were nearly all old and dilapidated, the streets narrow and filthy, and the people, when in best attire, not half dressed."[26]

The question for Sam Bean, and anyone else with the wherewithal to ask, is how to make money in this forlorn place. There are few commodities to bring home beyond furs and deerskin, blankets and some wool. The new thing here are large flocks of sheep that the better-heeled landowners have been driving into town, but the creatures seem ill-suited for the Santa

---

26 James Josiah Webb, *Adventures in the Santa Fe Trade 1844–1847* (Lincoln: University of Nebraska Press, 1931; 1995): 92.

Fe Trail. Sam sees a glimmer of opportunity, however. He unknowingly agrees with the verdict of Webb: "The only chance I could see of getting any portion of it was from the little that might be in the hands of a very few who might want to start a little store . . . or might indulge in the national propensity of gambling."[27]

That's a dream for another time, if ever. Sam's mind is bent on getting home, to see chimney smoke curling from American-style houses instead of these mud-hardened adobe boxes. His job is done—he doesn't have to tarry to see the goods and wagons sold. Instead of waiting for September to join an eastbound wagon train, he decides to head back immediately. "There were eight of us, all young Missouri boys, who formed a party to come back to 'God's country.'"[28]

The cadre stocks up on hard bread and dried beef, uses their pay to buy mules to ride, and sets forth on the Santa Fe Trail back to Missouri, eight young souls with more bravery than common sense, as Sam will concede: "We were all young and without experience, having never been from home before and never beyond the sight of houses or beyond the pale of civilization."

Somewhere on the Cimarron River
September 1845

The proud youths of Missouri are eight lumps beneath wet blankets. Sam peers through the sheets of rain and sees the mules standing together, heads down. We've been reduced to that, he thinks. Dumb brutes huddled together in sullen acceptance, helplessly battered by rain and lashed by

---

27 *Rio Grande Republican*, quoted in full in Sonnichsen, *Judge Roy Bean*, 17–26. Sam Bean didn't enjoy gambling or drinking but had no problem with profiting from these vices.

28 Ibid., 25. In his write-up, Sam Bean said he associated chimneys with the United States and home.

wind. The man pressed next to Sam jumps a little every time the thunder cracks. So does he.

The Apache didn't massacre them, the desert didn't kill them, but this evening storm on the Cimarron River might just do it. The trip home for Sam's party until now has been fast and, for the Santa Fe Trail, easy. Without wagons, the distances just don't seem as far. A small group can keep a low profile from Indians and are of little interest to ones looking to steal larger amounts of pack animals and freight. Still, there are plenty of examples of traders in groups of two or three being picked off, so having seven other guns nearby seems safer. Except tonight, when an entire gang of desperadoes could be feet from them and they wouldn't know it. If they get the drop on us tonight, they deserve our wet mules, Sam thinks despondently.

When the rain tapers off, the temperature drops and Sam can feel the man next to him shivering. He is too. There's no hope for a fire; what little wood was nearby is long gone to trail traffic. ("Not enough wood within fifty miles of the place to make a toothpick of," Sam complains.) There is a lot of fuel underfoot in the form of buffalo crap, but the torrential rain has soaked it through.

So again, there's nothing to do but endure the creeping hypothermia and watch the horizon, feeling a thin shell of ice harden on their blankets. The night "seemed to be a month long," Sam puts it. "But that long night with its horrors had an ending, and the boys shouted 'Glory to God' as the sun come out in great splendor in the morning. The sun warmed us up, dried our clothes and blankets, and we began to feel like we would once more tread Missouri soil and see our friends."[29]

The mood remains bright as they leave the lush river bottoms for the ocean of scrub, since home gets closer with each mule step. The songs resume, the young men putting their own variations on the teamsters' lyrics. One hundred miles after the storm, after breakfast, someone thinks to do an inventory of their provisions. The dried meat and hardtack stores are

---

29 *Rio Grande Republican*, quoted in Sonnichsen, *Judge Roy Bean*, 26.

almost gone, not nearly enough to last the four hundred miles ahead of them. Now they face the prospect of slow starvation, paying dearly for a stupid greenhorn mistake.

There's only one solution to assuage the fear and prevent fatal panic: ride east. They run out of food within days. The hunger pangs subside after two days without food, but the young men are exhausted all the time and struggle with even simple tasks.

On the third morning without food, Sam Bean and his seven companions slowly rouse after a short sleep for what may be their last day on earth, spent on the backs of mules. Sam slowly sways with each step, shaking his aching head when his vision blurs. He finds that he cares less and less about keeping an eye out for Indians or bandits, but he guesses he'd spot a lizard worth eating at fifty paces.

Sam snaps to attention when he hears the joyous whoops of his companions, hope transmuted into pain-numbing adrenaline. There, stretched out in the dirt, fresh wagon tracks intersect the Santa Fe Trail. A caravan has recently steered onto the roadway, heading toward Missouri.

Now, to survive, Bean's party must catch that wagon train. It's an even-money race: their target should be moving slower than they are, but the starving Missourians' mules are staggering after long, desperate days without grazing.

They spend all day on the chase. Their desperation nears panic as the wagon tracks just continue, with no sign of their source. An almost physical blanket of doom settles on the party as the sun sets, visible in the body language of his fellow travelers, and keenly felt inside Sam's own dark thoughts. But they don't stop, using welcome moonlight to forge ahead in a make-or-break push.

Moonlight saves them when they spot the white sheets of canvas of the caravan radiating the pale light. The men start whooping again, and they're swiftly surrounded by dozens of Mexican gunmen. The scene quickly becomes what frontiersmen politely call "an interview." With a look, the Mexicans see that the half-dead Missourians pose no threat. The gunmen are escorts of rich merchants who are associated with the famous Armijo family, hauling cargo to Missouri. The ragged Americans accept an invitation into their camp, slavering over the smell of roasting buffalo meat, stewing beans, and spiced coffee cooked in a clay pot.

Once Sam gets his bearings, he takes in the wagon train. It becomes clear why these guys were so hard to catch. The vehicles are laden with hard sacks of gold and silver. The merchants, setting a furious pace, are traveling all night, worried they will be raided. It's the Santa Fe version of a treasure galleon, moving fast to avoid the chance of meeting pirates.

And as with the law of the sea, when a Santa Fe trader is in trouble, his peers can be counted on to help. This distinction doesn't know national lines. If anything, the relationship Mexican traders enjoy with American businessmen is warmer than the one they have with their own strife-riven government.

The Armijo merchants donate exactly fifteen days' worth of buffalo meat to the hapless youths, enough to last all the way to Independence. They arrive in Independence, "all in good health and spirits," to find locals and even some newspapermen already talking about their hard trip home. Sam Bean sees people looking at him when he tells the tales, and he realizes he's becoming one of the hard men that once fascinated him.

He has an opportunity to head back down the trail. James has organized a wagon train that he'll be taking to Santa Fe with a plan to bring mules back east. He leaves with a dozen wagons in September, but without his brother.[30] The near-death experiences have given Sam pause. "Whilst the memory of these were yet fresh in mind, I made a promise that I would never go across that fearful desert again, or beyond the confines of civilization," he says.

"But it only took a few months for that feeling to wear off."[31]

---

30 James Bean came back in a train carrying three hundred mules and $30,000 in specie after an "uneventful" trip. Louise Barry, *The Beginning of the West* (Topeka: Kansas State Historical Society, 1972), 565.

31 *Rio Grande Republican,* quoted in Sonnichsen, *Judge Roy Bean*, 26.

Independence, Missouri
Spring 1846

The news had quickly spread from Washington, DC, blaring from newspapers of every political stripe in Missouri: the United States on December 29, 1845, admitted Texas to the Union as a slave state. Even while the Santa Fe traders readied their wares for the spring season, the annexation of New Mexico seemed closer than ever. And so did war.

President James Polk tried a carrot-and-stick approach. He sent three thousand soldiers under General Zachary Taylor to the disputed area between the Nueces River and the Rio Grande to show American support for the Texans' claims. At the same time, his agent John Slidell worked in Mexico for months, trying to quietly negotiate a deal. Polk authorized Slidell to spend as much as $30 million for Texas, New Mexico, and California. The mission sputtered more than it failed, as diplomacy often does, and the president resigned himself to a war to annex New Mexico, Texas (to the Rio Grande), and California.

When the snow starts to melt, the traders start off for a new season on the trail. The gathering war clouds don't hinder them—just the opposite. They can beat the fighting, arrive in Santa Fe before the army to sell their goods to sympathetic business associates, and be on hand to help guide the conquest to represent their interests. There is short-term profit to be made, but there's also a generational opportunity. America is coming for New Mexico, and the men of Independence want a piece of the action. It's not every day that life offers the chance to create a commercial and political infrastructure in the new American land. It's a pivotal time and the merchants know it: Samuel Owens and Robert Aull themselves are caravanning into Mexico together this year.

Joining their usual group of teamsters and merchants will be Owen Meredith, who arrived in Independence from Baltimore, suffering from consumption (tuberculosis, or TB). As hard as the trail is, it still attracts ill people seeking benefits from the dry climate and sulfury natural baths of New Mexico. Meredith lives in the Owens house and promptly strikes up a flirtation with the married Fannie Harper.

When John Harper invites Meredith into his law office, the man from Baltimore doesn't see a polite way to decline. People in the street hear the gunshot just moments later; the young visitor doesn't have to worry about TB anymore. The lawyer claims that an argument escalated, but no one believes this because Harper had recently bought two pistols, and the shot was heard soon after the victim was seen entering the building. With Harper arrested and jailed, it seems that the attorney whom Samuel Owens hates so much may be out of his life.

That's when Fannie makes her move, visiting her husband in jail and smuggling a blade for Harper to use to dig free. She's got the mules and supplies ready, and the pair vanish down the Santa Fe Trail. Justice of the Peace James Bean's impromptu marriage ceremony has now blossomed from a personal embarrassment into the humiliation of a full-fledged murder scandal, accounts of which are printed in newspapers beyond Missouri. Owens is beyond distraught. His preparations for the coming trip only intensify, but he casts a maudlin shadow these days.

Sam knows the incident is a sore spot for his brother. James has put a lot of work into establishing himself in Independence, and, other than this very public misstep, the results have been impressive. He's acquired new partners (Thomas Pitcher and Robert Smart) and new property in downtown Independence along Rock Street, a short lane that ends at the town square.

If the Harper murder scandal has tainted his brother's name, Sam can't see it. Ambrose Owens, Bean family friend and Fannie's brother, doesn't harbor any grudges. But his father, the proud mercantile boss, can't possibly look at James without thinking of the horrible embarrassment. The amount of shame Sam Owens projects is a little scary. Maybe it's better if the big man hits the road, where surviving and mercantile empire building can occupy his mind.

The question for Sam is, should he join him? There will be streams of wagons heading west in 1846—the manufacturers in Independence alone report seventy-five new orders for vehicles. The traders are stocking up for an epic season, even by Santa Fe standards. How could he miss out on that?

One thing he knows, after having experienced months of life with James and his young family, sticking around Independence is not in Sam's cards. And he's worked in St. Louis as a stevedore and found the labor both difficult and uninspiring.[32] He's seen too much out west to domesticate in Missouri like his brother, no matter how successful he's becoming.

Hostilities begin in April, shortly after the Mexican army arrives at the Rio Grande to spar with Taylor. On May 13, 1846, Polk declares that a state of war exists between the United States and Mexico. The next day, Colonel Stephen Watts Kearny is placed in command of a fifteen-hundred-member detachment to be organized at Fort Leavenworth, comprised of the First US Dragoons and volunteer troops from Missouri. It's called the Army of the West.

Independence is whipped into a patriotic frenzy to go along with the commercial energy. Sam, always sensitive to his environment, is caught up in the hysteria. Soon after Kearny's command is formed, recruitment in Independence begins. The person in charge of inspiring the men of Jackson County to sign up is Alexander William Doniphan.

Sam knows him. Hell, *everyone* does, and not just in Independence, where the man lives. He's a successful, high-profile attorney who until recently represented Jackson County as a Missouri state legislator. He created three counties in two terms and once voted "nay" on a resolution offering Andrew Jackson "respect esteem and best wishes for his future happiness at his retirement." So, an effective politician with a talent for messaging. He won his elections as a Whig in a town hosting powerful Democrats, and by wide margins.

Doniphan is also a former state militia brigadier general, and as such he had his own involvement with the Church of Latter-day Saints. His grandest moment was refusing an order to shoot Joseph Smith and other prisoners, calling it "cold blooded murder." He later defended Smith and other high-profile Mormons in courtrooms and secured their release.

---

32 Bloom, "Shadows in Sam's Valley."

During one consultation, Smith told his lawyer not to accept land in town as payment for legal fees. "Wrath hangs over Jackson County," he intoned gravely. "God's people have been ruthlessly driven from it, and you will live to see the day when it will be visited by fire and sword."[33]

Being a Whig with sympathies for Mormons would appear to make Doniphan a natural enemy of Samuel Owens, but the pair hold wary mutual respect as fellow leading men of Independence. Doniphan's also very popular, having won elections by wide margins. (A good reputation can outweigh party loyalty, especially in small communities.) Even after he leaves the statehouse, Doniphan remains the town's premier attorney. He and Owens, the town's leading merchant, are now two sides of the same coin, one with troops to conquer New Mexico, the other with economic influence to do the same with freight wagons. Neither has any idea how closely those two efforts will merge.

An aggressive national pride permeates Independence. Everywhere Sam Bean looks, there are merchants griping about Mexican tariffs, toasts to the fallen at the Alamo, laments over the wasted opportunities in northern Mexico, and boasts about the superiority of American ambition over Mexican sloth.

When Owens and Aull leave in late May, Sam Bean watches the wagons go.

Sam and the rest of the city's youth turn out in Independence when Doniphan makes a rousing speech soliciting military recruits. The man is as persuasive as advertised, but the stirring emotions of the crowd pressed around him are equally energizing. Across Missouri, Doniphan finds it easy to persuade soldiers to fight for an expanded United States. "Patriotism," he later remarked, "was at a fever heat."[34]

---

33 B. H. Roberts, *Comprehensive History of the Church*, volume 1 (Provo, UT: Brigham Young University Press, 1965): 538.

34 Doniphan to D. C. Allen, quoted in "Sketch of Life," 1903, Doniphan Papers, Missouri Historical Society, St. Louis.

On June 6, Samuel Bean signs up with the Army of the West. He reports for duty with his own horse, saddle, and rifle, as required. There will be no uniforms, just sashes that identify the disparate men as a unit. The sashes are loathed immediately. (The common joke becomes "We didn't join up to look pretty" after a volunteer quips the line to an officer.)

At Fort Leavenworth, Sam is assigned to Company A of the freshly formed First Missouri Mounted Volunteers. "I enlisted as a twelve-months' volunteer soldier, to traverse not only the same but other deserts," Sam Bean will later say. "And endure more hardships, in a much longer voyage."[35]

35 Sam's writings about the trip appeared in the *Rio Grande Republican* and were quoted in full in Sonnichsen, *Judge Roy Bean*. Military records confirm his enrollment date, via the National Park Service's US Mexican War Soldiers & Sailors Database, accessed November 22, 2022, https://www.nps.gov/paal/learn/historyculture/search-usmexwar-detail.htm?id=sv3103.

JOSHUA

Louisville, Kentucky
June 20, 1846

Joshua Bean spurs his horse and edges the animal to keep its nose aligned with the one next to him. He glances around at the other soldiers; each of them is wearing the same light grey shirts, but he takes in the mishmash of the men's dark pants, boots, and wide-brimmed hats. Like the others, he has a long Springfield Model 1842 (muzzle-loaded, percussion cap) slung over his shoulder and a stunted saber jangling at his belt.

All the officers are dressed in dark blue and have matching hats. One of them gives the call, and the 853 men of the First Kentucky Mounted Volunteers begin the march out of Camp Owsley. The regiment's mission is to parade through downtown Louisville, where they were mustered just weeks ago, to show the populace that they're ready to seize Mexico.

As of June 9—three days after his brother Sam signed up in Missouri—Joshua Bean had become a private in Company D of the First Kentucky Mounted Volunteers.[36] Joshua's time in Kentucky has left no records; no

36 National Park Service's US Mexican War Soldiers & Sailors Database, accessed November 22, 2022, https://www.nps.gov/paal/learn/historyculture/search-usmexwar-detail.htm?id=sv3103.

property ties him to the state, and no census taker has captured him. Most of all, he's not married. In short, he's a man with nothing to lose, a ready-made militia soldier.

The line of horsemen tramp past the majestic Oakland House, which stands on the grounds in ivory-white opulence. This is the heart of the Oakland Race Course, established in 1832 on a fifty-five-acre plot on the southwest outskirts of the city.[37] The racetrack, like others before it, has faltered financially. Louisville just can't seem to get a classy horse-racing venue to stay open.

The track, under its new role as Camp Owsley, is now a mustering place for Mexico-bound troops. It's named for the current governor, who readily offered militia units to serve in the war. Enthusiasm is high; men from the surrounding area have flooded Louisville to enlist. Now the camp is bustling with these poorly disciplined volunteers.

The rush to join is so fevered that there will be accusations of political favoritism after throngs of volunteers are denied once the roster's been filled. There's been an outpouring of recruits from a generation of Kentuckians whose dreams of self-sufficiency were crushed by cholera and financial crises. In just weeks, these disaffected men have become cavalrymen worthy of a parade.

Joshua's company leader is Colonel Humphrey Marshall, a prominent lawyer, militia officer, and aspiring national Whig politician. The men can feel his affection for them, part of it being a projection of his own ambition. His pride may be too fragile since any perceived damage to it can easily turn into a duel-worthy offense. And by now the men know that Marshall is outspoken *and* has a temper.

Private Bean fills out a uniform well, being bearish and stout, but he's not handsome. He has wide cheeks, eyes that seem a little too close together, and a full beard that makes his expansive face seem even broader. He commands a physical presence, and in the testosterone-soaked life of a cavalryman, this is more useful than being handsome.

---

37 On the west and south sides of present-day 7th Street and Magnolia Avenue.

As a Kentuckian, he's got plenty of skill at riding and shooting. Now he's being asked to perform in a more precise way, and he enjoys the structure and challenge of learning. There's training twice a day, every day, practicing infantry and cavalry maneuvers. Learning the saber is among the least popular tasks, since their weapons are straighter and shorter than the officers' sleek, curved ones. The more educated men gripe that their blades look like Roman short swords, ill-suited for use on horseback.

Joshua pays close attention, not just to the lessons but to the way the officers handle the men. The clever ones are keen to preserve the new troops' enthusiasm, even as they impose uncomfortable discipline. One recruit has shot at an officer, luckily missing, and a group of drunken volunteers from the regiment recently fought the guards who arrived to fetch them from a whorehouse, wrecking the place.[38]

A parade is one way to maintain the relationship between the camp and residents. "Many of our most respected citizens have expressed a strong desire that the Volunteers now at Camp Owsley should be permitted to parade through the city," reads a June 17 item in the *Louisville Daily Courier*. "Such a movement, we should think, would be alike gratifying to officers, soldiers and citizens."

This display is as much a celebration of the positive war news as it is of the volunteers. Zachary Taylor is a new national hero after improbable victories at the battles of Palo Alto and Resaca de la Palma. With the much larger Mexican "Army of the North" of General Mariano Arista in retreat across the Rio Grande, Taylor (promoted to major general) is heading for Monterrey. He'll need more troops if he's to push any deeper. Everyone in camp expects the Kentucky volunteers to be in the vanguard of this phase of the invasion.

So do the citizens of Louisville, who greet the parading troops with decorative bunting, cries of patriotic slogans, and flowers waving in the hands of young women. "The display was a grand and imposing one," a

---

38 James A. Ramage, "John Hunt Morgan and the Kentucky Cavalry Volunteers in the Mexican War," *Register of the Kentucky Historical Society* 81, no. 4 (Autumn 1983): 343–65.

newspaper prints the day after. "Such a display of horse was never before seen in our city."[39] No one points out, in print, that six of the ten companies of the regiment are not equipped with rifles, courtesy of a supply snarl.

The regiment departs for war three weeks later, the missing rifles never issued. On the afternoon of July 7, the volunteers at Camp Owsley dismantle their tents, pack their personal supplies, draft final letters to families, and ride their horses to the river. There, five 180-foot steamships are waiting. Each will bear more than a hundred First Kentucky Cavalry volunteers and their steeds to their next stop, Memphis.

Like everyone with common sense, Joshua both loves and fears steamships. Their speed and convenience have already changed the scope of trade and immigration along America's inland rivers, but the technology comes with real danger. When something goes wrong, the results can be catastrophic: steamers have been known to capsize, and their boilers have a habit of detonating in massive explosions.[40]

It takes all day for the men and horses to load into the proper steamships. Colonel Marshall, with as much of his company as can fit, boards the side-wheeler *Diamond*. Another trip later in the week will fetch the remaining men. Bean sees that his ride will be towed behind the steamer *Diana*.[41] He settles in for a pleasant three-day trip to Tennessee.

On board, the party continues, as a fellow traveler in the *Diana* notes. "The men appeared to enjoy themselves exceedingly, having ample room on the two boats for their own accommodation without incommoding

---

39 *Lexington Observer Reporter*, June 21, 1846.

40 The *Glencoe*, one of the ships that ferried troops on July 7, 1846, suffered this fiery fate in 1852.

41 "City Intelligence, Military and Naval," *Evening Post* (New York), July 13, 1846. Besides the *Diana*, the *Diamond*, and the *Glencoe*, the other ships ferrying these troops were the *Bunker Hill* and the *Vesta*.

those who were unwell, some five or six in number," says the passenger, who wrote a detailed description for the *Louisville Morning Courier.* "Nor by singing and dancing did they disturb those who preferred quiet."[42]

Outside San Antonio, Texas
August 1846

It should be shocking to see a cavalry trooper riding with no pants, but at this point nothing would surprise Joshua Bean. He has seen some sad sights in the month since the regiment left Memphis, but this is somehow the most depressing.

Supply issues beset them as soon as they left the city. The quartermasters messed everything up, leaving the horses unfed and the regiment suffering during forced marches to race for their next meal. They reach Little Rock on June 26, traveling an impressive 160 miles from Memphis in just ten days. From there, they staggered into Texas.

The supply issues have only gotten worse. Now the troopers are also running out of food. Who would have ever guessed that there would be nostalgia for army-supplied pickled meat? Foraging has become a full-time occupation, and no nearby unattended goat or chicken is safe. The men also seek out locals and trade excess clothes for food and whiskey, something they regret when boots and pants decay under exposure to the harsh weather. There are no replacements, and these men must go without.[43] Joshua Bean doesn't need to talk to the pantsless trooper to know his story.

The ghoulish truth is that the man might get lucky if someone in his company dies and makes a new set of pants available. The regiment has already left a trail of ailing troopers behind like spent animals. Twenty-eight men are languishing in Memphis and another thirty in Little Rock. The number of marching sick swells that number that tallied at least sixty

---

42 *Louisville Morning Courier*, July 13, 1846.

43 Ramage, "John Hunt Morgan and the Kentucky Cavalry Volunteers."

ailing troopers on the trip between the two cities. One man in the regiment died of an unspecified sickness—far from the last.

There's a frightening lack of medical officers across the entire invading army, and those with the volunteers, in the opinion of Zach Taylor, "are entirely without experience as regards their duties in the field."[44] In the regular army, one-third of those who applied for service in Mexico were turned away for health reasons. The volunteers have never been subjected to this sensible screening—some of them have tuberculosis and actually enlisted so they could get a paid trip west to benefit from some dry air.

Travel is weeding out the weak. Surgeon General Thomas Lawson remarks in an 1846 letter that the volunteers are in over their heads: "Impelled by a feeling [of] patriotism, a thirst after military fame or the spirit of adventure, many of them recklessly enter the ranks and undertake to perform the duties of a soldier the toils, privations nor the self-restraint attendant on which are they in a frame of mind or body to endure."[45]

On the arid march from Little Rock to San Antonio, those struck down on the road are left behind with healthy caretakers to find shelter, often in the barns of sympathetic farmers. These stragglers are ordered to rendezvous with their units when they're able. Around them, dozens of men are dying, but those who can must march on.

Joshua Bean credits his family's hardy constitution for his health. He also uses common sense and what the surgeon general calls "self-restraint," which means avoiding eating unripe fruit or getting drunk all the time, two things that many troopers do regardless of the risk. Or maybe Joshua's just got good luck.

Soon the torturous drudgery of the march will end and they will reach San Antonio. The city is a war-torn mess, but it's home to a major resupply center for US troops. It's also where Marshall will report to General John

---

44 Zachary Taylor and William Holland Samson, *Letters of Zachary Taylor from the Battlefields of the Mexican War* (Rochester, NY: William K. Bixby, 1908): 42.

45 Quoted in Ramage, "John Hunt Morgan and the Kentucky Cavalry Volunteers."

Wool, and their combined forces will merge with the main effort, under the command of General Winfield Scott. The objective: Mexico City, for a knockout blow that will change history.

When they reach San Antonio, the First Kentucky Volunteer Cavalry will finally be in the war. Once they get new boots and pants, glory should come soon after.

SAM

Pawnee Fork, Kansas

July 1846

A chorus of harsh barks and yips greets the men of the First Missouri Volunteers as they march along the Arkansas River toward the Pawnee Fork Crossing on July 7. Men new to the Santa Fe Trail cry out as small brown heads appear in the brown dirt, like potatoes sprung to life to heckle them. For Samuel Bean, it's the familiar but welcome sight of a dog town. This one is an impressive, three-mile-wide network of warrens brimming with mammals smaller than rabbits. As the soldiers near, the furry faces vanish in the same instant, bringing delighted cries.

Private Bean is one of 166 soldiers in Company A, which is made up mostly of Jackson County men serving under David Waldo, a Santa Fe trader turned volunteer army captain. Waldo helped raise and equip the company, so it's his to run, as part of the First Regiment of Missouri Mounted Volunteers. At Fort Leavenworth the men elected Alexander Doniphan to be the colonel of the regiment. In turn, he and everyone else will answer to a familiar face: Gen. S. W. Kearny, promoted to brigadier general.

Company A was the first company to march from Fort Leavenworth on June 22 as the Army of the West started its soon-to-be-legendary expedition. It was preceded only by a detachment of regular army dragoons who were tasked with scouting the way and chasing reports of a trade convoy carrying weapons into Mexico.

Sam's already nostalgic for the early days when the enthusiasm ran sky-high. Since then, there've been too many dead horses, cold nights, and forced marches to maintain what you'd call high morale. The men's clothing is wearing out on the march to Mexico. They're forced to improvise, patching their clothes with deer hide, goatskin, and any other material they can find during the march. So much for "looking pretty." The entire regiment is lacking tents, a basic comfort whose scarcity Sam fears will cost lives if the quartermasters don't set something up.

Even worse, the paymaster is equipped only with government currency, which besides having been devalued will be useless in Mexico, where the men will finally be able to spend their wages. (Buying road provisions from Mexicans is impossible since locals accepting currency is evidence of collaboration.) Doniphan earns respect by refusing to allow his men to be paid in what he calls "worthless paper" and insists on waiting until a supply of solid coin arrives.

Considering the lack of support, Sam is proud of the way the soldiers are holding up. There's an innate stubbornness to the Missouri volunteers, even those new to the Santa Fe Trail. Doniphan builds on this with his ability to communicate and continually inspire them. Their tenacity is tested every day on the trail, in some way.

Today Sam knows the challenge will be clearing the notoriously tricky Pawnee Creek Crossing, which despite the name crosses a river. He well remembers how teamsters had to gang together to push each other's wagons up the slick, twenty-foot slopes. Luckily, the Pawnee is low enough to cross safely, although the supply wagons struggle on the steeps, and the poor infantrymen get dirty helping them.

The dragoons' camp is located about eleven miles past the far side of the river. Sam sees something unexpected: 150 covered wagons of a large trading convoy captained by none other than Samuel Owens and Robert Aull. They're in the army now, like it or not, and will be traveling with the troops all the way to New Mexico.

The caravan should have left sooner, Sam muses, thinking like a trader. Their late-May start meant being overtaken by Captain B. D. Moore, the head of the dragoon detachment and vanguard of the Army of the West. Moore was the one who had to break it to the merchants: they'd been requisitioned by the military and ordered to wait at the Pawnee Fork until the main body of Doniphan's troops arrived.

On the positive side, the traders should be protected from Indians and bandits, not to mention seizure by the Mexican military. But the merchants must now abandon the idea of selling their wares before the US Army appears, and it's unclear if there will be anyone left to purchase their goods. Their hopes all rest on the sympathies of the upper class of Santa Fe. Will they side with the invaders or their own splintered national government?

On top of this uncertainty is the route. The army plans on following the Arkansas River, where grazing is better for horses, and then taking the mountain route through a military outpost called Bent's Fort. This way into New Mexico is longer and contains steep roads that don't suit the traders' oxen and wagons. They brave the dry, dangerous Cimarron Cutoff for good reason: it's flat. The mountain route is a hundred miles longer in addition to everything. For the merchants, as is true for traders everywhere, distance is time and time is money.

The traders and soldiers mingle as they linger at Pawnee Creek, where Waldo's advance has been stalled waiting for the main body of troops. The men climb nearby hilltops to take in a sight that stuns even experienced hands. "Far over the plain to the west and north was one vast herd of buffalo, some in column [formation] marching in their trails, others carelessly grazing," one Company D soldier writes in his journal on July 7. "Every acre was covered, until the dim distance of the prairie became one black mass from which there was no opening and extending to the horizon. Every man was astonished." Men head into the herd and shoot forty, prompting fresh steak feasts cooked over dried buffalo-dung fires that night.[46]

On July 11, Waldo's men finally resume their step-by-step march down the Santa Fe Trail. Along the way, the troops are once again heralded by fields of prairie dogs. Sam studies the creatures' warrens as they pass and spies a rattlesnake easing into one of the holes. He's seen this before, but it hardly seems fair: the dog did all the work and now must share his space with a freeloading snake.

Outskirts of Santa Fe, Mexico
August 1846

Sam gazes up at the towering cliffs of Apache Pass and shudders to think about the fight that could have happened here. They're closing in on Santa Fe and are wary of an attack by thousands of Mexican troops.

This would have been the spot for it, Sam thinks as they snake through the pass on August 18. A small number of infantry backed by cannon could have ripped the entire regiment to pieces in the confines of this canyon. The soldiers are all talk about Mexican cowardice, but those with experience as traders know that there's little appetite for a fight mostly because the region has already fallen under the sway of American commerce.

During a three-day break at Bent's Fort in late July, the Army of the West had plotted its next move. General Kearny and his officers had gathered intelligence on conditions in New Mexico. Reports from spies and prisoners had raised hopes that Governor Manuel Armijo's gathering army may not want to fight. Kearny dispatched his agent James Maguffin, traveling incognito with his wife, Susan, in the trader's caravan, to seek out friendly officials who would vacate or surrender Santa Fe. The message Maguffin delivered to those who remained was that the invading Americans would respect the rights of former Mexican citizens.

On August 2, the army invaded Mexican territory, taking the tiny

---

46 Jacob Robinson, A *Journal of the Santa Fe Expedition Under Colonel Doniphan in 1846* (Princeton, NJ: Princeton University Press, 1932): 27–28.

village of Lower Mo and administering loyalty oaths. Then it was on to Santa Fe, the real prize. Apache Pass stood in the way, a perfect place to make a stand. And the Americans were ready to oblige any Mexican forces in the fight—or so they thought until they entered the canyon and took in the two-hundred-foot walls.

After clearing Apache Pass, the First Missouri Volunteers find themselves on a dusty plain, with no grass for the animals. A thirty-five-mile march tests their patience and their mounts' endurance. But the reward is the sight of Santa Fe that afternoon—and there's still no one blocking their way.[47]

The troops occupy Santa Fe as the sun sets, and an intrepid squad climbs the cathedral to plant an American flag over the tallest building in town. A very public loyalty oath ceremony is conducted. A major war objective has been achieved: Santa Fe is occupied. Now they have to make sure they can keep it.

Sam's heart sinks when instructions are issued the next morning. The troops have been ordered to camp outside town, where there's no wood, no shelter, and limited opportunities to buy or barter for much needed supplies. They are on half rations of flour and dried beef. There's no coffee, molasses, or rice. Tempers flare among the hungry men, and a volunteer named Haskins assaults an officer and is promptly court-martialed.[48]

Private Sam Bean may speak slowly, but his stoicism makes him dependable in tough situations. Doniphan orders him by name to be his orderly for the day, giving Bean valuable face time with his commander and boosting his morale, despite the dismal surroundings.[49]

New reports come in, verifying that Armijo has retreated to Chihuahua. Santa Fe has fallen, bloodlessly. The drive south to the important

---

47 Robinson, *Journal of the Santa Fe Expedition*, 29–30.

48 Ibid., 30.

49 Bloom, "Shadows in Sam's Valley."

commercial town of Chihuahua is sure to follow—but things are about to change for Doniphan and his volunteers.

Kearny breaks the news that he'll be taking the bulk of the Army of the West to conquer California, leaving the First Missouri Mounted Volunteers to occupy New Mexico. Doniphan is charged with serving as military governor in Santa Fe as he waits for reinforcements from Missouri to arrive, in the form of General John Wool. When Wool arrives—whenever that may be, considering his inability to organize—he'll take command of the march on Chihuahua. The Missourians will hand garrison duty over to another commander, Colonel Sterling Price, who'll march in from Veracruz.

Kearny takes the Army of the West toward the Pacific on September 25. The dust column rises along their route before settling, leaving the Missouri volunteers on their own.

JOSHUA

La Grange, Texas
September 1846

The ragged troops of the First Kentucky Volunteer Cavalry are just a hundred miles northeast of San Antonio when they receive an unexpected order. It contains a directive from General Zachary Taylor himself: divert the regiment and head to Lavaca, where they're to wait for further instructions. It seems the intention is to not to head south to the Mexican capital with Winfield Scott's main force, but instead to head to Veracruz to protect the rear of the advance.

The regiment is stunned. For the past starving, pestilent eight hundred miles, Colonel Marshall has rallied his men—and fortified himself—around the idea that they are suffering along the way to a historic assault on Mexico City. San Antonio is the first step to this glory. But going there also means a chance to resupply his men, whose clothes are deteriorating on their wasted bodies. The rations have been cut and cut again. Horses have died in droves.

There's no denying an order that comes from the top, and on September 18 the men head to their new base, soon dubbed Camp Calhoun, in a thick grove of live oak trees twelve miles away from any buildings. Being closer would risk temptations. Although a hamlet of only about 150 settlers, Lavaca is known for its liquor sales, faro tables, and monte parlors.

Gambling isn't an immediate priority anyway. The men snare trout from the Aquilla Creek and redfish from the nearby bay, while hunting parties stalk the trees to snipe deer and prairie hens. Deerskins are crafted into new clothes and patches for tattered garments and gear. The fly-infested camp isn't a luxury, but it is life.

At least for some. By the time Marshall's main force reaches Lavaca, 26 men in his 280-man regiment are already dead of disease. Many more have been discharged along the route. The only good news is that the rifle shortage is being alleviated by the newly available weapons of those who can no longer fight.[50]

If they see fighting at all, that is. Marshall makes it clear to all in earshot that he feels betrayed. His men certainly know his position. "He swears like a very trooper at the base uses to which, as he calls them, 'his gallant boys' are subjected, and frets in his harness like a wild mustang," comments one volunteer in a September letter to the *Lexington Observer and Reporter*.[51] Vitriol from the troops toward General Taylor will soon lead to duels between officers—including one involving Marshall himself.

The volunteers regard his ambition with their usual combination of bravado and skepticism. "Our colonel seems to think his men are ready to perform a journey as long [as nine hundred miles] again, if we should draw conclusions as to his opinions from the deep dissatisfaction he manifests at being halted on his march to the Rio Grande," writes the trooper turned columnist, who only signs his letter with the initial "J."

It's tempting to assign the writer's identity to Joshua Bean, but that's one person who can be ruled out. When Marshall's men finally break down their tents and march to where a twenty-ton schooner awaits to transport them to Veracruz, the letter writer is with them. Joshua remains

---

50 By the war's end, about fifteen hundred soldiers died of wounds. Nearly eleven thousand were killed by disease.

51 Reprinted in the *Louisville (KY) Daily Courier*, November 7, 1846.

in Lavaca, his certificate of disability effected on October 9, on order of Colonel Marshall. He's been discharged as another invalid trooper.

It's not clear what struck down the hale man—the army at the time was beset with dysentery and a mix of ailments stemming from malnutrition. It's a bad time to contract any illness, since it'll be nearly impossible for Joshua to reconnect with his unit once it sails away to Veracruz. Even a temporary sickness in Lavaca leads to a military discharge, whereas the troopers sickened earlier had time to recuperate and rejoin their companies down the road.

The regiment, and the war, will continue without Joshua Bean. When he's able, he starts the slow, disappointing return to Kentucky.

The dashed former soldier may not have seen it this way, but Joshua's luck may have been with him. There were many dark days ahead for the First Kentucky Volunteer Cavalry, starting with witnessing and contributing to the "Yawning Graveyard" of Veracruz, which held the corpses of fifteen hundred volunteers from various units. There, dysentery was joined by various lethal fevers and a plague of measles to ravage the volunteers at the camp in Camargo. A young officer at the time, George B. McClellan, summed up the plight of the volunteers in a diary. "It is really awful," he wrote in December 1846. "They die like dogs."[52]

But three days before Christmas, when Taylor gathered his forces in the hills south of Saltillo, readying to square off against General Santa Anna, the suffering First Kentucky Volunteer Cavalry marched from Camargo to be there. When the regiment finally saw battle, only 235 of the more than 800 original troops were there to fight.[53]

---

52 Ann Gabbert, "'They Die Like Dogs': Disease Mortality Among U.S. Forces During the U.S.-Mexican War," *Military History of the West*, Spring 2001. McClellan went on to be a Union general in the Civil War, a railroad executive, and the twenty-fourth governor of New Jersey.

53 General Santa Anna attacked Taylor with twenty thousand men at the Battle of Buena Vista in February 1847, leaving around seven hundred Americans dead or wounded at a cost of over fifteen hundred Mexican casualties. The Kentuckians did pretty well, holding together even when forced to retreat.

SAM

Brazito Creek, Mexico (thirty miles north of El Paso del Norte)
December 1846

It's just a slow Christmas Day for the First Missouri Volunteers, meant for watching the staked horses nibble on grass, fishing for the day's meal, or attending to their worn-out gear.

They're still recovering from their trip across the Jornada del Muerto. They survived its ninety waterless miles of desert to reach the village of Doña Ana by breaking the regiment into three parts, preserving the limited resources at the trek's end. Sam moved out with the first group. They marched through sunset, shivering and miserable, and only rested the animals for a few hours before sunrise. There was no wood or animal dung for fires, and the men had no tents anyway. They set a grueling pace of about thirty miles a day, reaching water at Doña Ana in just three days.

The entire regiment reunited near Brazito Creek mere days before the holiday. By then word had come from friendly villagers: a sizable Mexican force was assembling ahead.

Christmas or no, guards are posted outside camp. They're in perfect position to spot a dust cloud on the southern horizon. It signifies that a large force is on the march and, judging by the way it's growing, coming their way. A sentry races to deliver the news to Doniphan, who's playing cards. He stands, eyes the horizon, then insists there's enough time for the officers to finish their hands. The lawyer is never one to miss the chance to make an impression.

Across the camp, bugles blare for assembly. The men realize this isn't a drill—the dust cloud tells them all they need to know—and the gathering is more of a panicked rush. It's not a panic born of fear, but manic excitement. The regiment is forming a battle line regardless of company or commander. Still, they're organized enough to establish a line that not only faces the oncoming troops but bends at each end to prevent flanking attacks from cavalry. As an added defense, Sam Owens and his trading caravan have formed into a circle on the left flank as well, a fortified position to guard against breakthroughs.

That's *Major* Owens now, his having been drafted without legal basis as the head of a "trading battalion." Now the Santa Fe merchants, who left home for profit, are in a pitched battle for the future of two nations.

Sam Bean grips his Springfield 1842 smoothbore with slick palms as men fall in around him. In front of them, hundreds of Mexican troops in bright uniforms are doing the same, assembling before a series of looming buttes. He can see cavalry riding onto the plain on each flank and horses towing a cannon to the center. There must be more than a thousand of them, he reckons, which nearly doubles the number of Missourians. And the Americans have no cannon and few cavalry.

Sam watches as a solitary Mexican soldier rides into the space between them, carrying a black flag. The word quickly filters through the lines—the flag means what they think it does: "No quarter will be given."

The rider with the flag heads back into his lines, and soon the Mexican cannons boom, sending balls skipping harmlessly through the dirt between lines. With a blare of bugles and battle cry, the Mexican infantry and horsemen surge forward all at once. The Mexican commander, General Antonio Ponce de León, has ordered a full-scale attack.

Sam can hear the enemy gunshots sailing over his head, high enough that he doubts one would hit his raised arm. They sound like a swarm of insects passing overhead. But the order comes from nearby officers: "Lay down! Get down!" He throws himself to the ground, feeling a little ridiculous despite the looming danger. But from the wild cheers of the Mexican troops, he understands that they think the Americans are being cut down.

"They advanced closer, and continued to advance, pouring in volley after volley, till the sound of bullets over our heads reminded me of a hail-storm," one private in the battle later writes in his journal.[54]

When the Mexican line is just sixty yards away, another order comes: stand and fire. Sam takes a bead on the mass of rushing soldiers through the crude sight and pulls the trigger. A bloom of acrid smoke, one of hundreds, blinds him. He has no idea if he's killed anyone and doesn't care.

The first volley is devastating. Not only are the rushing Mexican troops surprised by the sudden resurrection of the Americans, but a wall of half-inch balls rips through them without mercy. The Springfields don't have rifled barrels, but their heavy .69-caliber shots are effective out to three hundred yards. The Missourians are much closer than that.

Sam's world is now consumed by one task—reloading. The sequence is familiar from a lifetime of practice: set the gunpowder percussion charge, drop in a ball on top of it, pack it with a ramrod. It's one thing to be able to do this fast enough to shoot three times a minute in training. Here, hands shaking with adrenaline, the air over his head creasing with enemy shots and sucking gunpowder fumes, it's a lot harder.

This is when the superiority of the Americans' firearms becomes bloodily clear. The Mexican army is using smoothbore flintlock muskets, the kind most call Brown Bess. When it is compared to the quickness and reliability of a percussion-lock weapon, the advantage is clearly on the side of the invading Americans.

The second volley is irregular, but the storm of balls rattles through the Mexican center and left, and before most men reload a third time, they see the enemy forces in retreat. The volunteers set after them, howling wildly.

---

54 Robinson, *Journal of the Santa Fe Expedition*, 66–67.

The Mexican cannon can't fire without hitting their own troops, so the Americans overrun the big gun and kill its defenders. One is said to be a female volunteer from El Paso del Norte.

On the American left, the Mexican cavalry sweep around their flank and attack the wagons. Owens and his teamsters fire from their ad hoc fort, driving off the charge. Ponce de León's army retreats in disarray, soon becoming prey to Navajo and Apache warbands who wait nearby to continue their trademark aggression against Mexicans.

The victory is one that couldn't have been hoped for. Seven Missourians have been wounded and none killed. In comparison, the battlefield is littered with an estimated two hundred Mexican dead, with more undoubtedly wounded. In writing about the battle, participants on both sides scratch their heads over how it happened—mixed signals, poor marksmanship, superior weapons, the willingness to fight—but the men of Missouri generally figure with Anglo pride that they're just *better*. Deserving to run Mexico because its being wasted under current management is the bedrock tenet of annexation. This battle is just their latest example.

Sam, like everyone else in the regiment, enjoys the rest of his Christmas Day feasting on captured supplies. The lopsided victory has made them feel invincible.

El Paso Del Norte, Mexico
December 1846

Sam has seen many mountain men in his travels, but very few legends. He can't help but gawk as the Scalp Lord strides through camp, clad in clean white buckskin and riding a beautiful tan-brown Arabian mare. The black leather of the man's "Mexican saddle"[55] and holsters is striking against the pure white clothing—Sam can't understand how the man

---

55 For Sam Bean, this meant the saddle had "a slim, carved poniard case under the leg strap well against the saddle tree. No Mexican went with his knife far from where his hand swung as he rode along." Bloom, "Shadows in Sam's Valley."

has kept his garments so clean on the trail. He grips a Jake Hawken rifle nonchalantly in one hand, the weapon's stock swirled with a complex silver inlay.

A severe, weathered face peers from beneath a floppy Mexican hat. His beard is greyed, more than that of most fifty-four-year-olds. But James Kirker has seen and done a lot in his years to make him age. Just last July, he and more than a hundred volunteers invited an Apache chief identified as Reyes to the town of Galeana, where they enjoyed whiskey together, and then the volunteers slaughtered 148 of the band for their scalps. It's part of his current core business: taking human pelts and selling them to the Mexican government.[56]

Kirker came to Mexico in 1824, marrying a local woman and thereby gaining the right to operate a business. His life since then had become a lucrative mix of trapping, self-promotion, and political maneuvering. Opportunity knocked in the form of a bounty issued by the Mexican government on Native American scalps, particularly after 1844, when the Apache declared a peace treaty null because the Mexican governor who'd signed it was deposed.

Kirker quickly turned his trade from hunting animals for their pelts to skinning people for theirs. The appalling work helped him build a small empire in northern Mexico, where he became "the Terror of the Apache," "the White Barbarian, "the Scalp Lord," "Don Santiago," and, under one newspaper photo at the time, "King of New Mexico." For all that, he arrived at the American camp as a man without a nation—and with a price on his head.

The prior year Kirker had ridden into Chihuahua expecting to be paid $30,000 for scalps that were strung on the poles carried by his horsemen like ornamental flags. Instead of paying him, Governor don Ángel Trías repudiated the claims. There was talk of Kirker's arrest on charges of scalping Mexican peasants (which were likely true). Then Trías tried to enlist

56 Hal Jackson, "Don Santiago Kirker, the King of New Mexico," *Wagon Tracks: Quarterly Publication of the Santa Fe Trail Association* (November 2006).

Kirker to fight with the Mexican army as a colonel, but the mountain man refused; the governor placed a $10,000 bounty on his life. The danger forced him away from his wife, son, and daughter, who were at Corralitos in northwestern Chihuahua.

James Kirker shows up at the volunteers' camp the day after the battle of Brazito, backed by a frontier praetorian guard of six Delaware and Shawnee warriors, to join Doniphan. Kirker's reembrace of the United States will influence Samuel Bean's life in ways he can't currently imagine.

"Here was a man among men," Sam Bean later recalls. "Murderer or no."[57]

The troops are fascinated by the man and his retinue, but Doniphan is not as certain. He assigns Kirker to Captain Thomas Forsythe's platoon of mountain men, a motley crew gathered along the road from Kansas, and quietly tells the captain it's okay to shoot Kirker if he's revealed as a double-dealer.

For his part, Kirker likes the young Missourians. He shows up in journals of officers and common soldiers, using a gritty charm and hard frontier charisma to win respect. It's his knowledge of the terrain that makes him so useful—and that includes the political turf. When Doniphan plans to move into El Paso del Norte, Kirker rides ahead to find that the Mexican army has retreated. He canvasses his contacts there and secures a peaceful surrender. On December 26, a delegation from the city's well-heeled citizenry rides outside of El Paso, where Doniphan and Kirker wait. These prominent residents concede the town, swear allegiance to the United States, and that's that.

When Doniphan marches his men through town, Sam likes very much what he sees of El Paso del Norte. For a city of twelve thousand it's remarkably clean and well tended. He's struck by the trees lining the wide streets, the well-kept homes, the bright dress of the seemingly friendly population who turn out to see them. There are stores and markets, and the

---

57 Sam Bean described his reaction to Kirker, his horse, and his dress in Bloom, "Shadows in Sam's Valley."

men drool thinking of the food and liquor inside. The town's layout winds along the banks of the Rio Grande, and so does their march. The column of weary troops leaves the town, heading south to make camp. Happily, they find their campsite will be amid orchards and lush fields, all fed by a network of irrigated canals from the river.

Doniphan may find himself busy passing decrees and chasing anti-occupation plotters, but for his men this camp becomes a paradise. Sure, there are patrols and house-to-house searches for weapons, and the ever-present threat of a Mexican army rally, but the important thing is that they are stationary and fed. That's not to say there isn't any anti-American sentiment, but there are no rebellions, attacks, or violent confrontations on either side, beyond the knifing of a soldier by another American.

Doniphan encourages local Mexicans to establish a market for his men to purchase goods, but the men are still unpaid and have long ago bartered away anything of value for food or supplies. A bigger success are the balls that Doniphan encourages between his occupation forces and the upper crust of El Paso. No alcohol is served, but the presence of women and promise of rampant gambling are enough to bring in the troops, who spill out of the dance halls into street parties that block traffic. There are few merrier places to ring in 1847 than downtown El Paso de Norte.

On January 5, Kirker and the men of Company A cross paths. Captain Waldo selects a squad to join the famous mountain man for a patrol. They're looking for Mexican patrols or bands of Apache on one hand, and on the other it's a foraging party to seize any stock animal they come across. They spend more than a week prowling the Rio Grande, camping under the stars, and trading their most hair-raising stories. It's more of a sporting trip of gentlemen than a military expedition. One day they spot Mexican soldiers, likely stragglers, and the band of Americans gives an energetic but fruitless chase.[58]

---

58 Ralph Smith, "The 'King of New Mexico' and the Doniphan Expedition," *New Mexico Historical Review* 38 (1963): 39–55.

During this time, Sam Bean is assigned as Kirker's adjunct. On their first meeting, Kirker notes that the private's eyes are shaped like question marks, and they make him look like an owl. Sam decides not to take offense, since the jibing seems to be given without malice. During their time together, Sam calmly defends Doniphan when Kirker vents his frustration with him, earning the respect of the famous mountain man.[59]

In mid-February Doniphan musters the men. They shuffle uncomfortably, wondering what could prompt such a gathering. It's not good news: he tells them that no reinforcements are coming. Now the volunteers have a stark choice. They can wait here for a possible counterattack, or they can march south and take Chihuahua, the goal of the campaign.

Doniphan spells out the situation and does the unthinkable. He puts the decision to a vote. He is a masterful orator, but Doniphan's real skill is reading people. The men choose overwhelmingly to continue to Chihuahua and finish what they started.

Sacramento Pass, Mexico
February 1847

The Missouri volunteers are obviously walking into a trap. Sam is just a private, but the situation is bleakly obvious to him as he marches alongside a supply wagon on the El Paso–Chihuahua Road on February 28. The high terrain ahead is swarmed with Mexican troops, well prepared for the Americans' arrival.

General José Heredia has locked down the road to Chihuahua by sealing off this crucial spot, where it crosses a raised peninsula with a jagged, steep border. The edge traces a dry arroyo route to the Sacramento River and a formidable obstacle for the American army. A long line of breastworks blocks the road itself, connecting steep hills that are now home to four- and nine-pound cannons. Heredia has ten field pieces and six lighter fixed guns to protect these redoubts.

---

59 Bloom, "Shadows in Sam's Valley."

He's also gathered two hundred cavalry, as many infantry, and fourteen hundred volunteer rancheros armed with lances and machetes to repel the invaders. Morale is not an issue—citizens of Chihuahua have melted church bells to make a cannon for this fight. El Paso was an embarrassment, and the Mexican army massed at the Sacramento River is eager for redemption.

Thanks to Heredia's careful positioning, every direction Doniphan can take to cross the river will be met with deadly resistance. The worst option is to just continue along the road, straight into the wolf's teeth. But that's exactly what the First Missouri Volunteers are doing.

Sam licks his lips, huffing dust from the three cavalry companies riding ahead of the regiment's formation. He's happy for the swirling grit—the lines of horses are meant to screen the wagon train from view. The less the Mexicans can see from those heights, the better.

The regiment isn't marching in long lines vulnerable to ambush. Instead, Doniphan has devised something else. The wagons are streaming toward Chihuahua in four columns, with the artillery crews and infantry marching in the gaps between. (The cannons were liberated during the occupation of El Paso and surrounding forts.) Now if Heredia attacks, the men can form the columns into a fortress of wagons.

Sam feels like a small part of a very large moment. History will be made here today, one way or the other. And if there's one thing the young man has learned during his time out west as a soldier, the closer you are to history, the less your life is worth.

Sam jumps when the order is given, maybe because he's been expecting it. The column suddenly breaks west, increasing pace to gain distance from the looming fortifications. The regiment swings south, heading for their safe spot (out of range of the enemy cannons) at the top of the raised peninsula. There's no easy way up, though. Sam and the other soldiers put their backs into cutting down the steep banks of the arroyo with shovels, then pushing the wagons up the newly created inclines.

Now atop the peninsula, the American army reforms into a battle line, with the artillery standing in front of the infantry and Owens's trading caravan and supply wagons circled in the rear. Sam finds himself on the right wing. The enemy probably thought we were running, he thinks, but they know better now. Indeed, he sees the Mexican cavalry arriving to face them on this plateau, soon joined by artillery and infantry, ready to push them off.

The cannon across from them barks. The three pieces of the nearest hilltop battery are also vaulting cannonballs their way. Sam watches the incoming cannonballs fly with a sick fascination. It's got to be some trick of the light and background, but he and the others can clearly see the balls sail through the air. He sees groups of volunteers ease out of the way of incoming shots in almost comic displays of nimbleness. After watching this, he finds the artillery less daunting.

And then comes the charge, Mexican infantry and cavalry leaping forward with rallying cries. The charge only withstands three volleys from the Missourians' cannons before faltering. Broken men and horses litter the ground as the charge staggers to a halt. The next volley routs them, and the infantry and cavalry stream back to the redoubts. This is only good news until Heredia's cannons on the plateau take advantage of the clean shots, and they again come alive.

But now the American cannon crews are returning fire. Sam has a front-row seat to an artillery duel. The battery, commanded by Meriwether Lewis Clark (the son of explorer William Clark), vaults shots at the artillery and infantry guarding it. Sam watches in disgust as cannonballs detonate harmlessly in the air, far from their targets. But others are landing true, enough to leave still and writhing men in their wake.

Sam hears a boom from the opposing side and sees the cannonball tear well over his head. He cranes his neck to watch it skip into the assembly of wagons, killing a mule. A nearby blast from the American battery whips his head around again, just in time to see the bloom of dirt and debris rise around a now wrecked enemy cannon. The duel lasts an hour before the Mexican troops fall back to their fortifications.

Now it's time to take the redoubts. Doniphan gives the order, and

Waldo gives his men their objective: they're to silence the three cannons on the hilltop. The men assemble, steeling their nerves and staring at the defenses facing them. It'll be an exposed dash to the foot of the escarpment and a vulnerable climb to fight for the summit.

As Sam watches, a line of cavalry winds up toward the redoubt on its own. It's Captain Thomas Reid and his troopers, acting without orders (or, at best, unclear ones). Another figure is riding at their forefront, wearing a bright white shirt and charging heedlessly to the very brink of the Mexican battery. And then he's swallowed by gun smoke. When it clears, he and the horse are dead. Reid's men struggle at the hilltop before seeing that they've charged alone, and then retreat.

Now Waldo commands Company A to charge. Sam's feet seem to act on their own as they propel him closer and closer to the dangers above. The banks are steep, but when the troops above do shoot, they stick the barrels of their long guns over the side and fire blindly. Company A labors up the incline, unscathed.

Still, there's no avoiding the infantry when they get to the top. Luckily, many are armed only with machetes. Sam Bean faces a medieval hand-to-hand fight, but against men with little training and plunging morale. Pistol shots ring at close range, the long guns are swung like clubs, knives plunge into desperate masses of struggling men. In a span of minutes, Sam and the men of Company A are exhausted, blood spattered, and victorious. They've beaten off the Mexican defenses without any loss of life.

Attacks on Mexican positions elsewhere end in similar successes. Three hundred dead Mexican troops lie scattered on the peninsula and hilltops. Amazingly, there are scores of American wounded but only one death. While taking in the view of the battlefield from the hard-earned redoubt, Sam hears the news. The man riding into battle in the white shirt was Samuel C. Owens.

The theories are already flying. The most charitable holds that Owens was taken with martial zeal and charged the lines with the cavalry. The less flattering one is that he wore bright white and rode into the guns because he was suicidal over his daughter's scandalous behavior.[60]

Sam listens to the stories about Owens's death with interest. He's certain that James Bean will want to hear the particulars. After all, if you believe the rumors, the justice of the peace may have helped kill Sam Owens when he signed Fannie's marriage into existence.

60 For example, Santa Fe trader James Webb writes in a memoir that one of Owens's men told him that the major probably courted death because of "family troubles." Webb, *Adventures in the Santa Fe Trade, 1844–1847*, 274.

JAMES

Pawnee Fork, Kansas
May 15, 1847

James Bean has done everything right to make his trip down the Santa Fe Trail a success. He's gathered his stock during the winter and aligned himself with experienced outfits in Independence and St. Louis to make a joint trip. With the war still on but the road to Santa Fe open, leaving early was a priority, and he was able to organize himself for an April departure of his trade caravan of fifteen wagons and thirty-four men.

It's becoming clear that his calculation included two large mistakes. One was disregarding the low temperature, which has sapped his team's energy and enthusiasm from the day the group left Independence. The other was forgetting that the spring rains can create impassible rivers from what should have been dry creek beds.

On May 15, James finds his wagon train one of several stranded on the riverbank. Among the discussions during the wait for the water to recede at Pawnee Fork are distressing reports about the latest Indian attacks. Things are getting worse. American travelers have already been assaulted and killed, and some are saying that a force of more than a thousand Indian warriors is gathering along the Arkansas River.

There's not much to be done except be vigilant. James's caravan is large enough to ward off a small band, but it would be helpless against such an overwhelming attack. So they circle the wagons, set guards to watch the oxen tied to stakes in the grass, and pray for the river to calm down.

His companions include Thomas Hereford, a doctor from St. Louis. He's also new to the trail, as he makes plain in a letter he writes from the road to his wife, Margaret. "I have two excellent men and good drivers. You would be astonished to see how well I get along. I have kept my temper well. The weather has been extremely cold since we left & I have worked harder than I ever did. Can drink a quart of coffee and thirst for more, I am dirty and ragged but think it is the best way of regaining health to remain so."[61]

Luckily, there are more experienced wagon hands than Bean and Hereford in this train, including those who operate the freighters of the established St. Louis firm of Bullard, Hooks and Co. Of the Independence men, Thomas G. Clarkson, a thirty-two-year-old property owner with three children and four slaves at home, is the most seasoned. Clarkson becomes the Independence trains' go-to guy on all things trail-related. It's embarrassing for James to defer to the two-man teamster crews, and besides, many of these hired hands are new to wagon travel as well.

James has left a young family in Missouri—his newest child, Leon, was born earlier in the year—and a growing footprint in the county. In 1846, he bought farmland outside the city, the next step in becoming the model citizen of Independence, in other words a successful trader and civic-minded landowner. He deeded a parcel to his father-in-law, Sam Carson.

Samuel Owens may be gone, but his mercantile spirit lives on. The war has not shut down the Santa Fe Trail; the stream of military troops and supplies makes it busier than ever. And with American occupation of

---

61 Thomas A. Hereford to his wife, Margaret Hereford, written at Diamond Springs, Kansas, letter dated May 17, 1847, courtesy of the Manuscript Collection WN 1385, Huntington Library Art Collections and Botanical Gardens, San Marino, CA.

Santa Fe, there's never been a better time for the traders to unload goods there—and to scope out the chances to build something more.

Gunshots and screams break James from his reverie. He dashes toward the sounds, which come from a nearby pasture where he knows the oxen are tied. Dozens of men are milling around, long guns and rifles at the ready, staring into the bush. Indians, he's told. A band snuck into camp, trying to snatch the animals. If the guards hit any with gunfire, the Indians took their wounded away.

Clarkson gets a description from the guards. He frowns when he hears that several had large feather bonnets and carried fourteen-foot war lances. They sound like Arapaho or Cheyenne warriors, and he can count on them to remain aggressive.

Without an actual fight, it's hard to gauge their intentions. Those lances are sharp, their stone tips having long ago been replaced with metal. They can be lethal weapons when jabbed, usually one-handed, into a buffalo or a person. But they're also the tool of choice for "counting coup"—getting close enough to an intruder to touch them (without causing harm) as an act of bravery. The real issue here is that the Arapaho and Cheyenne believe that stealing an enemy's horse or livestock is an act of bravery equal to counting coup, which the enraged traders say is just a way to justify base thievery. Losing animals is a threat to their livelihoods as well as their lives.

James is no grizzled Indian fighter, and he wants to know what they can expect. Clarkson predicts that the small groups of braves will go for the animals and that the chances of a massacre are remote. They will try to steal or bluff some supplies from the traders with martial displays, but even these awkward encounters usually end with a bribe or a mutually advantageous deal. Stealing livestock is not only an accepted military practice, but now a practical way to survive.

Clarkson has only previous experience to guide him, which is of limited use because things are changing on the Great Plains. The caravan doesn't know it, but they've ventured out on the Santa Fe Trail just as it's becoming a low-intensity war zone. Native Americans here are realizing the extent of the American push westward—the scope of the ambition and the amount of damage being done. The ongoing slaughter of buffalo and loss of land has already pushed tribes into each other, causing warfare and even more displacement. But now, all the tribes of the Great Plains—Kiowa, Pawnee, Cheyenne, Comanche, and Arapaho—have formed ad hoc alliances to jointly harass the Santa Fe wagon trains.[62]

James and the traders finally continue across the Pawnee Fork and rattle southeast, crossing Little Coon Creek and the larger Racoon Creek by late afternoon. A trail caravan always crosses a stream before making camp, since oxen won't easily wade into water in the morning. (This is wagon train gospel.) It's easier to accommodate them than lashing the animals into cooperating.

The creek is a good place to camp, so the men form a circle with the wagons and place the oxen inside, light buffalo dung campfires, and watch with amusement as Dr. Hereford as usual helps to prepare chow, proud of how he's learning the recipes. Despite the hard ground and lingering uncertainty, exhaustion brings sleep quickly.

Big Racoon Creek, Kansas
May 19, 1847

James Bean knows there's something terribly wrong even before he opens his eyes. There are the distinct sounds of panic inside the wagon camp: shuffling feet, profane swears, openly uttered prayers, guns loaded.

He gazes at the ground near their camp to see the stuff of Missouri nightmares: hundreds upon hundreds of Indians have formed their own ring around the camp. The traders are completely surrounded and pathetically outnumbered.

Clarkson has already gotten a head count—seven hundred Comanche and Arapaho, four hundred of them bearing long lances. More than enough to storm the camp and cut down the thirty-four men guarding it. The threat of a few firearms will do nothing to deter the warriors; their

62 During the summer of 1847, bands of Kiowas, Apaches, Pawnees, and Comanches killed forty-seven Americans on the Santa Fe road.

bows are just as effective at the same ranges. Hell, it'd take cannons to even begin to even the odds.

The teamsters take defensive positions among the wagons, and the captains huddle. Clarkson admits he's never seen anything like this. Obviously, if they wanted the traders dead and their goods stolen, it could have happened already. They must want something else or at least are uncertain about what to do. No one has come to parley, which is just as well. With the numbers of warriors assembled, it would be more like blackmail or a call for surrender than a negotiation. "They're testing us," Clarkson says.

He reasons that, numbers aside, the motives for this demonstration are the same as for any other: the warriors want to gain honor and steal livestock. That means launching attacks that will be less than a full-scale assault. If the traders don't regain some initiative, the situation could get out of hand. The traders could end up captured for ransom or be killed and left to rot.

The siege drags on for two days. James Bean has never felt such gut-wrenching fear, and it only gets worse as the hours drag on and the war band acts more aggressively. Handfuls of warriors charge them on horseback, only to retreat with whoops that set his teeth on edge. These half-hearted assaults stoke James's anger at being victimized. All he sees around them are marauders who want to steal his future.

On the third day, a band of young Comanche and Arapaho form up, rallying each other with a fervor that makes the traders ready their weapons. Then they charge, unaffected by the gunshots aimed at them, sweeping directly into camp between gaps in the wagons. Ignoring the people, they immediately start pulling the stakes holding the oxen and driving dozens of them out of the protective circle.

Clarkson charges the warriors who've penetrated their makeshift wagon fort, unhorsing a young brave with his hands. After the warrior is pinned by the other traders, Clarkson aims for another, throws him down, and disarms him.

James now gets a close look at their foes. The pair are younger than he realized. Blue tattoos are traced across their arms and chests, which are bare under buckskin vests. These details confirm them as Arapaho.

Their breechcloths are drawn between the legs and tied around the waist. Necklaces dangle from their necks, and twin braids fall from their heads. Their faces are carefully stony, but he can tell from their eyes that they're frightened—and shifty.

When one of the young men makes a break for it, James Bean is ready. The brave only travels a few steps before a rifle barks, and the youth sprawls to the ground, motionless. The report carries, and everyone inside the wagon fort tenses, shooting James Bean murderous looks. If there's a reprisal, it will come now.

Instead, it seems the bounty of oxen and the loss of two braves have given the Arapaho reason to reconsider the siege. The mass of horsemen retreat, enabling the wagon to move on.

This incident has been recorded in precious few places, but the details all agree that Clarkson took two prisoners singlehandedly and James C. Bean shot one. Still, a report casts some doubt on certain facts; it came from a famous frontiersman, Alexander Barclay, who crossed paths with the trader just days later. In his diary, he wrote that "Bean annoyed by Indians and killed one Arapaho."[63]

The truth, like the identity of the executed Arapaho, is lost to history. But it should be noted that the next time the Arapaho saw the other captured prisoner, he was in good health, set free from the traders' camp wrapped in a new blanket.[64]

Fort Mann, Kansas
May 29, 1847

The wagon train never expected much from Fort Mann. It was only established in April, as more of a government-run waystation than a military

---

63 George Hammond, *The Adventures of Alexander Barclay Mountain Man,* Fred Rosenstock Old West Publishing Company, January 1976, 148. The book contains Barklay's diary.

64 Lewis Hector Garrard, *Wah-to-yah and the Taos Trail* (H. W. Derby & Company, 1850): 316.

base. And indeed, it's just four flat-roofed houses connected by fifteen-foot, slanted walls of timber, encasing an area just sixty feet in diameter.

It seems pathetically small compared to the new neighbors, a city of tipis that has somehow grown three hundred yards away. And when they get closer, James can tell by bitter experience that the tribe here is Arapaho, the same that harassed his caravan. Some of the tipi peaks are higher than twelve feet; the taller the tipi, the more horses its owner must have to move it, and the wealthier they are. Arapaho villages are entirely mobile and can pack up to relocate within an hour.

The traders are incensed. Once the military hears what happened, maybe they'll use that cannon and some soldiers to burn the village to the ground. That's their mood not just after the three-day siege, but following a week of harassment along the road. The Comanche and Arapaho trailed them, getting uncomfortably close and backing away, a mental torture that only ended after seventy miles, when the Comanche and Arapaho warriors melted away.

Now the Arapaho are back, and smugly settled next to the American fort that the traders had hoped would protect them. But the traders have been diplomatically outmaneuvered.

The wagons encamp and the captains walk inside Fort Mann's two-foot-thick wooden gates, perched on wooden hinges. Thomas Sloan is there to greet them, ready to relate the fort's sad story.

Sloan is the post's blacksmith, put in command of the fifty men here—teamsters, not soldiers—after his superior left just a week following his arrival. The outpost is thinly garrisoned, badly supplied, and was harassed by Indians during construction. Truth be told, his men have been in a worse bind than the traders since they are a stationary target.

May has been a violent month here. Comanche raiding parties attacked the fort's animal pens, forcing a stampede that drove away fifteen oxen and forty mules. The same war band also lanced one soldier to death while he was fishing. And then the Arapaho arrived.

There were just ten of them at first, Sloan says, and they did their best to run off stock. The troops saw them coming and rolled their six-pound cannon to the gate and took defensive positions. In a sudden but not surprising turn of heart, the Arapaho offered to parley, expressing friendship and asking for food and tobacco. It was a classic tactic for a scouting party.

Yesterday, they learned who those Arapaho were scouting for: Chief Warratoria and his entire village. He's a great diplomat of the plains. At this moment he's in an alliance with the Cheyenne, operating under a new pact with the Comanche to support raids on caravans and under treaty with the Americans. Cooperation with the whites has not been working, but open warfare is suicide. So Warratoria is trying a carrot-and-stick approach—raids on one hand, peace on the other.

Warratoria is playing a dangerous game. Raiding alleviates the pressure felt by his frustrated people, keeps tribes from killing each other, and may give leverage with the Americans. It can also bring extermination. So he's let his warriors freely raid with the Comanche, but he also seems to have put some limits on their actions to avoid retaliation. It's the best reason why the siege didn't end with the slaughter of James Bean's caravan; that was never the intention.

Bringing the entire village to Fort Mann was a stroke of genius. Overnight, the fort has become the temporary home to three hundred Indians in eighty lodges, and an estimated eleven hundred mules, oxen, and horses. Women, children, and dogs pose no threat, yet the sheer numbers gathered are a show of strength.

There's someone else inside Fort Mann—a government employee named Lewis Garrard. A new arrival (as of May 15), he devotes himself to keeping a log of events. He was also on hand when the Indian chief arrived at Fort Mann's gate. "When Warratoria came, he was admitted though Sloan much distrusted him," he says. "I made his acquaintance in the Comanche village [in a prior visit] and I knew his friendly disposition toward the whites, and the good effect it would have to treat with him in confidence. Shaking hands as old friends, and inviting him into the mess room, we sat before him coffee, bread and the long pipe."[65]

The day after, the soldiers at the fort could hear the celebration over the return of the traders' young prisoner. The captured raider's presence is direct proof of Warratoria's double game of raiding and civility.

The Santa Fe traders simply can't believe what they're hearing. There's a cannon nearby and a tribe of hostile Indians. Surely there's a way for the men at Fort Mann to back the traders in some attempt at restitution—or revenge. Sloan won't hear of it. There will be no trouble tolerated between the village and the fort. They are barely hanging on as it is; there's no way Sloan is risking his men for the sake of stolen oxen. The team captains return to their camp, seething, but they do agree to sell Sloan six gallons of whiskey.

At three in the afternoon, a US military wagon train pulls up to the fort. It's in bad shape, to no one's surprise. The unskilled drivers hired by the government lose about three times the oxen and wagons on trips as an experienced private sector Santa Fe trader; government contracts have already adopted penalties for excessive losses. This "rickety" (Garrard's word) and poorly supplied train has been harassed by Comanche who not only stole oxen during raids, but also hamstringed animals they couldn't take. "One well proportioned six-footer proposed, with the cannon, 'to rake the village,'" relates Garrard. "We at once refused the use of our gun—and told them they should take it by force alone."

Massacre averted, both caravans leave the next day, the traders westbound and the government train heading east, taking all but ten of Fort Mann's teamsters with them. Warratoria's village also departs, leaving a spooky silence over the outpost. Soon they'll repel a concerted attack by three hundred Comanche warriors by spraying them with grapeshot from

---

65 Quotes in this section from Lewis Hector Garrard are from his book *Wah-to-yah and the Taos Trail* (H. W. Derby & Company, 1850): 310–18.

the six-pound cannon. Sloan's men will endure privation and sporadic attacks until June, when they'll abandon the outpost.

James's caravan moves in twin columns, a defensive posture that is soon proven to be needed as Comanches appear. The harassing raids resume and last a week. After that, the weary caravan moves into the Jornada del Muerto, light on oxen. The remaining animals are worn out from hauling heavy loads and move slowly, a signal to anyone watching that these traders are an easy target. Indeed, packs of brigands appear while the train is crossing the desert, and the wagons must stay in their double-line defensive formation and post guards all night.

But it's the environment, not bandits, that takes its toll on the wagon train. By the time they reach water at the Point of Rocks, they've left the carcasses of twenty oxen along the trail. The traders have no option but to stagger onward with their remaining beasts.

It takes until the end of June for them to reach Santa Fe. They find a city embroiled in commerce and hedonism. The occupation under Sterling Price, now a brigadier general, has degenerated into what a correspondent for the *Independence (MO) Expositor* who's there in late July calls "the most miserable state of society that exists upon the globe."[66]

There's gambling everywhere the soldiers make camp, and whiskey flows whenever they can get it, so that's no different. But the sight of exposed flesh has put the good men from Independence on edge and influences them to cross gentlemanly lines. "Lewdness in both sexes exhibits itself in the most glaring and shameless forms," sniffs the *Expositor.*

Now that the front lines have moved south, the soldiers are enjoying the loose atmosphere of occupation, maybe too much. "There are many

66 The item from Mexico was reprinted in the *Palmyra (MO) Weekly Whig*, September 16, 1847. Price was elected to the US House of Representatives in 1844. He resigned from Congress and accepted a commission as colonel of the Second Regiment, Missouri Infantry. Colonel Price put down a rebellion against the American occupation of Santa Fe in January 1847. He became Missouri's governor soon after the events related here.

of the officers and privates who are gentlemen and hold themselves aloof from the vices and dissipation that are so contagious, of which the atmosphere seems composed," the *Expositor* correspondent describes breathlessly. "But alas! For the large majority, they have expended more than the amount of their wages and are, indeed, a reckless, ragamuffin band."

Those who worked commercial freighters have no officers to sneer at them. Santa Fe has become a warren of Mexican merchants, cash-rich teamsters, sodden occupation soldiers, leering prostitutes, accommodating barkeeps, and gambling den operators. It takes weeks amid the chaos for James Bean to secure his wares in warehouses and negotiate deals to vend them.

He's plotting a trip home—this time he'll be joining a military convoy that should arrive in early September—when news comes from the capital. Winfield Scott has captured Mexico City.

SAM

New Orleans, Louisiana
June 1847

The First Missouri Mounted has been discharged. The newspapers are ranking its three-thousand-mile-mile trek as one of the most successful marches in military history. There will be balls and parades ahead. And how do the bulk of the released men celebrate? With a trip to the slave market.

Sam Bean recoils from slavery—as he's gotten older, his distaste has grown. He sees no point wallowing in that misery. Instead, he walks back down to the docks, where the military boats are being loaded. He's not alone; James Morton falls into step with him. He was an assistant surgeon with the First Missouri, where the men called him Young Doc Morton.[67]

There's only one direction Sam can go: on a steamship to St. Louis, and then on to Independence. The thought of this seems empty; he has

67 "James F. Morton," National Park Service, U.S. Mexican War Soldiers & Sailors Database, https://www.nps.gov/paal/learn/historyculture/search-usmexwar-detail.htm?id=sv37655. Sam Bean recalled his postrelease dockside stroll and its result to Maude Bloom in her unpublished manuscript, "Shadows in Sam's Valley," the source for the quotes in this passage.

family there, but he's never considered it home. His time in Mexico with Doniphan exposed him to an entire new universe, one of adobe walls, mysterious mountains, trade-worn roadways, and untapped potential.

The pair saunter to where the horses and mules are being loaded on a ship bound for Veracruz. "Poor beasts," says Sam, thinking of the animals' brutal lives ahead in the swamps and deserts of Mexico.

But Doc Morton's mind is going in a different direction. He fixes his companion with a frank stare. "I'll go back if you will."

The suggestion hits Sam like a jab to the nose. It's absurd—reenlist in the regular army, don a uniform, and head back into occupied Mexico? Turning their backs on American civilization sounds crazy, but the appeal is obvious now that it's been proposed, given the enslaved masses, crowded cities, and ruthless competition here.

Morton sees the choice made in Sam's face and knows him well enough to not wait for him to speak. "Well, shall we?"

Reenlisting is as easy as finding an officer and hopping on board one of the Mexico-bound ships. There's no time to be issued a uniform. The pair disembark at the mouth of the Rio Grande, where they take a series of wood-fired river steamers upriver. At night the crews and passengers go ashore and sleep under the stars, pestered by gnats and flies. Leaving the ship at San Elizario, Sam Bean and Doc Morton make their way to El Paso.

Here, their impromptu partnership ends. Sam's made a quartermaster sergeant, assigned to run a supply depot on a roadway on the outskirts of the city. He'll be working there alone—Morton is stationed in Santa Fe. Doc rode with him to the depot (with eight others). Sam watches them recede once he reaches the old corral, which was used by Americans during the Doniphan expedition.

He finds it littered with broken wagons, busted harnesses, and worn-out mules and horses. Instead of being disheartened, he sees a chance to fix the place up. His Santa Fe Trail experience is more useful than his soldiering, and he likes it that way.

Sam reaches out to the locals of El Paso. First on his list is Don

Guadalupe Miranda, a known friend to Americans who famously saved a group of invading Texans and local merchants from being massacred in Taos in 1841.

The pair chat in English and find a mutual respect. Like many, Miranda has a bifurcated view of Americans. "I tell my friends, be disposed to keep the eye open to distinguish between a Yanque and our ancient enemies, the Tejano," Miranda tells him. "Not yet has any Yanque been faithless to his word, although they may lack many other qualities one might desire. But as to Tejanos, there is a different breed. Wild cruel men."

Sam waits for the man's verdict. "You, my young friend, are a Yanque."

JAMES

Independence, Missouri
November 1847

The city is asking, What has happened to Squire Bean? Since his return from the Santa Fe Trail, the JP hasn't performed any wedding ceremonies. His last was in April 1846, just before his trip west. Maybe he feels less sentimental after experiencing the violence of the trail, including his killing of an unarmed man. Or maybe he's stung by the Owens affair, which has only grown in prominence.

The accused murderer, Sam Owens's son-in-law John Harper, was captured and is facing trial. None other than Sam Bean's former commander, Alexander Doniphan, a new national hero, is defending him. Promising to be a sensational case, it will be held in Platte County after Doniphan argued successfully for a change of venue from Jackson County.

James Bean is not retreating from Independence, however, and is actually pondering new ways to extend his influence. Buying a newspaper seems a logical step, both financially and to increase his public stature. On its pages, he can advocate for the local traders, deliver news for them, and assert himself into Democratic politics. He's already prowling town for a new business partner. And he's got another vision of purchasing farmland outside town, where he can raise his family.

The Harper trial begins in late November, playing to a packed courtroom. The military hero argues a passionate but strange defense based on the court accepting that infidelity was a crime, which basically sanctions Harper's act. When the accused is found not guilty on November 25, a crowd carries Doniphan out of the courthouse on their shoulders.[68]

Please, James Bean prays, let this be the end of the scandal.

68 *Columbia (MO) Herald-Statesman*, November 26, 1847; and Greg Maynard, "Alexander William Doniphan, the Forgotten Man from Missouri" (master's thesis, Brigham Young University, 1973).

JOSHUA

Near Veracruz, Mexico
November 1847

After ten hot days spent camping outside Veracruz, the Third Kentucky Volunteer Infantry is finally marching toward Mexico City on November 26. It's a moment of extreme danger: guerilla bands have struck the National Road supply line with regularity, targeting marching columns with horsemen who melt away after an attack. With no matching cavalry, the US forces can't hope to catch them.

Private Joshua Bean is finally facing the enemy in Mexico. Feeling stung by his early exit from the war, he's back in uniform, this time in the infantry. He mustered into another year's commitment with the Third Kentucky Volunteers, Company D.

He's not expecting glory. The war continues as the diplomats flail, but all the major fighting is done. The company's assignment will be garrison duty, securing the capital so that realistic peace talks can happen. With the Mexican military shattered, the nation lost the stabilizing role it played, and rebellions and political upheaval follow. The United States does not want to occupy all of Mexico and does not want to see it ruined—the US needs a central government to negotiate a deal, demarcate the terrain it has won, and enable the pullout from bandit- and guerilla-infested central Mexico. In the meantime, soldiers fall to crippling bouts of fever and diarrhea. Men are swilling cayenne pepper tea in efforts to sweat out the sickness.

The Third Kentucky Volunteers are marching behind Major John C. Breckinridge, a Lexington lawyer who comes from a well-connected but indebted family.[69] So far, he's appeared to the troops as both humane and capable, a mix they appreciate. Breckinridge has been spotted letting sick soldiers ride his horse as he walks alongside.

Joshua doesn't like what he's seen from the quartermasters here in Mexico, however. This morning, when the men assembled, they discovered that the wagons only had four days' rations for a trip that could take a month. The men are assured that more wagons are following and that there are supply caches along the way to Mexico City. At two p.m. the troops finally start their march from the coast through central Mexico.

By day three the men are pleased to climb onto an elevated plain and reach the main, thirty-foot-wide artery of the National Road. "The road is as hard as our paved roads," notes one soldier in the Third Kentucky Volunteers, Captain Leander Cox. "I am not certain it has been paved with cement or hardened by long travel and the action of the sun upon [the] soil." Later he'll marvel at the road's drainage and stone and brick bridges, calling it "a masterpiece of public improvement."[70]

The landscape has few trees, scrawny thickets that stand among the wide mats of chaparral. Some of the gently swelling hills have ranches on top and a few seemingly temporary seasonal structures. And among them, nearly a hundred horsemen, observing the column below. It's the soldiers' first glimpse of the guerillas they all fear, but the men keep their distance and eventually vanish. The sick volunteers march even when their

---

69 He's also the future Democratic vice president under James Buchanan.

70 Charles Hinds, "Mexican War Journal of Leander M. Cox," *Register of the Kentucky Historical Society* 55, no. 3 (July 1957).

stomachs are rebelling, risking dehydration with each step. But becoming a straggler is an invitation to fall prey to the guerillas.

The men make camp at a creek called the San Juan, the first military waystation of many on the road ahead. The night brings alarms by nervous guards. Mexican army irregulars have proven adept at accessing American camps to steal livestock or quietly kill isolated guards. Paranoia quickly becomes routine. "We expect an alarm tonight as usual," Captain Cox writes. "The men will occasionally shoot & you can't find out the man."

The military occupation here in central Mexico under Winfield Scott is very different than the one handled by Zachary Taylor's men up north. Scott wields better discipline, leading to fewer atrocities and better overall relations.[71] But the guerillas in the south are professional, mobile, and well organized. In the summer, they all but shut down the American supply lines around Mexico City, prompting Scott to dedicate bigger escorts and more guards for the wagons.

On the morning of November 28, the column of Kentucky volunteers is winding across a bend in the road eleven miles from San Juan when gunfire erupts ahead. The regiment's lieutenant colonel, Thomas Crittenden, calls to the men, "Close up and front face!" The Kentuckians shuffle into a line, clutching their rifles in trembling anticipation. Joshua Bean has waited his entire military career for a moment like this, standing in a battle line to face the enemy and to hear the commanders firm up their troops with calls to "stand firm, every man to his place."

The men pass the word through the lines: the soldiers at the tip of the column spooked a deer and chased it off with a hail of balls. They'd been ordered not to fire until instructed, and Colonel Crittenden is furious. "The Col. was very indignant & intended to punish the men responsible, but I believe he never ascertained who they were," writes Cox.

---

71 An 1847 massacre and mass rape by US troops at Puebla is one very notable exception. As revenge for the outrages there, four thousand guerillas descended on the city in October and trapped Colonel Thomas Childs and his men for weeks.

Joshua is disappointed and relieved. Even if a skirmish occurred and he were killed, would anyone in the United States notice or care? The war is slipping from the national attention, except for divisions over the way to end it. Occupation is already proving to be all risk and no reward.

Río Frío, Mexico
December 1847

The Third Kentucky Volunteers can now gripe like seasoned veterans. They have a lot to complain about this morning, December 17. The pork that the regiment bought in Puebla has spoiled, and beef has been hard to come by. Now the men hear that the quartermaster slew some cattle, but there's no time to cook it for breakfast.

Rations have been thin, the weather frigid, and the men dying of sickness. There have been no enemy attacks, which is just as well because many soldiers are too weak to fight.

Today's march, made while the men are hungry, offers sights that stagger Joshua Bean with their dramatic beauty. He knows *río* means "river," but the Frío proves to only be an unimpressive stream. Still, the mountain pass it flows through fills him with awe. Sheer walls rise on either side, thick with pines, cedars, and firs. The column is moving between the peaks of two volcanoes, both of which can be seen by the men gawking below. As Joshua watches, smoke curls from the active caldera of one of them.

The column walks steadily uphill as the regiment follows the Frío upstream and then through a pass. Through it is the great valley of Tenochtitlan. The massive plateau is covered in lesser peaks, cultivated fields, and the occasional lake. Blocked by a small mountain range is Mexico City, once the capital of the Aztec empire, target of Cortés and his native allies, new-world headquarters of the Napoleon family, seat of the Mexican national government, and currently under the control of the United States of America.

Now the march becomes a steep descent into the valley. The men find a spot near a lake and bed down, having cleared twenty-five miles of the steep terrain. The worst of the march to their post is over. The next day, they'll tramp "to the very gates of the city, it's domes, spires and trees in full view."[72] The city is a busy but war-battered metropolis of more than two hundred thousand residents.

Mexico City is mostly pacified when Joshua arrives. That means the soldiers who get killed are the ones who go off alone to drink or find prostitutes. Otherwise, it's a daily routine of military discipline mixed with the occasional foray to see something interesting. There are arrests and false alarms, but Mexico City remains relatively tranquil compared with the rest of Mexico.

The real action is happening behind closed doors. Scott has implemented a new tax that's targeted at the revenue still streaming to the exiled Mexican government. This policy has had the dual effect of hitting some of the elite in their personal pocketbooks, and more importantly impairing their ability to raise funds to support resistance.

The regiment finds itself quartered inside offices, barracks, and monasteries, any public building where they fit. They quickly learn how Scott runs things here. There are drills every morning, and the officers surprise the men with sudden roll call assemblies.

Joshua is impressed with Scott's organization and oversight of the lower ranks. He's established a standardized system, with each regiment assigning a captain of the day, who wanders the men's quarters for signs of disorder, inspects the mess to keep it clean, runs the drills, and counts the men during roll calls. The responsibility is clearly assigned but shared over time.

The harsh discipline meted out to soldiers who report to duty drunk, desert to become city policemen, or assault citizens is passed from soldier to soldier and written about in the English-language newspapers being printed in occupied Mexico City, the *North American* and the *American*

---

72 Hinds, "Mexican War Journal of Leander M. Cox."

Star. Percy Doyle, the British chargé d'affaires who's there at the time, notes that the troops have a "rough character" but behave well: "General Scott has made severe examples, which seems to have had a most salutary effect."[73]

73 Piercy Doyle, Jan 13, 1848, *Dispatches to Palmerson,* as cited in Thomas Spahr, "Occupying For Peace, The U.S. Army In Mexico, 1846–1848," The Ohio State University, 2011, 264.

SAM

El Paso Del Norte, Mexico

January 1848

As the months go by, Sam realizes that the army has forgotten about him. No one's come by to make use of the depot, deliver supplies, or deliver a report. Or deliver any pay, for that matter. Sam reckons that his being assigned guard duty here was a gesture by a bored quartermaster officer, two hundred miles away.[74]

By the time he reaches these conclusions, it doesn't matter. He wears civilian clothes like those of the locals: a short-sleeved hickory shirt, stone-washed jeans, and hand-sewn moccasins. His blond hair grows shaggy. He's content to run the depot, which doesn't see a military visitor for five months.

Sam doesn't miss the company of his crass army brethren; he much prefers the Mexican residents and travelers whom he interacts with on a day-to-day basis. He now sees a distinct difference between the *ricos* who ran the nation and the rest of the Mexican people. Immersed alone in

---

74 These thoughts are contained in Maude Bloom's "Shadows in Sam's Valley" and appear to have come straight from her interviews with Sam Bean. The direct quotes in this chapter are also from this source, which is an unpublished manuscript.

El Paso, he's exposed to viewpoints that might shock his comrades back home. Sam now has sympathy for Mexican patriots, even foes like Governor Ángel Trías and General José de Urrea, who are still attempting to muster forces against the Americans. No matter what happens as this war ends, Sam can see what lies ahead for the region: a new territory where slavery is legal. More greedy *ricos*, but this time ones hell-bent on replacing working men with human cattle.

This tour with the army has shown him a different face of the conflict. "It wasn't a war us common men had any stomach for," Sam will later say. "A wholesale Texan land grab that kept getting more and more plain the longer we stayed."

Sam is content but conflicted. He can't think of a more pleasant place to serve as a soldier—that is, if he still is one. When army troops finally do visit, the run-ins are ugly and humiliating. One colonel asked if he was an American, doubted his word, and said he looked like a "renegade." Visiting soldiers tell him that the nickname for this forlorn supply depot is "the morgue." The encounters reinforce Sam's feeling of isolation, from the army and from the United States.

He finds it hard to admit, but what Sam wants to do is simply desert. This seems incomprehensible for a Doniphan man to consider, but he knows it's true. Sam asks himself what he'd do if ordered to pick up arms against Mexico, and he's forced to admit he'd rather be court-martialed. But desertion is not his style, even if in his heart he considers himself a traitor.[75]

"By January I knew I loved Mexico," he says. "I'd come to know that if both sides behaved themselves, we'd turn out to be good neighbors. That, as time passed and the old border feeling cooled with our greying heads, our two nations could be good friends for keeps.

"Never changed my mind, neither."

---

75 Bloom, "Shadows in Sam's Valley." These strong emotions were expressed by Sam Bean directly, who said his divided loyalty created a "crushed feeling of disgust in my breast."

JOSHUA

Mexico City

February 1848

President Polk's former peace commissioner, Nicholas Trist, is still at work in Mexico City despite having been dismissed by the administration months ago. He has stuck around, working with the few Mexican government officials left who actually hold sway, and drafted a treaty to end the war. To everyone's surprise, especially Polk's, it's accepted.

On February 2, 1848, the Treaty of Guadalupe Hidalgo is signed in Mexico City. The document cedes control of Texas (to the Rio Grande), California, New Mexico, and Colorado to the United States. The nation is now 525,000 square miles larger than when the fighting started.

Mexico receives $15 million, less than half the amount the US offered before the war. Washington, DC, also assumes the $3.25 million in debt that the Mexican government owed to US citizens, another nod to the international commerce that helped feed the conflict, and an absurdly aspirational guarantee for the United States to prevent Indian raids into Mexico.

The war is over, for a relieved nation and even more so for the Third Kentucky Volunteers. The garrison leaves Mexico City in June. (The US had controlled the capital for about nine months.) Joshua's service is done without his having experienced a fight—he'll muster out on July 21.

He's released at the forefront of an epic population surge to the west. But it's not just the newly won lands that are attracting people. In January, prospectors found gold at Sutter's Mill. News of the find has been followed by accounts of poor people striking it rich in the foothills of the Sierra mountains. The result is the California Gold Rush.

In the spring of 1848, men of ambition were turning their attention to the West Coast. Among them, Joshua Bean.

SAM

El Paso del Norte

March 1848

The end of the war brings a surprise for quartermaster's sergeant Sam Bean. One is the appearance of Major Ben Beall of the US First Dragoon Regiment. Sam stands before the officer in his moccasins, not knowing what to expect. He's ready to plead his case for the back pay the army owes him.

What he gets is the deal of a lifetime: an honorable discharge and the possession of all the equipment and animals in the yard. "I know all you men can't wait to get home," says Beall, who's shivering with malaria. "Think it over a couple of days."

Sam signs right away, first his discharge and then a bill of sale. The gear and horses—Billy-Boy, Jim-Dandy, Peter the Great, and the rest—are now his. "You're doing me a great favor," says Beall happily. Then he almost guiltily adds, "It's not a happy fate to be tied down to this wild borderland. I advise you to clear out as soon as you get your money back."[76] Sam's intention is exactly the opposite. Now he's got the seed money and, with some work, a team strong enough to start a new life.

---

76 Unless otherwise attributed, narrative and quotes in this chapter come from Bloom, "Shadows in Sam's Valley."

Off the Camino Real, Mexico
April 1848

Sam and his four-man crew, headed by an older hired hand named Zoro, are perched on a bluff where they can use field glasses to observe anyone approaching. They've been followed by two different parties—a group of ten horsemen they suspect to be bandits and a solitary rider who seems oblivious to any danger.

Their wagons and mules are hidden nearby, laden with supplies. Sam's on a freighting job that he took to help fund his aspiration to open a store. He's hired a small group of guards to avoid attracting attention, but that tactic has clearly failed.

Under observation, the lonely man rides up toward the camp, waving at the crew emerging from the bushes. "Is this the Bean train?" he asks.

Sam scrutinizes the rider. He's shorter than Sam, but broad-shouldered and with dark hair that spills out under his floppy hat. "We'll have no strangers in camp tonight," Sam warns.

"Sam, you she-devil," the man responds. "It's Roy!"[77]

The whereabouts of Roy Bean, now twenty-three years old, after he departed Kentucky will remain obscure. He left no discernible mark over the intervening seven years except for his own stories. And his tales of river journeys, leaping from steamboats, and courting highborn ladies can't be trusted.

Later in his life, Roy will tell people that his brother James entrusted a wagon train to him when Roy was fifteen. That would have been around 1840, before even Sam first trekked west.[78] Yet Sam doesn't mention his

---

77 There is much conjecture over when and where Roy reunited with Sam. Various authors have placed the reunion in Kentucky, Missouri, San Antonio, and New Mexico. Sam in the *Rio Grande Republican* article states that he and Roy made a trip "across the great American desert, now covered by the rich state of Colorado." Sam also related a detailed version of the Bean brothers' trailside reunion to Maude Bloom in her "Shadows in Sam's Valley" manuscript.

78 *Pittsburgh Press*, September 25, 1893. This is one of several falsifications in the interview; Roy took elements of his brothers' biographies as his own.

brother being on the trail with him in 1844, nor is there any other proof to back up Roy's claim. It seems doubtful that James would send his teenage brother to captain a wagon before he himself journeyed down the trail in 1845. Roy also claimed on occasion to have been a teamster with Doniphan during the war, borrowing from his brother Sam's résumé. But that claim may have actual roots in his having worked on wagon teams traveling from San Antonio through El Paso del Norte to Chihuahua.

"Things I didn't like about San Antone," Roy says to Sam the day they're reunited, as they're surveying the land around them for approaching bandits, "are mutton and Mexicans."

This comment raises Sam's hackles. One thing he hates about his fellow Americans is a superior attitude. He lets the comment slide as Roy explains how he heard about his brother, the soldier who stayed in Mexico to go into business. "They say you're crazy in San Antonio," Roy adds.

The reunion turns to more pressing matters, like the danger posed by nearby horsemen. Sam has just gained a gunman, bringing their forces to six. It's an even match, if the traders can get the drop on the bandits. "Isn't it weird to rely on Mexicans to fight other Mexicans, for an American?" Roy asks, eyeing Zoro suspiciously. "That old fellow looks like a pirate."

It's time to confront this. "Brother, you're new to this country," Sam says slowly. "If you want to stay around me, and I want you to, I hope you'll leave off that Mexican-American talk. These men are my friends."

"I'm just shooting off my mouth," Roy says defensively.

It's dusk when the bandits approach, moving slowly and cautiously, not knowing they're being observed under the teamsters' field glasses. When they get close enough, the teamsters open fire, driving the approaching men into panicked flight.

Sam and Roy's new partnership has been sealed in gun smoke.

SAM

Outside Chihuahua, Mexico
May 1848

The spring that Sam and Roy Bean open their roadside trading post, three thousand wagons and twelve thousand people move over the Santa Fe Trail. Those who make the effort to reach the lucrative markets of Chihuahua find an oasis of rest and pleasure, owned by two American brothers, just outside town.

A frontier post was more than a single store. It was more like a stand-alone hamlet catering to the transient. There were living quarters, cabins for travelers, and separate buildings housing the store and tavern. Outside were grain storage sheds, stables, and corrals for livestock. There was a lot to offer a traveler, from a safe night's sleep to an all-night gambling bender.

There was also a lot to defend. Any building with a window could be sealed with shutters cut with firing ports. Apache preyed on isolated residences and wagon trains, striking at the lifeblood of any frontier trader in need of supplies, as well as customers.

Soon after he's started freighting operations, Sam crosses paths with James Kirker on the road. Kirker is leading a wagon laden with household goods, and a veiled woman rides alongside on a mule. It appears to be an abandonment in progress.

Kirker has gold fever. He's left the hotel business in Santa Fe, where he lives, and left his family in El Paso del Norte—his second family. He abandoned his first wife back east when he married his current Mexican spouse, Rita García. Now he's heading out with a new partner.[79]

This is not an abstract crime for Sam. While passing through El Paso, he visited the Kirker family and met Kirker's three sons and fourteen-year-old daughter, Petra.[80] He feels obligated to ask about them. Challenged, Kirker prompts his mules to move before answering that his wife and children have been provided for.

"Besides," the retired scalp hunter says craftily as they roll away, "I told them to look you up if necessary."

Sam is boiling mad as Kirker waves a hand in farewell. "You'd better never come back," he cries to the departing figures.[81]

---

79 Hal Jackson, "Don Santiago Kirker, Apache Scalper, Part II," *Wagon Tracks* 21, no. 1 (November 2006): 5–12.

80 Petra Kirker was born on August 22, 1834. The sons are Rafael, Santiago, and José.

81 Maude Bloom, "Los Dos Frijoles Summary." The Maude McFie Bloom Manuscripts (NMSU Archives and Special Collections, Las Cruces, NM) include condensed summaries of books she envisioned, including one about Roy and Sam called *Los Dos Frijoles*. They read like modern book proposals, and this one includes information directly from Sam Bean.

ROY

Chihuahua, Mexico
April 1848

Roy Bean watches the towering tips of the jagged mountain ranges catch the last rays of sunset, creating gold-tipped pyramids from their rocky slopes. He's still taken with the dramatic landscape of Mexico. Here the layers of rock, once as malleable as clay, folded on themselves, pushed up into mountain peaks, and became sculpted by eons of weather.

Chihuahua also looks alien to him. It's a jumble of one-story rectangular buildings, the skyline only broken by looming cathedrals on either side of town. One is a basic dome, but the other has two spires that can be seen for miles. Roy has no interest in the holy places.

The market of Chihuahua is more to his liking—a den of merchants selling wares spread on colorful blankets, *zacateros* lounging on their hay bales, and women strolling around balancing baskets of melons on their heads. The heart of Chihuahua, like that of all Mexican towns and cities, is the main plaza. There he can always find people, and occasionally even a bullfight or a dance. The small city's delinquent underbelly is never too far away. There are gambling halls, saloons, and cockfight rings where Mexican soldiers, American traders, and Chihuahua residents all mix.

Frustratingly, he doesn't live in Chihuahua. The store is positioned on the roadside outside the city to service travelers, not locals. Life there can be interesting when customers come through, bringing tales of adventure as well as intelligence from the Santa Fe Trail and beyond. But the usual day is a dull wait interrupted by restocking or settling accounts. Working the sales desk can also come with risks, the most vivid example being the September 1847 murder of Missouri businessman (brother of Rober Aull and a partner of Sam Owens) James Aull, who was stabbed to death by thieves at his store in Chihuahua.[82]

Memories of that murder make all storeowners in Mexico nervous about their customers. One early evening a Mexican man walks into Roy and Sam's store. He's got a rough desperado look that Roy doesn't like, and he asks the sole patron in the store to leave. The tone is demanding. Heated words are passed, the man flashes a knife, and young Roy shoots the man in the head with a revolver.[83]

The dead man, whom Roy describes as "a Mexican of the lower class," becomes a rallying point for anti-American sentiment. A crowd of more than a hundred angry residents gathers outside the store, assembling in what could easily become a lynch mob.

By then, Sam Bean has rallied reinforcements among a "small number of Americans sojourning at that time in the town—less than a score of them, all told," according to Roy's later estimation. Armed with shotguns, they take positions in and around the store, promising a fight.

Something awful seems ready to happen when the crowd parts and a detachment of Mexican regular army troops appears in a column and forms a line facing the crowd. A young officer steps into the store and addresses Roy: "I am promising you equal justice, on my honor." Given little choice, Roy submits to arrest by the Mexican government.

The rest of the Americans congregate at the nearby mining town of

---

82 *The Washington Union,* September 13, 1847.

83 Roy Bean relates the circumstances of the killing in the *Pittsburgh Press,* September 25, 1893.

Jesús María, where William Sanford operates a store. The mob follows and ransacks the building, driving off Sam and the other Americans in a half-hearted, bloodless skirmish. Sanford and the rest make for Santa Fe—the merchant will be bound for California soon—but Sam must return to Chihuahua in hopes that his brother hasn't been lynched.[84]

Roy's cell in Chihuahua is dank and fetid, and from it he can hear crowds outside the ramshackle building. If not for the dozens of nearby guards, Roy figures they'd just walk in and stab him to death. Indeed, the young officer who brought him in appears and drapes him in a serape. Disguised, Roy slips out of the jail with his escort, and the pair walk through the mob, which is even now loudly discussing ways to rush the facility.

Roy moves to a new home in a military guardhouse, and the officer arranges thirty soldiers to keep him safe, although none know who he is. The next day, when the officer grouses about missing a bullfight, Roy swears to behave, and the two head to the plaza, the prisoner again under a serape. At one point, the officer runs into his belle of a cousin and finds that he has to pull his incognito prisoner off her arm.

Things seem alright with captivity until Roy is taken before a Mexican judge and levied a $20,000 bail. He's now facing a murder trial.

---

84 Horace Bell also described the countryside being in an uproar over the killing, leading to near riots and many Americans fleeing the Chihuahua area. His source was Roy Bean. Horace Bell, *On the Old West Coast* (New York: William Morrow, 1930): 224.

JAMES

Independence, Missouri
May 1848

There are a lot of reasons for James Bean to stay in the city this spring. The thirty-four-year-old owns property in town and has business associates with stellar political pedigrees. Along with his partner, John W. H. Patton, he's the new proprietor of the *Independence Expositor*, the county's stalwart Democratic newspaper.[85]

Things at home are pressing as well. Mary is just a month away from giving birth to the family's fourth child. The eldest, Aubrey, is just five years old. Mary has help: her father, Samuel Carson, has given a slave to the family to help her with the children. Some gift. James's father-in-law may have purchased the nanny, but it's James who has to pay for her upkeep.[86]

85 *Boon's Lick Times* (Fayette, MO), April 22, 1848.

86 A deed for at least one slave was transferred in 1847 to James Bean from Samuel Carson. No one by the name of Carson registered slave ownership in 1850 on the "slave schedule" census form that shows James C. Bean's ownership record of two

There is enormous pressure to head down the Santa Fe Trail again, however. Every shipment's success is vital these days as competition rises in Missouri. For all the traffic in the storehouses of downtown Independence, on the roads of Jackson County, and in the offloads at the Blue Mills and Wayne City landings, Independence is losing its footing. The bulk of the military and civilian activity has now shifted to Westport, a few miles downriver, which has eclipsed Independence as the crucial gateway to the west. The trail action at the town of Kansas, which is quickly becoming a city on its own, has also outgrown Independence's and is giving its neighbor Westport a run for its money.

Conditions at the landing at Blue Mills are getting worse. The sandbar left in the river by the epic flood of 1844 is a permanent fixture. The uphill road from the Wayne City landing is steep and often slick. "The road was so bad on our way to Independence, Missouri that all of the men got out of the carriage and clung to the side wheels to keep the carriage from skidding down the side of the hill," writes Rebecca Mayer, who passed through on her honeymoon. "I remained in the carriage and enjoyed the excitement."[87]

All the battered roadways between the town and the landings are in dire need of repairs, and the ones leading out of town to the frontier are even worse. The much-maligned condition of the county roads is a sore spot for James Bean; he served as county road commissioner in 1844.

Keen to protect his interests, James is headed back across the prai-

---

enslaved people: a fourteen-year-old boy and a twenty-five-year-old woman. No names of the enslaved people are recorded.

87 Rebecca Mayer, "The Memoir and Diary of Rebecca Mayer on Her 1852 Honeymoon Along the Santa Fe Trail and Down El Camino Real with Her Merchant Husband Henry Mayer, Fifty Men, and Five Hundred Mules," Joy Poole, ed., National Park Service, accessed October 29, 2023, www.nps.gov/safe/learn/historyculture/upload/Mayer-Diary-and-Memoir-508.pdf.

rie and the Jornada del Muerto, bound for Chihuahua.[88] At least he has family there—it will be good to see how his brothers are faring in their adopted land.

Chihuahua, Mexico
July 1848

James and Sam Bean mill around the city square as they wait for their brother's attorney to arrive. James arrived in Chihuahua to sell a load of goods, only to find Roy in jail and his other brother agitating for his release.

For Sam, this episode means the end of his shop business in Chihuahua; the Beans would be sitting ducks for any revenge killers who felt like dropping by. His plan is to spring Roy and retreat to Santa Fe with whatever they can carry before the trial even starts. The only thing delaying them is $20,000 bail.

For James, it's not so easy as just getting out of Mexico. He's got standing business operations in Chihuahua, and his reputation needs to survive this incident. Now he's affiliated with a criminal—and if the Bean brothers have the chance, a fugitive.

The lawyer's name is Guillermo Curtis Skinner, an American working in Mexico. He's smiling, so the news must be good. To start, he tells them that his gambit to bring in a doctor to examine their brother has worked. The medico told the court that the jail's bad air was sickening the prisoner, an argument he made to get the steep bail slashed. The court agreed, and then Skinner posted the amount with a guarantee from James Prewitt Hickman.

Hickman lived in San Antonio, but he launched his increasingly successful commercial ventures in Mexico from Independence. He probably

88 Reports from May 1848 mention that the westbound trade caravans encamped between Missouri and Council Grove included James Bean. Kenyon Riddle, *Records and Maps of the Old Santa Fe Trail* (Stuart, FL: Southeastern Printing, 1963). Also, Louise Barry cites records of James Bean's leaving Independence in her comprehensive *Beginning of the West*, 750.

didn't know Roy too well, but he did know James and Sam from their shared line of work. He was also a Kentuckian, born in Bourbon County. Hickman's involvement in Roy's legal case appears to have been a professional courtesy extended to fellow Americans in need, since there's no record of business between him and the Beans prior to these dealings. (That will change.)

In short, Roy Bean is getting out of jail. Step one is complete. "The prospects looked very dark if Roy remained in Mexico to face his trial, and his brother James at once on his liberation began to plan escape for Roy across the Mexican boundary line," Roy later relates to a reporter.[89]

The getaway is simple: James arranges a horse and some supplies, while Sam rides ahead to Santa Fe. Roy then sneaks off, hops on the horse, and rides north on his own, planning to meet Sam at a predetermined shallow crossing of the Rio Grande.

When he gets there, he finds the river swollen with rain and too high to safely cross. It takes two days of waiting until the water lowers enough for him to cross to the American side. Roy later says there were Mexican soldiers guarding the ford, and that he had to shoot down two of them in order to cross the border. It's only based on his word that this happened, and it likely didn't.

James stays behind in Chihuahua to clean up the legal mess. Says Roy, "James, the eldest brother whose property interests compelled him to stay some time longer in Mexico, after a good deal of trouble affected a compromise with the Chihuahuan courts regarding his brother's flight." James's ability to trade in Chihuahua can continue unhindered, but at a cost in fees or bribes that no one ever speaks about for posterity.

Roy and Sam split up in Santa Fe. Sam plans to go to Juarez to find Petra. Roy can only shake his head at this romanticism. It's 1848 and there's an entire West Coast to explore. It's time to look up brother Joshua.

There's every reason to believe that James Bean met his brother Roy in

---

89 *Pittsburgh Press*, September 25, 1893. In this account, Roy cites Hickman and Skinner by name.

Santa Fe on his way home and funded Roy's trip to California. That's certainly the impression that will endure for decades in the collective memories of Jackson County, where "the old-timers will tell you that James Bean gave [Roy] enough money for a trip to the west. And that he never returned."[90]

90 *Lexington (KY) Herald-Leader*, February 12, 1939. The reporter visited Missouri to look at the Beans' history there. The article contains several biographical mistakes, but this tidbit from "old-timers" seems worthwhile emotional history.

PART TWO

Our inheritance will be turned to strangers.

—JUAN BANDINI[91]

91 Quoted in the *Southern Californian* newspaper, April 11, 1855.

JAMES

Mississippi River, Missouri
January 1849

The steamboat creeps innocently upriver, sternwheel churning a wake that shimmers in the moonlight. The vessel is loaded with passengers from New Orleans, where an insidious disease is emerging among recent immigrants there. And some on board, destined for the docks at Kansas City, are contagious.

Pestilence has come to Jackson County.

Life and ambition continue for Independence's unsuspecting traders. James Bean has diversified his freight business by carrying mail. Congress authorized a Santa Fe post office in 1847 but still hasn't set up an official mail route. Until that contract is issued—expected this fall—it's an open market. James hopes to be in a position to bid for the work, so he becomes a mail carrier, ferrying letters and military correspondence to Santa Fe. On return trips he collects hundreds of letters from California that are awaiting shipment to the post office in Independence or Fort Leavenworth.[92]

Mail stages are not like freighters; they're a faster, much more sleek, and nearly sophisticated way to travel. There are six mules per coach, each

92 Barry, *Beginning of the West*, 1094.

carrying eight men with colt rifles and pistols. "The stages are got up in elegant style," writes one newspaper reporter. "The bodies are beautifully painted and made water-tight, with a view of using them as boats in ferrying streams."[93]

James also has a tangential stake in the newest project in Jackson County: a 6.5-mile rail line connecting the Wayne City landing to downtown Independence. The apparatus traversing the track won't be a locomotive, per se, but a wheeled coach that will be pulled along a smooth wooden track by a pair of mules. It's the work of the Independence and Missouri River Railroad Company, incorporated in 1849, which built a large warehouse on the 100 block of Maple Street in Independence, near the square, to store cargo.

James has positioned himself to benefit from this project by opening a restaurant at the Wayne City landing, a perfect place for a passenger to spend some time waiting for the car or steamboat to arrive. Construction on the tracks is underway, and its expected debut this year will make it the first rail line west of the Mississippi.

In July 1849, James leaves for the trail again, carrying hundreds of letters and military correspondence.[94] By then, plague has already seized Missouri. It's spreading fast in Kansas City, and in Jackson County it's reaping a grim harvest in the slave shacks of the county's biggest slave trader, Jabez Smith.

James is leaving his family in the path of a growing catastrophe. Cholera, the scourge of the Bean family in Kentucky, has found them in Missouri.

---

93 The reporter from the *Missouri Commonwealth* newspaper saw contemporary stages in July 1850 and is quoted in Henry Inman, "The Old Santa Fe Trail," Crane and Company, Topeka, 1916, 145–46, and cited in Robert Utley, "Fort Union and the Santa Fe Trail," U.S. National Parks Service, December 1959, 11.

94 An August 1849 roster of traders returning to Missouri from Chihuahua and Santa Fe included James Bean, who was a contract mail carrier bringing more than four hundred letters that had been sent from California to Santa Fe, plus a large amount of mail for Fort Leavenworth.

SAM

El Paso Del Norte
March 1849

It's hard to meet the desperate eyes of Rita García as she sits across from Sam Bean. James Kirker, her husband, is not coming back, and the funds he's provided aren't holding out. The family has been frozen in place in El Paso since the patriarch and breadwinner hit the road.

Now she's here to offer her fifteen-year-old daughter's hand in marriage.

Sam is in no shape for such an offer; in fact, he's heartbroken. Sam had plans to marry the daughter of a Mexican man who hired him to move their family away from the American border, but she died just after Sam secured permission. His days lately have been spent riding aimlessly, his nights spent without food or company.

Sam has always imagined marrying a Mexican woman, from his early days hearing about them from Santa Fe traders. They come with citizenship rights, making it possible to buy property and operate businesses in Mexico. But Petra Kirker comes with none of these benefits.

The pair have met before, but their reacquaintance is made awkward by the pressure of marriage. The mutual shyness gives way as they spend some time, and Sam he finds that the teenager is as deliberate and spirited as her frontier-famous father. She's pretty, but he sometimes catches a glimpse of her father's features in Petra's face.[95]

Sam is moved to action. Days later, he decides to marry Petra. "Although the girl knows he does not love her yet, she pleases her mother by marrying Sam," relates Maude McFie Bloom, who heard the story from Sam Bean.

There's no basis for love, but serendipity and circumstance have pushed them together. On March 11, Reverend Benigno Cardenas marries the couple in El Paso del Norte's Guadalupe Church.[96]

---

95 Bloom, "Los Dos Frijoles Summary."

96 Katherine Stoes, *Las Cruces (NM) Citizen*, February 10, 1955. Stoes knew the Bean family, but researchers have not found records of the marriage at that church, and Cardenas was at another church at the time. Benigno Cardenas later became a renegade Catholic priest after he converted to Methodism; in 1854 he preached the first Protestant sermon in Socorro.

JAMES

Outside Independence, Missouri
October 1849

From horseback, disease seems to have reduced the county to the medieval era. Tents are scattered throughout the area, the result of a mass exodus from various cities into the countryside. Now the fields are thick with refugees and the grey smoke from innumerable small campfires. At night the specks of flame can be seen flickering for miles.

James detects a stench and winces. He rides close enough to see the telltale column of black smoke; someone has burned a plague house. The county is now pockmarked with these destroyed homes, where family members buried their dead kin, burned their belongings, and fled. The charred remnants are all that remain of them. James has heard that some of the familiar, nearby Indian villages along the Santa Fe Trail have fared even worse and are now entirely destroyed.

He's heading west to see how much wagon train traffic is avoiding town. When he's close enough to glimpse the trailhead, he sees long lines of white canvas and brown-skinned animals: westbound settlers, gold-struck bands headed to California, and freighters bound for Mexico. Business in Jackson County is virtually frozen, but the trail is still open. The caravans and steamboats avoid the landings at Independence if they can.

James spurs his horse and turns toward town, not really wanting to head back for fear of what he'll have to face. He's worried about his family since cholera is especially adept at killing young children,[97] but it's Mary who hasn't been feeling well.

James returns to find that his wife is unable to stand. She is stricken with crippling "rice-water stools" and has started vomiting, leaving her dehydrated and vulnerable to painful muscle cramps. There's a mad look in her eye, a panic he's seen in scared pack animals.

Finding a doctor isn't easy—they're overworked and exhausted. They're not much help anyway, since the cause of the disease is unknown. The doctor measures her low blood pressure and probes her dry mouth with clinical but grim efficiency. She's got cholera, and with no cure they can only chase symptoms by administering morphine and compounds of mercury (which often makes patients sicker). The newspapers recommend bathing at least once a week, staying out of damp weather, avoiding fish and vegetables, and shunning public gatherings.

The actual cause of the disease is the *Vibrio cholerae* bacterium, which contaminates water and food. Those sickened by it produce vast numbers of the organisms, easily passing them to new victims through oral contact with human waste—an all-too-common occurrence in an unsanitary era—or even through the handling of tainted clothes or bedsheets.

In just a few days, the mother of four is reduced to a shell of a human. Mary's heart starts to flutter from hypovolemic shock, and her struggles mercifully cease. James Bean is now a widower at age thirty-five.

---

97 Children's lack of stomach acid makes them vulnerable.

SAM

La Mesilla, Mexico
November 1849

The village is not much to look at: the citizenry live in jacales, with walls made of wooden stakes and woven twigs and branches, all lathered with mud. This design has been around since prehistory, but it's decidedly ugly. The buildings are arranged in a square, like an infantry formation fighting cavalry. Which makes sense, since the tightly clustered buildings double as a small fortress during raids by Apache horsemen.

This is an unimpressive, traditional village, but its geography is perfect for Sam's ambitions. Mesilla is an undeveloped stop on the El Camino Real de Tierra Adentro, which runs between the US and Mexico. The "Royal Road of the Interior" was the earliest Euro-American trade route in the United States, but the puebla itself is a new creation.

When the Mexican-American War ended in 1848, the Mexican government, eager to make sure the new border wouldn't shift, founded new towns by decree as a hedge against incursion. Cura Ramón Ortíz, a local priest turned "commissioner of emigration," in 1849 helped Mexican citizens from Doña Ana County relocate to the Mexican side of the border, a few miles south of the boundary created by the Treaty of Guadalupe Hidalgo. They called the new town La Mesilla, or "little table."

The treaty used the Rio Grande as a national boundary, and in fall 1849 its path changed. The river routinely shifts channels during heavy snowmelts, a fact that the engineers should have seen coming. But they didn't, and now there's a new international crisis because towns in the state of Chihuahua like Socorro, Isleta, San Elizario, and Mesilla are now technically on the US side. It's a loophole that the United States wants to use to take more land—particularly at sites where the tracks of a transcontinental railroad could run.

Sam leaps through this loophole.[98] However, he's hardly an interloper. The trader is already known in La Mesilla and has a reputation for being, well, nothing like the Texans that Mesilleros hate. He despises slavery, as most Mexicans do, and doesn't talk down to anybody.

The area is disputed terrain, so an American with some vision can set roots here without facing too much competition. Sam's choice is a testament to his enduring appreciation of Mexico. Another Doniphan veteran, former army clerk Thomas Bull, came to Mesilla in 1849.[99] However, he left as soon as the Mexican government started pushing back on American claims with troop movements and threats.

Bull leaves for American territory; Sam Bean stays. In early 1850 Sam brings his teenage bride and their one-year-old daughter from El Paso del Norte to their new town—and a new start.[100]

No matter what flag will fly overhead, Sam's dream for La Mesilla is straight from the Bean family economic-conquest playbook. The first step's been done: set up a freighting business, a familiar profession to Sam and a lucrative one here. His next move will be to buy property and establish

---

98 In later testimony to the US Court of Private Land Claims, which examined the town's national status, Sam said he came to Doña Ana County in 1849.

99 Bull testified in the same court case as Sam Bean.

100 He'll also enable the three sons of James Kirker—Rafael, Santiago, and José—to join them in Mesilla.

some sort of combination store and boardinghouse to capitalize on the traffic along the camino. With enough profit, he could even open a saloon.

All of this can be achieved from the humble town. Given time and some international peace, this hamlet could grow to be a powerhouse. As is true for Sam himself, Mesilla's position between two nations could be its greatest strength.

JAMES

Independence, Missouri
February 1850

Downtown isn't the same place that James and Sam Bean enjoyed in 1844.

The familiar wagons are still present, stuffed with families of Mormons or East Coast economic refugees, and so is the occasional wagon crammed with goods for resale in Mexico. But these prairie schooners are now joined by throngs of gold hunters. That means handcarts, two-wheelers, or pack animals without wagons. And instead of families, the would-be prospectors are bachelors and wandering husbands. They're rougher, louder, and drunker.

James watches the action, feeling bitter. There's not enough traffic in Independence these days, as busy as it can seem on the Westport Road. But especially when compared to other places, Independence and even Kansas City are slumping. The competition is booming at places like Oregon Crossing and Weston, while cholera-stricken Jackson County is still considered best to float past or roll through as quickly as possible.

St. Joseph is the biggest winner of the epidemic in Jackson County. In 1850 the population there exploded to three thousand permanent residents. About ten thousand emigrants live in "Gambling Hells," a makeshift camp outside town. Until spring, this rootless bunch will settle—and spend—in St. Joe. That kind of windfall should be dropping money here, James thinks. But the fact that it's not is just one way that cholera has ruined his life.

James, a victim of the collapsed local economy, has suffered a serious business reversal. The federal mail contract to Santa Fe has been filled, and not by him. Downtown outfitter stores aren't making the money they used to. The novel mule-borne train line hasn't revived Wayne's Landing as hoped. His trading expeditions don't seem to make up the shortfalls; Jackson County records from the time are marked by a series of James C. Bean property sales, including parcels of farmland outside town.

Among the deeds is one for the sale of his five slaves. In September 1849, James sold two men and a woman—all in their early twenties—to the county's biggest slave owners, Jabez Smith and Samuel Lucas. Their farmland south of town houses hundreds of slaves in so many free-standing shanties that the locals call the property "Nigger Hill."[101] It's a terrifying place for the Bean family's slaves to be sent, since a resale can be out of state, into a cruel agricultural job or, for the young woman, into forced prostitution.

Sam Carson, James's father-in-law in Shelby County, has taken in the youngest slaves. He'll buy some outright the next year, paying $7,000 for a ten-year-old girl named Margaret and an eleven-year-old named Adeline, the deed citing "the natural love and affection he has for his grandchildren" as motive for the purchase. (It's a chillingly discordant document.) Clearly, he's doing what he can to help James get back on his feet, but the accrued debts must have been steep. In the 1850 census, James lists his property ownership at just $500.

In the wake of Mary's death, James has given up his children. Aubry, Roy, Leon, and Gordon are staying here in town with John and Bettie

---

101 Kristen Kimberly Epps, "Bound Together: Masters and Slaves on the Kansas-Missouri Border, 1825–1865" (PhD diss., University of Kansas, 2010). Lucas and Smith were atypical as big brokers; Missouri slaveholders typically "rented" slaves to do nonagricultural work or hired them out to their neighbors.

Smarr, who are renowned for their expansive charity. James lives nearby, sleeping at the restaurant he manages. It's owned by Ambrose Owens, who also lives there with his wife, Helen, and their newborn child, Samuel C. Owens.[102] Clearly the son of the slain trader doesn't hold a grudge over the scandal and infamous trial involving his sister's marriage.

For the moment, James Bean has lost his home and his children. The once ambitious thirty-six-year-old has also lost his identity as a Santa Fe trader. When a census taker asks his profession in 1850, James Bean responds, "Restaurateur."[103]

---

102 A census record lists household members Ambrose G. Owens, twenty-one; Helen Owens, twenty; Samuel C. Owens, less than one year old; and James C. Bean, thirty-six.

103 On the census, he uses the term "Restorator."

JOSHUA

San Diego, California
April 1850

Joshua Bean walks out of the Gila House, savoring the sunset view of the harbor, the rolling hills of the Mission Valley, and the mountains stretching off to his right. A dirt road from Old Town follows the north bank of the valley to Mission San Diego. The open land surrounding San Diego is crawling with roaming cattle, and every so often he can spot vaqueros in sombreros and loose-fitting white shirts, trailing the herd on horseback or lounging in the shade of trees.

"The only food a Californian cares for is beef & milk—with the exception of the short space devoted to this repast, and sleep, the rest of his time is spent on horseback," writes one twenty-three-year-old government official, Robert Patterson Effinger, a member of the US Boundary Commission, which mapped the national border the year before.[104]

Cowhides and tallow exports have been the backbone of the San Diego economy for decades, and the nearby herds prove there's still a market.

---

104 The San Diego Historical Society has all eleven of Effinger's letters. See also: Carol Schille, "Robert Patterson Effinger: Letters from San Diego, 1849" (master's thesis, San Diego State University, 1986).

But things are changing, now that San Diego is under the American flag, and the rancho phase is facing its end.

The hotel is the newest fixture in Old Town, which was formed around the city plaza and is the location of the flagstaff where the handover ceremony made this city a part of the United States. A pair of artillery pieces currently flank the pole flying the stars and stripes. Two blocks of Old Town are occupied by the US Army; one block holds a depot and barracks, the other stables and a stockyard, but the army is building a new fort in another part of town.

San Diego is a village of around 650 people. (By comparison, the Native American population in the surrounding areas is estimated to be ten thousand, but no census focuses on them.) Still, the port and the presence of military facilities grant this hamlet a lot of potential for development. The discovery of gold is swelling the number of transients, many coming by steamship and most of whom head straight to the Los Angeles area to seek their fortunes. San Diego needs to find a way to retain some of that commerce if it's to grow into an actual city. Right now, it's just a small but festive waystation.

The Gila House is a two-story, wood-frame hotel with an adobe kitchen that stands apart from the main structure. It's the newest and nicest lodging in town, built in Old Town San Diego by Juan Bandini, the town's former mayor and largest property owner. Or as they say here, he's the "*alcalde del puebla y un rico.*" His hotel is also a status symbol—120 feet tall and 62 feet wide, with an eye-catching zinc-plated roof. Bandini, disgusted by internal national Mexican politics, supported an American takeover during the war. Now the don is backing a cabal of Anglos who are plotting San Diego's future—and their own.

Joshua knows all about the cabal; he's a very active participant. He's serving as San Diego's *alcalde*, the mayoral position once held by Don Bandini himself. There will be city elections once the state legislature gets its act together, and Joshua Bean is poised to become the first mayor of American San Diego. Indeed, he's even now off to an election-night fiesta at the Bandini mansion.

How did this recently dismissed private become a prominent politician and businessman in California? There are military men at the head of the cabal, but none are known to have served in Mexico City with Joshua, nor are there any known links between him and those who had family in Kentucky. Joshua's rapid rise was a blessing of being at the forefront of the Gold Rush. He arrived straight from Mexico, before the hordes of other fortune seekers. This early arrival enabled him to establish himself before the competition and to more easily ingratiate himself with the top men of San Diego. He was also a large, capable man with a military bearing and a willingness to lead. Within less than a year of his arrival, he was already turning a brisk business as a store-saloon owner, listing $5,000 worth of property ownership in 1850. But he was also the front man for the cabal of Anglos, backed by the Mexican *ricos* of San Diego, to create a modern port city from this humble town at the dawn of American ownership. Create it—and control it.

It's just a three-block walk from Bandini's Gila House hotel to his mansion. The home is a grand example of the Spanish style, custom built to evoke the regal mystique of a don. It has two wings with fifteen rooms total. People on the patio are milling under a veranda held twelve feet high by specially ordered redwood posts, each nearly a foot thick.

Joshua reaches the heart of the party as soon as he enters the open front doors and steps into the mansion's *sala*, a thirty-three-by sixteen-foot space with a white pine floor, now famously scuffed from the boot scrapes of previous dance parties. Guitar players in black and silver suits are serenading two women, who twirl and stomp in bright-patterned dresses. And there's Don Juan Bandini himself, earning applause from onlookers at tables as he and Doña Refugio (his second wife) also gracefully sweep past. The pair are renowned dancers.

Joshua takes in the brute symbolism of the foyer's decor. There's a towering Yankee clock case, a picture of George Washington, and an American flag. The Bandinis host a lot of lavish parties here. "Our house would be full of company; thirty or forty persons at a table; it would have to be set twice. A single fiesta might cost a thousand dollars," Doña Refugio later recalls. "But, in those days, receipts at my husband's store might pass

$18,000 a month."[105] Her husband is currently the biggest landowner in the county, and her name is on many of the deeds with his.

This party marks a special moment in the aspiring town's history. Today was the first county election in San Diego's history as an American possession. Of 650 residents, 157 are registered voters, and 136 of those have arrived since the invasion.[106] The conclusions of the election are pretty much known ahead of time.

Guests are watching from tables, dancing, or ignoring the entertainment to huddle in discussion. Election winners abound. Joshua greets John Hays, a Gila House resident, who's been elected county judge. He shakes hands with Agoston Haraszthy, a Hungarian immigrant who's establishing a vineyard north of town, for his win as sheriff.

Joshua eases away to work his way deeper into the party and up the hierarchy of San Diego power players. He aims for Thomas Sutherland, one of the only attorneys in San Diego and among its most prominent citizens. Joshua trusts him for his competence and respects how professionally he's sidled up to the wealthy Bandini family to become an indispensable man. Sutherland served as an "acting *alcalde*" for Bean earlier in the year to more easily scheme property deals for many of the men in this room—including Sutherland himself.

There's another wealthy Californio holding court: José Antonio Estudillo, a major landowner who today has been elected county assessor.[107]

---

105 Quoted in Victor Walsh, "If Walls Could Speak: San Diego's Historic Casa de Bandini," *California History* 88, no. 4 (2011): 22–70.

106 William Smythe, *History of San Diego, 1542–1908* (San Diego: The History Company, 1908). "The national census of 1850 gave San Diego County a population of 798. (Indians weren't counted.) There were 157 registered voters, eighty-eight in Old Town and sixty-nine at La Playa, of whom 136 had arrived during or since the conquest." Part 2, chapter 9.

107 Californio (noun): One of the original Spanish colonists of California or their descendants. *The Merriam-Webster Dictionary*, 2023.

He's also Don Bandini's brother-in-law, embodying a lesson in family-business dynamics that's not lost on the ambitious Anglos. The Bandinis are "*gente de razón*," landowners who rule as feudal lords, control politics and commerce, and enjoy being called "Don" by respectful serfs. It's an elevated status that these American transplants aspire to.

Standing with Estudillo is Lieutenant Cave Couts, a West Point officer and nephew of a secretary of the treasury under President Polk. He came to San Diego assigned to lead the boundary commission that drew the national line in 1849. Couts now lives with Don Bandini here in the mansion, and under his tutelage has risen to become a success. Couts is already the largest Anglo landowner in San Diego with $15,000 worth of land and stock.

Couts, in essence, wants to become the American analog of his host, Don Bandini. To that end, he's summoned his younger brother William and twenty-seven-year-old cousin Henry to San Diego to help run the town. This history opens up the possibility that Joshua Bean went to California with Couts's younger brother and cousin after mustering out of the army in 1848, if he returned to Kentucky. (The record does not say where his enlistment ended.) Henry Couts lives at the Gila House, and William resides in the Bandini mansion.

A young, booming voice draws Joshua's attention, belonging to perhaps the least likely resident of the Gila House's august list of residents. His brother Roy has come to join the Californio party.[108]

He arrived in 1850, wrung dry after the long overland trip from New Mexico. His stories of commercial businesses, narrow escapes from danger, and brotherly comradery have the clear overtones of a nepotistic job interview since Roy intends to hitch himself to Joshua's progress in San Diego. Roy says he was "received by him with open arms."[109] Joshua quickly put

108 The two brothers appear together on the 1850 federal census in San Diego.

109 *Pittsburgh Press*, September 25, 1893.

his brother to work at the store, where he tended the saloon and learned how to run the gaming tables.

It's hard to imagine that Joshua is as thrilled as his brother imagines. The elder Bean is proud, aspiring, and ambitious, on the verge of a once-in-a-lifetime bid to be a founder of an American city, with all the rewards that follow. He's also a bachelor who's had only himself to worry about for his entire adult life. Now he has his young brother to tend to, one whose wild side is gaining strength as he recovers from his journey west.

Roy, a loudmouth who drinks too much, seeks both thrills and attention. He's also quick to escalate a situation just to make a scene, something Joshua Bean has always considered a liability no matter where he's been.

San Diego is a bad town for people like this. Men have been stabbed to death here over a glib insult. "You can form no idea of what a desperate Country we live in, without law, order, or the gospel," laments young Effinger. "Americans at San Diego . . . having nothing to engage their attention and plenty of whiskey to drink, have neither the fear of man nor God before their eyes. The wonder is that crime is not more frequent."[110]

In private, even Don Bandini admits to becoming disillusioned. "Liberty, the one guarantee the citizen can make use of in civil affairs, has become licentiousness," he writes to a friend and business associate. "Thus, one sees in the towns nothing but drunkenness, gaming, sloth, and public manhandling of the opposite sex."[111]

In other words, San Diego is Roy's kind of town.

Despite the drawbacks, watching his brother revel in the California scene lifts Joshua's spirits. There's a charisma to Roy's chaos, and a spirit of mischief to the strong, handsome youth that softens reactions to his manic behavior. Joshua is a long way from his ancestral home, surrounded by strangers posing as friends. His brother is a wild card and often a pain in

110 Effinger's letters, San Diego Historical Society archives.

111 "Bandini to Stearns," June 7, 1947, Abel Stearns Collection, Box 6, Huntington Library, San Marino, CA.

the ass, but it's nice to have a more familiar face at the ambitious fandango that is late 1840s California.

San Diego, California
June 1850

On June 16, the cabal becomes the city government, and *alcalde* Joshua Bean is now the first elected mayor in San Diego's history.

The results of the election for municipal officials have some other familiar names. Sheriff Haraszthy is now also the city marshal, Charles Johnson (a Los Angeles businessman who relocated to San Diego, moved into Gila House, and is romancing one of Bandini's daughters) and Charles Haraszthy, father of the marshal, are on the city council. José Estudillo is elected as treasurer, while Juan Bandini won for assessor (he'll resign before taking office). Thomas Sutherland is now city attorney.[112]

On top of being mayor, Joshua is also a major general. In May the state legislature created four military divisions of state militia and named Joshua Bean as the head of the Fourth Division. It comes with status: in San Diego they start calling him "El General Frijole."[113] The militia exists primarily as protection against local Native American tribes. And Joshua leaps into action against the threat, in a way. Within days he delegates a state-mandated anti-Indian expedition to the newly named quartermaster J. C. Morehead. He also authorizes him—without permission—to draw

---

112 Most of these men were Masons, but it's not clear that Joshua Bean was. In 1942, the *San Diego Union* will note of the early Masons, "More than 90 years ago, they quietly began taking over the new government of the little Spanish pueblo around Old Town plaza." Ruth Taunton, "Lodge Has Colorful History of Pioneering, Progress," April 19, 1942.

113 Letter from Governor Peter H. Burnett, in San Jose, to Major General Bean, June 1, 1850, telling him to raise forty men in Los Angeles and twenty men in San Diego to form a company to proceed to the Colorado River ferry and punish Indians there and protect immigrants. Online Archive of California, accessed October 29, 2023, https://oac.cdlib.org/findaid/ark:/13030/tf4779n694/dsc/.

from the state treasury to pay for supplies and dispatches him to the Colorado River. The troubles there are exaggerated, and by early September the governor will write the militia major in San Gabriel directly, complaining that Joshua Bean hasn't given any updates and ordering him to disband the expedition.[114]

Meanwhile, Joshua can focus on running the city. The first official acts of the San Diego Council are to approve maps of San Diego and its tidelands, made by Couts and Bean, and to certify the legality of certain grants of land made when Bean first became the *alcalde*. During that time, there was a fire sale of land speculation for the puebla's property among friends and family of members of the city administration that needed to be rubber-stamped.

The city councilmen are chiefly supporters of Old Town, where the Gila House, Bandini mansion, and army facilities are located. But a New Town extension has been established by a rival cadre of property owners. Even more galling, the army has chosen New Town as the site for a new depot.

If there were to be new neighborhoods, the Old Town players wanted to control them. From this was born a scheme to create "Middletown." In May 1850, city attorney Sutherland and his partners purchased the 687 acres between Old and New Towns for $3,187.[115] The group of investors included Sutherland; *ricos* Estudillo and Bandini; Cave Couts; Sheriff Haraszthy; City Councilmen Atkins Wright and Charles Noell; and boundary commission official and Gila House resident Oliver S. Witherby.

Now Mayor Bean has made those real estate machinations official under US jurisdiction.

The other city business shows the flavor of the Anglo ambitions for the

---

114 Letter from Burnett to Bean, written in San Jose, September 4, 1850, Online Archive of California, accessed October 29, 2023, https://oac.cdlib.org/findaid/ark:/13030/tf4779n694/dsc/.

115 *San Diego Deed Book B*, 110, 75–76.

town. The council creates a committee to investigate ways to divert the San Diego River into False Bay[116] and enable Native Americans in jail to be "let out to" local industries as laborers. Those with saloons welcome licensing fees for new gambling houses. The council also issues a steep $5,000 contract for building a new jail to Councilman Haraszthy's son, the sheriff.

It's almost funny how quickly the members of the city council forget their lofty preelection talk about serving only for the honor of serving. Mayor Bean and his council have their first schism soon after he takes office when the council votes for their own salaries. He publicly upbraids them for the move. In the city's official record he reports that he's given the matter "some days for mature reflection and [has] arrived at the conclusion that the ordinance granting such a large amount of the city's funds would at this time [be] not only wrong but prejudicial to the best interests of our growing community." Over his objections, the salaries are approved.[117]

Hostility from the city council is the last thing he should be courting. Joshua has acquired land titles for himself and Couts, including for the very buildings that contain the city offices. The *alcalde*'s move was simple: convince an old woman with the last name Amada to sell her Old Town land at community-friendly prices, claiming it was for the good of the growing city. He does something similar with an army captain named Hayden Turning, and Couts is even now building a hotel on that property. Joshua's assumption of the properties' titles and the absurdly cheap sales to Couts (reportedly as low as $2.50) might have attracted less attention had the pair not set about evicting city staff when they took control of the property used as municipal offices.

Now the city council has an issue with which to strike at the mayor: that he tried to literally sell city hall to his pals. Councilman Charles Noell,

---

116 Mission Bay.

117 July 20, 1850, City of San Diego official records, accessed October 29, 2023, https://www.sandiego.gov/sites/default/files/1850a.pdf.

a beneficiary of the Middletown annexation, leads the public charge. The well-off San Diego merchant crusades against the deal, calling for an investigatory commission to plumb its details. Lawsuits and arbitration are soon to follow.

Mayor Joshua Bean is only a few months into his historic term, and he's already embroiled in a scandal.

San Diego
October 10, 1851

> THE FOLLOWING REPORT FROM THE COMMITTEE APPOINTED TO CONFER WITH MESSRS BEAN-COUTS FOR THE PURPOSE OF MAKING AN AMICABLE ADJUSTMENT OF THE DIFFICULTIES NOW EXISTING BETWEEN THE COUNCIL AND THE SAID BEAN-COUTS WAS RECEIVED AND ADOPTED AS FOLLOWS:
>
> MESSRS BEAN-COUTS SHALL HAND OVER TO THE COUNCIL THE AMADA DEED AND SHALL RESIGN ALL THEIR INTEREST RIGHT AND CLAIM THERETO AND THEREBY;
>
> SAID MESSRS BEAN-COUTS SHALL QUIT CLAIM TO THE TOWN THE TOWN HOUSE LOT ON WHICH IT STANDS THE LINE OF SAID LOT TO COMMENCE ON THE OUTSIDE WEST OF THE CHIMNEY OF SAID TOWN HOUSE;
>
> SAID BEAN SHALL LIKEWISE HAND OVER TO THE CITY COUNCIL WITH THE PROPER ENDORSEMENT THE DOCUMENT GIVEN BY CAPT HAYDEN TURNING OVER SAID HOUSE TO HIM;
>
> THE CITY COUNCIL SHALL RELINQUISH TO THE SAID BEAN-COUTS ALL THEIR RIGHT TITLE AND INTEREST . . . ON WHICH THE NEW HOUSE BUILT BY BEAN-COUTS NOW STANDS AND THE GROUND

> EAST OF THE BUILDING AS FAR EAST AS TO THE CHIMNEY OF THE TOWN HOUSE;
>
> ALL SUITS NOW PENDING BETWEEN THE CITY COUNCIL AND THE SAID BEAN-COUTS SHALL BE FORTHWITH WITHDRAWN AND CANCELLED EACH PARTY PAYING THEIR OWN LAWYER THE COSTS BEING EQUALLY DIVIDED.[118]

San Diego, California
November 1851

Even as San Diego reels from economic and political uncertainty, a new crisis descends on the city. Earlier in the year, Sheriff Haraszthy decreed that local Native Americans were obligated to pay local taxes and started to confiscate land and property of the San Diego County tribes.

This is the spark that propels Antonio Garra, chief of the Cupeño tribe, into insurrection. His ranch at Agua Caliente, located in the Valle de San Jose, sits directly on the route taken by travelers to San Diego from the desert. Since the Cupeño are a branch of the nearby Cahuilla tribes, he believes he can garner support from them if he strikes first. Garra also knows how disgusted Californios are with American management and expects at least some *gente de razón* to support his crusade.

It starts violently. Garra joins forces with a Yuma raiding party, ransacks a large herd of sheep west of the Colorado River, and kills five of the six Americans herding the animals. The Cupeño and Yuma argue over the spoils, and with that Garra's hope of a united uprising starts to unravel.

On November 21, Garra rallies a party to attack a store and settlement five miles away called Warner's Ranch. Although he stays behind due to illness, his men (including an Anglo store owner who operates in Agua Caliente) slay five people in cold blood.

---

118 City of San Diego official records, accessed October 29, 2023, www.sandiego.gov/sites/default/files/1850a.pdf.

News of the murders sweep the state. The idea of an Indian uprising is so terrifying that any hint of it inflames passions. Garra is having a hard time finding active supporters for his war, but the California politicians respond as if thousands are gathering to reclaim the West Coast. On November 26, martial law is proclaimed in San Diego. The town becomes a fortress. Sentinels stand on twenty-four-hour guard at every approach to the city.

The US Army deploys forty-five soldiers under the command of Captain Samuel Heintzelman to counter any uprising, but the legislature feels it's time for the state militia to again swing into action. Major General Joshua Bean is tapped to quell the Garra uprising.

The army is spoiling for a fight, but there's a diplomatic aspect to Joshua's mandate. Ideally, he'll find some way to cajole the Native Americans into a treaty that soothes the anger stirred by the state's property tax laws and land-grabbing county officials. It's not a job for brute force, no matter how bloodthirsty the calls for extermination that come from the Anglo community.

On December 2, Garra writes to Juan Antonio, chief of the Cahuilla: "If we lose this war, all will be lost—the world. If we gain this war, then it is forever. Never will it stop; this war is for a whole life."[119] But his pleas fall on deaf ears. Instead, the crafty chief sees an opportunity.

He lures Garra to his ranch, knowing that the Cupeño outlaw is desperate for wider support and will risk a meeting. As he arrives, Garra and his men are seized and stripped. Juan Antonio then sends word to all his affiliated Cahuillas, as well as to the Cupeños, that he's captured Garra and the rebellion is over.

The next word he sends is to Joshua Bean: he's got Garra held prisoner and is ready to negotiate a deal that secures his ranch and his people's

---

119 Antonio Garra, Sr. "Letter to Cahuilla leader Juan Antonio," December 2, 1851, quoted in George Phillips, *Chiefs and Challengers: Indian Resistance and Cooperation in Southern California, 1769–1906* (University of California Press, Berkeley, 2014): 105.

property. "His course was influenced beyond a doubt by the hope of gain, and he had made a pretty nice calculation as to which side would pay the best," the *Los Angeles Star* opines at the time.[120]

Joshua is elated. With this one stroke, his mission has basically been fulfilled. Peace is not fully restored to San Diego County—Captain Heintzelman and his soldiers attack the Cahuilla at Los Coyotes Canyon after Garra's arrest—but the crisis is over.[121] The state accountants are horrified to see that the militia expedition cost $120,000 in supplies and salaries, authorized by Major General Joshua Bean.

Joshua then negotiates a treaty with Juan Antonio stating that the chief can keep his lands as long as he continues to play nice with the new regime in California.[122] The treaty is proven worthless in the long run, due to legislative interference, and white settlers will eventually occupy all of his land.[123]

It might be assumed that Joshua Bean, as a major general and a mayor, has become a serious and respected man. Yet on November 26, a crowd forms in the plaza in San Diego to watch him duel. A drunken doctor is insisting on squaring off against him for a perceived verbal slight. The

---

120 Quoted in William Evans, "The Garra Uprising: Conflict between San Diego Indians and Settlers in 1851," *California Historical Quarterly* 45 (1966): 339–49.

121 At Los Coyotes, four of Garra's accomplices are captured and tried on the spot: Juan Bautista or Coton, Jacobo or Qui-sil, and Luis E. Alcalde, all of Agua Caliente; and Francisco Mocate, chief of the rancheria San Ysidro. All four are executed at Los Coyotes.

122 Jeff Smith, "An Indian Chief Envisions the Mother of All Warpaths," *San Diego Reader*, July 3, 2002.

123 Throughout California from 1851 to 1853, federal treaties reserved 7.5 million acres to the tribes of California state. A variety of political forces successfully lobbied against Senate ratification of all of them. Juan Antonio died of smallpox on February 28, 1863.

doctor accepts a pistol from one of Joshua's friends and takes his position. The crowd parts, staying close enough to see but out of the line of fire. The doctor draws and shoots, the explosion startling him nearly as much as Joshua's dramatic collapse to the ground.

General Frijole rises, slowly facing the doctor and aiming his pistol at the doctor's head. Joshua's opponent drops his weapon and runs off, pelted by peals of laughter from the crowd. The guns have been loaded with blanks, a prank that's celebrated with appropriate seriousness in that week's *San Diego Herald*: "If the Medico will recur his early reading, he may chance to remember the account of the aspiring boy who, in his efforts to get to the top of a tall *Bean*, met a tall fall."[124]

Maybe some of Roy's theatrical sense of humor is rubbing off on his brother.

San Diego, California
January 1852

By New Year's, the deal Joshua Bean had struck with the city council has unraveled, and the matter has gone to the courts. None other than fellow Gila House resident Oliver S. Witherby serves as district judge and settles the matter on January 7. Bean and Couts must relinquish their claim to the properties.

Interestingly, Couts is allowed to keep the building he constructed on the purloined property, which will become a successful hotel called the Colorado House. It's a symptom of how the scandal settles—with Joshua Bean being the fall guy and Couts coming through virtually unscathed. He'll go on to become the new don of San Diego, while Mayor Bean quits office.

On January 10 Antonio Garra is tried by a court-martial composed of volunteer officers and presided over by Joshua himself. Cave Couts serves as judge advocate. Not surprisingly, at three p.m. Garra is sentenced to be shot. At four p.m. the sentence is scheduled to be carried out. Joshua

---

124 "Duel," *San Diego Herald*, November 27, 1851.

borrows weapons and ammunition from Thomas Sweeny, a US Army lieutenant stationed in San Diego, so his men can complete the punishment. "He died like a man," Sweeny remarks of Garra.[125]

It's Joshua's final act in San Diego. He knows of a place where the competition won't be too stiff yet that has enough life to support an ambitious businessman: Mission San Gabriel, just outside Los Angeles. The mission itself once flourished as a ranching operation that supplied food to dozens of other missions throughout California, but it's fallen from grace since being secularized in 1834. As a nexus for travelers to and from Los Angeles, it's a perfect place for a saloon.

Joshua closes his businesses in town and leaves before the end of January. He was pushed, but he was also ready to jump ship. San Diego's time has not come. As John Bartlett, of the US Boundary Commission, observes at the time, "There is no business to bring vessels here, except an occasional one with government stores. There is no water nearer than the San Diego River. . . . Wood has to be brought some eight or ten miles; nor is there any arable land within four miles."[126]

The cabal's attempts to build San Diego falter. Middletown won't work out, falling victim to a flat lack of interest. It and rival New Town both remain "paper" towns, empty lots left for some future generation to build on. The town's population will peak at 250 during 1851 and then start to decline.

The cabal members' quest to become *gente de razón* continues unabated. Cave Couts marries Ysidora Bandini, daughter of Don Juan, on April 5, 1851. The wedding party lasts three full days. He'll leave the army

---

125 "The Journal of Lt. Thomas Sweeny, 2nd Infantry," 1854–1855 Thomas William Sweeny Collection, MS 154, San Diego Historical Society Research Archives, San Diego, CA.

126 John Russell Bartlett, *Personal Narrative of Explorations and Incidents in Texas, New Mexico, California, Sonora, and Chihuahua* (New York: D. Appleton, 1854): 97.

in October, making his home on Guajome Rancho, a wedding present to his wife from her L.A.-based brother-in-law, Abel Stearns. Cave's brother William marries a daughter of Santiago Arguello.[127]

They find Don Juan Bandini hollow. He spends lavishly, but behind closed doors he operates in the red. He's waning as a power in San Diego, and his sons-in-law are taking over his hotel, his businesses, and his town. With no profits from his store, falling cattle prices, and mounting debts, Don Juan in April 1851 mortgaged his family home to Adolfo Savin for nearly $13,000. Bandini's son-in-law Charles Johnson, a former Gila House resident who married Dolores Bandini, arranged a loan to repay the debt to Savin.

Politically, Californios lost control of San Diego as of the first 1850 elections. Not counting the election of Estudillo and Juan Bandini, only three or four Californios will run during more than one hundred elections over the next six years. As a result, the city's policies fail to take these residents into account. The taxes that are imposed are ones many Californios can't meet, as the beef tallow trade ebbs and the land proves too arid for most agriculture. They are clear losers in the transition to American leadership.[128]

When Joshua leaves town for San Gabriel to set up a new saloon, he leaves his brother Roy behind. The crass, fun-loving town may be stumbling economically, but it's the kind of place Roy revels in. The Bean family is not yet done with San Diego.

---

127 Richard F. Pourade, *The Silver Dons, 1833–1865*, vol. 3, *The History of San Diego*, San Diego History Center, accessed October 29, 2023, https://sandiegohistory.org/archives/books/dons/ch9/.

128 When California was admitted to the Union as a state in 1850, resident Californios became American citizens with full voting rights. Don Bandini renounced his US citizenship but moved back to the United States to live out his remaining years

ROY

San Diego, California

February 1852

The dances in town usually start at ten p.m., leaving Roy Bean time to find a place to drink whiskey beforehand.

There's nothing in Chihuahua or even New Orleans that can hold a candle to a California ball. All the women of the area, white or Mexican, seem tutored in the fine art of the waltz and the polka, leaving clumsy-footed teamsters and horsemen to only gape until a country dance begins. There are bare legs and exposed bodices, curled hair and perfumed wrists, sly glances from under eye makeup. "The greatest sport in this country is dancing," says Robert Effinger, proving that this boundary commission stick-in-the-mud isn't immune to a room full of bouncing women. "All the California women waltz beautifully. They commence dancing here in the evening and keep it up until broad daylight in the morning."[129]

Roy heads for the plaza, the center of the action in San Diego. He's adopted the local style, wearing flared trousers and bright neckerchief during the day, and embroidered jackets and pants at night. The pearl-handled Bowie knife and pistol on his belt are ever present.

---

129 Effinger's letters, San Diego Historical Society archives.

On most evenings the plaza is busy with drunken immigrants and soldiers, but on weekends it plays home to traveling card sharks setting up monte bank tables for epic bouts of street gambling. Fights break out, usually between the soldiers and the recently arrived forty-niners, or the soldiers and Mexicans, or the forty-niners and Mexicans, or within these groups. "The gambling and drinking of the officers here and their exceedingly supercilious manners to the immigrants is very reprehensible," notes H. M. T. Powell, an artist who worked in San Diego at the time to earn enough money to mine gold. "Gamblers and gambling rife here, Sunday or no Sunday. Everybody gets drunk."[130]

Nightlife here is dominated by the fringe classes of San Diegans. Transients and immigrants from across the United States, Mexico, and the world are drinking, betting, and beating each other in a never-ending revelry that matches Roy's own impulses. Hanging over the scene are women—everything from curious señoritas to dime-a-dance workers to outright prostitutes.

Without Joshua around, it's safe to say that Roy has allowed chaos to take over more and more of his life. The absence of his mayoral sibling, and the way he left town, has left Roy at a disadvantage. He has no name for himself in San Diego, just the reflected glory and ignominy of his departed brother. Now he's insecure, eager to prove himself, and without any moderating influence.

What specifically provoked a confrontation between Roy Bean and John Collins, a Scottish immigrant chasing the Gold Rush, one night in San Diego? It could have been anything—a response to card-table bragging, making fun of the man's accent, peacocking for nearby women, or just the animosity that naturally develops between two large, proud men in close, drunken proximity. One version specifies that it started when the men began bragging about their shooting prowess. Once words got heated, a bar fight or even a stabbing could be expected. But that doesn't

130 Quoted in Pourade, *Silver Dons*, chapter 9, https://sandiegohistory.org/archives/books/dons/ch9.

speak to Roy's motivations. He wants spectacle. So he challenges Collins to a duel.

Dueling was an illegal but accepted part of southern culture, and it was imported wholesale to the frontier. The idea that personal integrity had actual value was not abstract in the American South; scholars say that the word "honor" there was culturally synonymous with "creditworthiness." The fact that dueling persisted until banks created standardized lending criteria seems to back this theory.[131]

But there was no financial angle in the case of Roy Bean and John Collins, only a psychological one. Roy may have been looking to impress the new Anglo elite of San Diego, many of whom were southerners, but securing his future was not his intent. If it had been, he wouldn't have set such absurd conditions for his duel with Collins. He challenges the man to a pistol match, on horseback, riding through Main Street. Not only is that location ideal for maximum visibility, but it also makes sense because the street is often used for horse races. This won't be a hidden shoot-out on the outskirts of town; it'll be a public performance. Roy is on a narcissistic quest for fame, and he doesn't care who gets hurt.

Such blatant lawlessness actually flies in the face of what the town's elite is trying to do with San Diego, which is to promote it as the West Coast's premier port. Roy is not surprised when Sheriff Haraszthy comes by the Gila House and warns him against the public duel.

But what is the young man supposed to do? Backing down is unthinkable to his self-image, the one he wants to project to the citizens of San Diego. He has promised a show, and when Roy Bean does that, no one can say he doesn't deliver.

And the truth is, he'll enjoy throwing a pole in the spokes of the wagon

---

131 According to a 2020 study, dueling behavior in the United States declined as state capacity (measured by the density of post offices) increased. Jeffrey L. Jensen and Adam J. Ramey, "Going Postal: State Capacity and Violent Dispute Resolution," *Journal of Comparative Economics* 48, no. 4 (2020), https://www.sciencedirect.com/science/article/abs/pii/S0147596720300378.

wheels of the hypocritical elites who chased off his brother. There is a part of Roy that justifies his actions by assuming moral positions that transcend the limits of written law. Dueling is illegal but socially acceptable, so it falls right into Roy Bean's intellectual sweet spot. He often takes the low road but justifies it with the rationale of higher principles. It'll be a part of his persona that only grows.

Sending an intermediary, Roy sets the date of the duel for Tuesday. Word of Collins's acceptance comes soon after.

The turnout on February 24 is better than Roy Bean could have hoped. One side of Main Street is lined with spectators, providing a mid-week boom for downtown businesses. Soldiers, women, drunks, gamblers, immigrants, and well-to-do merchants are lined up to witness the human blood sport. Roy finds the crowd's attention intoxicating.

He's dressed to the nines, aware of the eyes taking him in as he gallops to one end of Main Street. John Collins has also arrived, awaiting him down the thoroughfare. Sheriff Haraszthy rushes over, hair looking more clumsily upswept than usual.

"Sheriff Haraszthy pretended to regard the approaching duel between Roy Bean and the French [*sic*] gallant as a sort of joke," remarks Horace Bell, a California arrival from Indiana who includes an eyewitness-supplied account of these goings-on in his book *On the Old West Coast*. "Indeed, it would have been quite an impolitic act to call it off because news of the impending show brought rancheros swarming to town, the rancheros patronized the stores and cantinas and there ensued lively prosperity, for the moment at least."[132]

Now the sheriff is in a bind. He can't stop the duel before it starts, and a part of him hopes the men content themselves with a few missed shots to

132 Horace Bell, *On the Old West Coast* (New York: William Morrow, 1930): 225–227. He heard the details from witness and future state treasurer Guadalupe Estudillo. Bell came to Los Angeles in 1852 to visit an uncle, Alexander Bell, who had settled there.

satisfy their honor and back away bloodlessly. But these idiots are planning a shoot-out on a crowded city street.

"If you hit anyone in the crowd, I'll arrest you both for murder!" the sheriff cries to Roy. Roy waves off the comment and spurs his horse to a gallop. The crowd's murmuring escalates and then drops to a whisper. Collins also races ahead, drawing his pistol as he approaches.

What follows is more like a naval skirmish; neither rider wants to stay still and get shot at, nor can he take an accurate shot while in motion. Their strategies are foiled by the crowd. Whenever one of the men lines up a shot, the intended target can turn so that the spectators are behind him, spoiling any shot.

After several awkward, wheeling passes, Collins pulls his reins and takes two shots. They both miss by wide margins. Roy takes his own shot, but the ball whizzes past Collins's head. The Scotsman doesn't turn but just takes off, away from his opponent, likely hoping to end the duel with a draw.

Roy turns his mount to get behind Collins and shoots twice. The first shot punches into Collins's leg, the other kills the horse. Man and beast tumble to the ground as the crowd cries out in alarm and exhilaration. Roy Bean is triumphant and wants to hear as much from the crowd, but instead he finds an incensed Haraszthy preempting any such celebrations.

The sheriff arrests both duelists for attempted murder. Collins is taken to a doctor while Roy Bean is taken to jail.

The jail is certainly nicer than the one he stayed at in Chihuahua—not that that's saying much. It's also newer and seemingly modern, being the first stone jail in California's history. It measures thirty-four by twenty-four feet, with ten-foot-tall cobblestone walls. Inside are a long hallway and two separate holding cells. The windows allow plenty of air but are slatted with iron bars.

Haraszthy's had a tough time building the jail. After the first attempt collapsed (done in by poorly poured concrete and heavy rains), he received another $2,000 from the city council to try again. For $7,000, the new jail ought to be the pride of San Diego. But it's already proving to be vulnerable to escape—in February, two Native Americans arrested for disorderly conduct climbed out through the bars of a window and ran off.

Roy spends a month in the jail, with only drunks, Indians, and (kept in a separate cell) a limping John Collins for company. It's a tight spot, but Roy finds that the sheriff isn't averse to inmates buying privileges. "The sheriff would accompany inmates to a hotel," San Diego attorney G. A. Benzen writes a friend in 1852, "[to] jointly take their eye-openers, bitters or nightcaps, as the case may be."[133]

The pair are arraigned before criminal court judge John Ames (also the publisher of the *San Diego Herald*) on a warrant for attempted murder. The warrant is signed by county judge Withersby, Roy's neighbor in the Gila House. The duelists are bound for trial, with a bail set at $1,000 each, a steep amount neither can afford.

Given the lack of guards and the accommodating attitude toward prisoners, it shouldn't be a big surprise that Roy Bean decides to break out of the San Diego jail. All it takes is a friend willing to pass him a small blade so he can dig out the edges of the mortar near the window, and to tie his horse nearby so he can make a quick getaway.

Later, Roy will say that the local women were so moved by his gallantry that they passed him a knife inside a cake; in another version, the señoritas smuggled the implement in a bouquet of flowers. People's reactions to celebrity are strange; either of these stories could conceivably be true.

Of course, Joshua Bean also has friends in San Diego. No one else for certain could be counted on to care what happened to Roy. Joshua also has employees and confidants in San Gabriel who could have ridden south to liberate his brother. There's no evidence that this happened, but it makes more sense than an outpouring of female emotion for the reckless youth.

---

133 Randy Dotinga, "Dispatches from History Man: Jailbreak," Voice of San Diego, August 13, 2009, https://voiceofsandiego.org/2009/08/13/dispatches-from-history-man-jailbreak.

In any event, *someone* tethered Roy's horse nearby for his flight from San Diego.

The jailbreak is a municipal scandal, the second caused by a Bean family member within the year. In the aftermath, city officials are facing charges of nepotism and conflict of interest stemming from a big jail construction contract given to a family member of a city councilman. By April San Diego is seeing its funds dry up, and municipal bankruptcy is looming. The shoddy jail is a lightning rod for dissatisfaction with the greedy, incompetent city officials. (The state legislature will within months revoke the city charter and organize a board of trustees to administer public affairs.)

As for Roy, he heads to the one place he knows he'll be safe: at his brother's side in San Gabriel.

SAN DIEGO HERALD

April 17, 1852

Present, his Honor John Hays, Judge. After impaneling the Grand Jury, the District Attorney, J. W. Robinson, Esq., addressed them at some length on the nature of their duties and the law by which they would be governed in their deliberations. The Grand Jury presented bills of indictment against John Collins and P. R. Bean for an assault, with intent to murder, and for sending and accepting a challenge.

The Court adjourned over from day to day, till the 13th, when the Grand Jury presented the annexed report, together with bills of indictment. . . . Bean having broke jail and escaped, Collins was arraigned on the 14th, on the indictment for an assault with intent to kill. He pled not guilty.

Collins was arraigned on the charge of challenging to fight a duel. The case was given to the jury on the evening of the 16th, and in about twenty minutes, they returned a verdict of not guilty, and were discharged.

And we will take occasion to remark here, that there seems to be a cadre of persons in our community, whose sympathies are on the side of reckless and lawless men, and so long as this feeling prevails, there will be no such thing as order in society or safety for life or property.

JOSHUA

Mission San Gabriel, California
July 1852

In the foothills just east of the town of Los Angeles, at the crossroads of three important trails, once stood the "Pride of the California Missions." For hundreds of years starting in 1771, the Mission San Gabriel served as a refuge for the pious and the site of generations of Native American conversions. The Gabrielino-Tongva Indians built the Moorish structure, painted the stations of the cross inside, and worked the cattle and crops that fed a network of twenty other missions across the state.

But the last Franciscan left town this year. The rowdies have taken over San Gabriel.

In the southwestern corner of the former mission building stands Headquarters Saloon. Its owner, Joshua Bean, whitewashed the outside wall and painted the establishment's name in large black letters. It can be hard to see the letters through the crowd; there are nearly three hundred people clustered outside the saloon, lined up to watch the straightaway horse race matchups.[134]

---

134 Horace Bell, *Reminiscences of a Ranger; or, Early Times in Southern California* (Norman: University of Oklahoma Press, 1881; 2000): 92–93.

Horace Bell dubs Headquarters "the most aristocratic" of the three saloons in San Gabriel, not that that's saying much. "Old Jackson, the village pettifogger, stood behind the bar dealing out whiskey to the American, aguardiente to the Mexican and Indian, angelica to the feminine angels therein congregated, and a miscellaneous mixture to the squaws who were just beginning to get 'hellarious,'" he describes after a visit. "Two Monte games were in full blast in the Saloon, cockfighting and a Mexican circus going in the rear, and a horse race about to come off in front."[135]

When it comes to organizing these events, Roy is proving to be a natural. You can't miss him, dressed in full glittering finery, collecting bets, riling up the crowd to make emotional wagers, and generally creating a buzz. He's a showman, a spark of vitality in a crowd, impossible to ignore. He's replicating all the fun witnessed in San Diego, but now he and Joshua are serving as purveyors and beneficiaries of the chaos.

Accounts mention Headquarters offering "a woman for a time." This isn't surprising, but it's not necessarily prostitution. Joshua employs saloon girls, who are on hand to entertain the men and above all keep them drinking. It's hard to get a saloon girl drunk, because bartenders slip them colored water instead of whiskey and charge customers the full price. Some accept a dime for a dance. Few of these women are actually sex workers. In the parlance of the time, prostitutes were found at "bawdy houses" or "sporting lounges," separate business entities from saloons and dramshops.

Joshua has chosen his location well. The human stampede toward the gold mines has surged demand for beef, and purchasers who've exhausted their local supplies are now coming to Los Angeles. "The streets were thronged throughout the entire day with splendidly mounted and richly dressed *caballeros*, most of whom wore suits of clothes that cost all the way from $500 to $1,000, with saddle and horse trappings that cost even more," says Horace Bell. "Everybody in Los Angeles seemed rich; everybody *was* rich."

---

135 In a Mexican circus, traditional routines blended acrobatics, pantomime, clowning, singing, dancing, comedy routines, and dramatic monologues.

The cattle action pumps new blood into San Gabriel. As Roy makes money from public spectacles, Joshua keeps the store stocked, runs a stagecoach line, and prepares ways to parlay his role as major general of the state militia into a political career. Unlike in San Diego, a budding municipality is growing around the fallen mission, and this year San Gabriel has become the first official township in Los Angeles County.

But it's also a rough town. All of the county seems gripped with a murder fever, and lives are lost with incomprehensible frequency. The small puebla of Los Angeles alone records more than thirty-one homicides between September 1850 and 1851. San Gabriel is bigger and rowdier than Los Angeles, in large part courtesy of the grogshop that stands in the remains of the mission. "The place was certainly the 'Headquarters' of all the *lazzaroni* of the country," Bell opines.[136]

Local legends maintain that Native American blood sports involving clubs were what inspired the name of Headquarters Saloon. For Joshua Bean, the bar is literally the epicenter of his continuing rise as an important man of California. After all the years of marching, seeking, compromising, wheeling, and dealing, he finally has a piece of the West to call his own.

---

136 He's referring to the "homeless idlers of Naples who live by chance work or begging," per Merriam-Webster's online dictionary.

ROY

Mission San Gabriel, California
November 1852

Roy likes to tend bar. It's the one place in a saloon that everyone at one point or another must pay attention to. He can hold court, tell jokes, spin yarns, and keep his ear to the ground for gossip and brewing schemes. It's a natural position from which to flirt with women. What's not to like?

It's past eleven p.m. on November 6, and he's expecting an inflow of people coming back from a rope-dancing show. With three saloons in the immediate area, some of the business is bound to go elsewhere. With no competing show at Headquarters tonight, he'll work behind the bar, giving Old Jackson the night off.

News comes rushing in breathlessly from the saloon doors: Joshua Bean has been ambushed and shot down in the street.

Roy scrambles outside and races to where a crowd is gathered. He reaches the scene to see a dead horse, sprawled and bleeding in the roadway. He recognizes his brother's horse and saddle. "Where is he?"

Joshua is lying in a nearby house owned by a man named Juan Rico. A gunshot has punched through his torso: in the chest and out the back. Shock has set in, and he's barely conscious. A doctor is on the way, but if there's one thing Californians by now know, it's gunshot wounds. And this one looks serious.

The militia general can't describe who shot him. Two blasts came from the darkness as he rode for his home in the old mission building. One struck him in the chest, knocking him from the saddle; the other went wide. Another fusillade killed his horse, but by then Joshua had drawn his own pistol and fired three shots into the shadows, and the assailants fled. The man or men were on foot, accounting for the shot's trajectory upward into his chest.

Joshua Bean languishes through the night, swimming in and out of a morphine haze. He dies the next day.[137]

Los Angeles, California
November 1852

Roy Bean takes his place at the head of the crowd stuffed into Abbott's Bath House in downtown Los Angeles. It's hard to breathe against the densely packed mass of bodies, a crowd that extends into the street. This is the day, at long last, when his brother will get justice.

Roy spent the month of November agitating the so-called vigilance committee, formed by merchants and ranch owners, to make arrests in his brother's murder. The formation of such committees is a common reaction to spikes in crime, with private property owners taking up the law-and-order slack left by local governments.

This ad hoc California justice is frustratingly hypocritical. On the one hand, it's entirely illegal. But on the other, the process is nevertheless slow and procedural, going through pathetic versions of legal justice even as men are under threat of being hung without benefit of an actual trial or defense attorney. It's a well-orchestrated form of frontier justice, a slow-motion lynching.

There's a roundup of seven suspects in Los Angeles County. In San

---

137 *Nevada Journal* (Nevada City, CA), November 26, 1852, and *Placer Herald* (Rocklin, CA), December 4, 1852.

Gabriel, the illegal arrests sweep up Juan Rico, owner of the home where Bean collapsed, and a cobbler named Cipriano Sandoval. Hoodlums like Reyes Feliz and Jose Alviso are taken into custody at the behest of local landowners who are pretty sure they're horse thieves. (Revenge for the murder is being used to eliminate other area troublemakers, a response to the rising crime.) All the men arrested are Mexicans from Sonora except one, Felipe Reid, the Native American and Scottish son of a well-heeled Los Angeles politician.

Rico and Alviso are questioned and released. The rest are to be delivered to Los Angeles for a simultaneous investigation and interrogation under a self-appointed court, a "popular tribunal" that gives the veneer of fairness. Acceptance of these extralegal organizations is widespread. "It is not improbable that these persons will be tried by a people's court, and the guilty ones punished as they deserve," says the *Los Angeles Star* on November 27. "There can certainly be no objection to this mode of procedure when we hear our very court officers acknowledge that the law is utterly incapable of bringing them to justice."[138]

The prisoners spend a week being grilled about the crime. Horace Bell, another gawker somewhere in the crowd with Roy Bean, asks around about how the investigation unfolded inside an adobe house in downtown Los Angeles:

> The [investigating] sub-committee had been in session for about a week, endeavoring to extract confessions from the miserable culprits by a very refined process of questioning and cross-questioning, first by one of the committee, then by another, until the whole committee would exhaust their ingenuity on the victim, when all of their separate results would be solemnly compared, and all of the discrepancies in the prisoner's statements would be brought back to him and he be required to explain and reconcile them to suit the examining committee; and the poor devil, who

138 *Los Angeles Star*, November 27, 1852.

> doubtless was frightened so badly that he would hardly know one moment what he had said the moment previous, was held strictly accountable for any and all contradictions, and if not satisfactorily explained, was invariably taken by the wise heads of the said committee to be conclusive evidence of guilt.[139]

Worn down after days of these proceedings, Cipriano Sandoval makes a confession. On the fatal night, he was walking home from the *maroma* show when shots rang out in the darkness. The sound of coming footsteps ended with a collision between Sandoval and Felipe Reid, who was out of breath and holding a pistol. The two knew each other, and Reid said, "Cipriano, I have just shot Bean. Here is five dollars; take it, say nothing about it, and when you want money come to me and get it."

The motive was Bean's romantic pursuit of Reid's Native American mistress. This theory is entirely plausible to Roy Bean. His brother, like other important men, seemed to think that he belonged with any woman he wanted, including Reid's paramour. But seducing her wasn't worth Joshua's life.

The crowd hushes as a committee member solemnly reads the report as it relates to Sandoval. The self-appointed judge is none other than Don Bandini's son-in-law and creditor, Abel Stearns. He's so ugly that people in Los Angeles call him "Old Horse-Face." Stearns gives Sandoval an opportunity to speak. He declares his innocence. The crowd murmurs its doubts. The proceedings continue.

"Gentlemen, the court is now ready to hear any motion," Stearns says, his words slurred by a section of missing tongue, bitten off during a fistfight over the sale of a cask of wine.

A disheveled guy that Roy would have guessed belonged on trial for banditry stands. "I move that Cipriano Sandoval be taken to the hill and hung by the neck until he be dead."

"All in favor of the motion will signify the same by saying aye."

---

139 Bell, *Reminiscences of a Ranger*, 25.

Roy's voice joins a loud choir of "Aye, aye, aye!"

The death sentence is to be carried out the next morning.

The committee and crowd must be in a hanging mood, because all the accused thieves are given the same sentence, even though only one, Reyes Feliz, has confessed to stealing horses. And the animals were in turn stolen by Indians, Feliz says, so he literally is dying for nothing.

Roy is ready for Felipe Reid, the man who pulled the trigger on his brother, to receive the same treatment. Instead, Stearns enters "a motion" that Reid be turned over to "the legally constituted authorities." And the sheriff appears and takes the man away to make bail.

The fix is in, and the crowd accepts it silently. Felipe Reid is the son of Hugo Reid, former Los Angeles city councilman, San Gabriel justice of the peace, and until 1847 owner of the Rancho Santa Anita. He's had some money issues but remains a prominent landowner with a serious pedigree; in 1849 he was elected as a delegate to California's first Constitutional Convention and signed the state's first constitution. So much for legal justice. After Felipe Reid makes bail, the charges are quietly dropped.

Roy spends the night drinking in Los Angeles, frustrated but hardly surprised. He should have shot Reid himself or seen that he was hung in San Gabriel. He's witnessed the failure of both the sanctified justice system and the organized frontier justice of a vigilance committee. In both cases there are too many people involved, too much influence getting in the way of common sense. Better that one man enforce what's fair, whether that agrees with the lawbooks or not.

The clanging of a dinner bell draws him outside the next morning. People pour into the streets to follow the grim herald, the gathering crowd trailing the man all the way up Fort Hill. At the top, silhouetted by a dark sky like a giant scarecrow, stands a newly built gallows.

At just after nine a.m., five doomed men file up the stairs morosely, escorted by the local priest. A light rain starts to fall as Father Anacleto Lestrade, priest of Our Lady of the Angels Church on the Plaza, offers prayers of mercy. "Would the condemned like to speak?" asks the executioner, who will soon parlay this role into a municipal groundskeeping job.

The men remain silent until Sandoval raises his voice. "May great God pardon my murderers just as I pardon, since I die innocent of any crime." Anacleto walks before each of the condemned and offers a crucifix, which the men kiss. Thunder rumbles dramatically as the nooses are looped over their heads. The four traps are held by the same rope, so when the executioner slices it, all five men fall through the open doors. The lucky die of snapped necks, the unlucky strangle. After the twitching stops, the crowd assembles at the nearest tavern—the Bella Union, owned by Mayor Alpheus Hodges—to share the titillation. "And so ended the first great lynching in this very moral and justice-loving community," Bell says.[140]

There was a coda to the murder of Joshua Bean that resonated for longer than anyone in Los Angeles could imagine. Although Reyes Feliz wasn't connected to the murder, he confessed to running off horses from Jim Thompson's Brea ranch in 1851. And he mentioned the name of an accomplice: Joaquin Murrieta. It was a name that meant little until the next year, when rising crime and stiffening resistance from disaffected Mexicans was causing outbreaks of banditry—and fits of paranoia. Pretty soon, state and local officials became convinced that "Joaquin Murrieta" was forming a bandit army to exterminate whites. Furthermore, he was the head of a band of five bloodthirsty bandit chiefs, each named Joaquin.

There's no doubt that crime was rampant in Los Angeles County, which was infested with bandits and outlaws who appreciated the proximity of the Mexican border. But the fears of widespread revolution graduated "Joaquin Murrieta" from an obscure horse thief to an existential threat. The governor soon offered a $1,000 reward for a man who may not even have existed.

The farce concluded the following year, when the state delegated a troop led by Harry Love to hunt them, at a salary of $150 a month per man and a share of the governor's reward. These California Rangers were the

---

140 Execution coverage that mirrored Bell's descriptions appeared in the *San Francisco Herald* and was reprinted in other newspapers, including the *Placer Herald*, December 18, 1852.

first statewide law enforcement organization in California history. They raided a gang of suspected horse thieves, severed the heads of the men they killed, and rode into Sacramento to collect the reward. The California Rangers then disbanded.

The head of Murrieta—whoever it actually was—made a tour of the state for paying customers. Months after the tour ended, a San Francisco publisher released John Rollin Ridge's book *The Life and Adventures of Joaquín Murieta, the Celebrated California Bandit.*[141] It created a dramatic backstory for Murrieta, whom Ridge portrayed as having been transformed by Anglo violence from a peaceful vaquero to a steely bandit. The novel's themes match the negative experiences of many Mexicans living under American rule, but the details are pure fiction. In 1919, the saga became one of the inspirations for the hero Zorro.

A murder became a miscarriage of justice, which spawned a legend and a media icon. Left in the aftermath of actual history was Joshua Bean, unavenged and forgotten, and the suddenly rudderless brother he left behind.

Los Angeles, California
December 1852

It's a still, cold night in the City of Angels. Dozens of men with rifles are preparing for action, Roy Bean among them. They're closing in on the plaza, rifles and pistols at the ready.

When John Raines and Roy meet, it's clear they'll end up either shooting each other or enabling each other toward new heights of hijinks. It turns out they're two of a kind. Together they engineer a hoax that is meant to shake the nerves of Los Angeles's best people to their cores.

Chief among their targets is Mayor Hodges, the affable man who owns the Bella Union. Horace Bell described him as "the junior member of the hotel firm, who was also Mayor of the city, and, like mayors in general . . . he just smiled all over, and all the time. It was a perpetual smile with genial old Hodges." Roy Bean and the toughs in town don't like the

141 Spellings of Murrieta's name varied.

man, deriding him as "a timid sort of fellow, in total dominion of his wife, a Spanish California lady."[142]

Roy and John Raines organize the town's rowdies into two sides and brief them on the plans. One side will play rampaging anti-American revolutionaries, the other will rush in as friendly reinforcements. Both drunken mobs load their weapons with blanks and surge into the night, taking their positions around the plaza, home to Mayor Hodges and other people of quality. The kind of people who let murderers go free.

Roy starts the men's fusillade with a rifle blast. Soon gunpower explosions and smoke clouds blossom across the city center, accompanied by shrieks of "Viva la Republica!" and "Muerte a los gringos!"

And into the plaza comes Hodges, calling out to the armed Americans nearby for help. He's heartened by an incoming rush of riflemen, who form a line and blast away into the darkness. Return fire fells them by the score, and they drop, writhing in pain. Hodges retreats, first to check on the well-being of Doña Maria, his wife, and then to spend the rest of the firefight sheltering in a wet culvert. The gunfire on both sides continues until the sky starts to lighten and the insurrectionists melt away.

"Hodges and the other town officials were kept in mortal terror the whole night long," Roy later recalls, cherishing the memory. "All the men he had seen bleeding and falling down mortally wounded greeted him with a derisive shout. . . . Not til then was he made aware that he had been the victim of an atrocious hoax."

In a conversation with a reporter, Roy will later credit the prank to the quality of the roughnecks who won the West: "It was a crazy exploit, dictated by that buoyancy of spirit and that love of mad adventure that characterized the American daredevils who then overran California." It's a comment entirely without self-reflection.

Pranks entertain and aggrandize the prankster as much as they diminish the victim. Roy will never question why he devotes so much energy

142 *Pittsburgh Press*, September 25, 1893. This article is the source of all quotes from Roy Bean in this chapter unless otherwise attributed.

to flagrantly denying, mocking, and subverting authority. He simply recognizes the hypocrisy of men in high places, and so they deserve what he dishes out.

LOS ANGELES STAR

January 29, 1853

Groceries and Liquers

The undersigned, having recently purchased the stocx of goods formally belonging to J. H. Bean deceased, inform the public of San Gabriel and vicinity that he will continue the business heretofore carried on by the said deceased, as the old stand. A well selected stock of the best Family Groceries and liquors will be always on hand, which will be offered for sale at the lowest prices.

ROY BEAN
San Gabriel[143]

San Gabriel, California
March 1853

The doors to Headquarters Saloon bang open early Sunday afternoon, and Roy Bean cranes his head to see who's there instead of at the nearby hanging. He's disappointed when it's not his employee but a large man in typical prospector's garb. It's none other than Horace Bell, the Indiana native (and future author) who visited Headquarters on his first tour of California.

Roy has a new job since Bell last saw him: sole proprietor of the Headquarters Saloon. The county's favorite crossroads for rampant gambling, Sunday horse races, grocery supplies, and excessive drinking is continuing

143 The notice ran again in the *Los Angeles Star* on February 26. The notice spells "liquor" two different ways, and spells "stocks" with an *x*.

under his ownership. And he's dressed for the part of saloon dandy, in a slick but disheveled black and white caballero outfit. A pair of the latest-model revolvers—six-shot Colt Revolving Belt Pistols, or "Navy Pistols"—hang from his belt.[144] Bell steals a glance at one of Roy's expensive red-topped boots and sees the silver handle of a sheathed Bowie knife jutting from it.

The two exchange pleasantries before Bell gets down to business. "Do you have barley for my horse?"

"Yes," Bean says. "As soon as Vicente comes in, when they get through hanging that fellow."

The crime story unfolding here isn't complicated; it's sadly typical. The man being hung is a Native American—no one asks from which tribe—who killed a companion in a drunken fight at the saloon the previous night. The crowd detained him and, this morning, took him before the justice of the peace, Judge B. F. Dennison. His Honor holds court at the rival grogshop of Frank Carroll, where Dennison sentenced the man to be hung. Now, about six hundred feet away from where they're talking, the still-sobering defendant is being strung from a tree in front of a crowd of men, women, and children.

A thought dawns on Roy. "Watch my front door and see that no damned thief steals my whiskey," he says. Then he dashes out the door, mounts his horse, and gallops off to watch the man swing, and to make sure the crowd comes to Headquarters to commemorate the occasion afterward. Which they do, drinking with an energy that's disturbing.

Bell likes the looks of San Gabriel from the outside, but the town's low value on human life unnerves him: "I saw a man go directly upward to the limb of a tree and there remain until an hour later, when, with a feeling in strange contrast with the exhilaration felt on approaching the pleasant looking place, I took my departure without getting the feed of barley for my gallant little charger."

Likewise, he rides away with a dim view of the new boss of Headquarters. "Roy Bean in all the pomp and glory of being the cock of the walk," he

---

144 This was a cap-and-ball revolver designed by Samuel Colt and in service 1851–1873.

describes. "Showing and assuming all the importance and brief authority of lording it over the Headquarters and all that reckless throng."[145]

But Horace Bell and Roy Bean are destined to the thrown together again, sooner than either one knows.

LOS ANGELES STAR

August 6, 1853

Public Defense—the Los Angeles Rangers

The people of this county have long felt the necessity of having among them an efficient military force, which could be brought out promptly in aid of the laws and for the protection of life and property. We are not only exposed to regular predatory visits from Indians from the neighboring mountains, who come here to feed on cattle and carry off horses, and who have never yet been even once chastised, and, consequently, are every day getting bolder in their forays amongst the ranchos; but, recently, we have seen an organized band of robbers, well mounted, and well armed, traversing the country unmolested, sometimes making no concealment of their movements, supplying themselves with the best horses with impunity, until it is universally admitted that the roads are unsafe to travel and a sense of utter insecurity prevails in house and field. . . .

A remedy for this state of things will, we conceive, be found mainly in the organization of the "Los Angeles Rangers." This corps consists of one hundred members, but only twenty-five form the active force, their horses to be furnished gratuitously by the rancheros as a loan to the company; forage for and the herding of, the horses, together with equipment (arms excepted) to be paid for by the county and private subscription. The horses, etc., will be kept in

145 Bell, *Reminiscences of a Ranger*, 351.

this city ready at a moment's warning. The members furnish their own arms until they shall be furnished by the state.

The Board of Supervisors have agreed to appropriate $1000 to this purpose, in the confidence that the urgent necessity of the case will cause the next Legislature to reimburse the county Treasury in that amount.[146]

San Gabriel, California
August 1853

Word comes into Headquarters, as it always does, in the form of someone babbling the news as they barrel through the front doors. There's been an attack at the Everton place, across the arroyo from Headquarters. The Los Angeles Rangers are gathering to respond.

Roy rushes out the door to his horse. Dashing into the night to chase outlaws is exactly why he joined the Rangers. Part-time crime fighting is a perfect fit for his ambitions as a public figure and sates his adventurous inclinations.

As far as posses go, this one is well organized. The Los Angeles Rangers operate under a chain of command, taking orders through their captain, who in turn is under orders from a sheriff or town marshal. This militia, the first official police force of Los Angeles, has Mexican and Anglo members.

Roy sees fellow Rangers gathering in the street, torches flickering. There's a familiar face illuminated beneath one: that of Horace Bell, one of the unit's twenty-five full-time members. He and the militia have been patrolling the paths around the county, what Bell calls "the bandit trail," and are in good position to respond to the crime nearby.

The details that Roy hears get his blood boiling. A gang broke into the Everton residence, seemingly taking advantage of the fact that Mr. Everton

146 *Los Angeles Star*, August 6, 1853. Accessed via the California Digital Newspaper Collection, a project of the Center for Bibliographical Studies and Research at the University of California, Riverside, https://cdnc.ucr.edu.

and the family's boarder, Doc Sturgis, were away, leaving his wife and teenage son alone. But they weren't as vulnerable as the bandits assumed, for sixteen-year-old Everett Everton interrupted an attempted assault on his mother by blazing away at the home invaders with a pair of old precision lock pistols he fetched from Sturgis's room.

Most believe that the outlaws are the same ones who recently robbed a whorehouse and its customers and assaulted the women. Now the ad hoc Ranger company will spend days scouring the county for the criminals, keeping an eye out for Indian bands while they're at it.

The men on the trail bond over firepits and shared bottles of whiskey. Bell finds his opinion of Roy Bean softening, a least a little bit, when he experiences the man away from the saloon. In the wilds, confidence, a capability for violence, and determination are survival traits instead of the liabilities they are in town. The seeds of a friendship are planted, although Bell never truly forgets his initial impression that Roy is a scoundrel equally capable of bravery and chicanery.

The chase for the Everton attackers goes nowhere. "The Rangers vainly endeavored to track this band of criminals to their lair, and a perfect reign of terror obtained for some months," Roy later relates.

For him, it's a perfect break from the drudgery of saloon and store ownership. Keeping the booze and merchandise in stock has proven vexing, to the point where Roy has to buy ads saying he has "replenished his store" and imploring people "to give him a call at his old stand, and he assures them he will be able to please."[147] In comparison, riding as an auxiliary Los Angeles Ranger affords the opportunity for a marginal man to gain some glory.

Alas, Roy's crimefighting résumé is fairly thin. His biggest claim to an apprehension comes in late February 1854, when Atanacio Moreno walks into the store, probably figuring it's a safe place. He's from a good family, but he "took to his heels" when his business went bankrupt. Wanted by creditors and desperate for funds, he gathers some accomplices and forms

147 *Los Angeles Star*, December 10, 1853.

a robber gang. Moreno also makes a brisk business by cashing in on the Murrieta craze and informing on other gangs, and then taking over their action. He even kills one of his own gang members for the reward money.

No one knows he's an outlaw and a murderer, but he's still wanted for his debts. Roy draws his pistol on the man as he shops and delivers him to the Los Angeles Rangers. Moreno soon confesses to banditry, and one of the many criminal gangs of Los Angeles County comes to an unlikely end.[148]

The source of this version of Moreno's story is Roy Bean himself—and he may have stolen it from someone else. *Los Angeles Star* publisher Benjamin Truman, in an 1889 history of Los Angeles County, ascribes the downfall of Moreno to another store operator.[149] The newspaperman says Charles Ducommun recognized a stolen watch and went to Marshal William Getman to identify Moreno as a thief.

Roy's other big anticrime effort smells more like an effort to put one of the county's wealthiest Mexican families in its place. The Lugo family was a beneficiary of the provision in the 1848 Treaty of Guadalupe Hidalgo that Spanish land grants would be honored since the families' wealth stemmed from having owned the massive tracts of land since the late 1700s. Don Antonio Lugo's ranch included the Casa de Rancho San Antonio mansion, one of the finest in the county.

The trouble started when two of the sixty-five-year-old don's nephews rode after Apache horse thieves, only to bump into a party of Americans on the way home. Their blood up from a fight with the Indians, the nephews got into a quarrel with the other party that resulted in the unwarranted shooting of two Americans, or so the Anglos in town claimed. Soon the Los Angeles Rangers were called on to respond. Roy said that he and ten Rangers rode out to Lugo's ranch, bluffed their way inside the mansion,

---

148 Atanacio Moreno, "From Los Angeles," *Placer Herald*, February 25, 1854.

149 Moreno was sent to a severely overcrowded San Quentin and pardoned in 1859.

held the Lugo nephews at sudden gunpoint, and made a quick retreat to Los Angeles with the prisoners in tow.

Roy ascribed the two men's eventual release to the "liberal use of bribes" and indicated that there was a trial. If a trial of two close relatives of Los Angeles County's richest man occurred, it somehow wasn't mentioned in newspapers.

Faced with lies and stories impossible to prove, it would be easy to toss out all Roy Bean's tales about his past. But there is something to be learned from the ones he chose to promote. They invariably feature Roy speaking some basic truth to power or exposing systemic corruption. Even while wearing the trappings of the system—being a part-time Los Angeles Ranger—he presented himself as antiauthoritarian. It'll be the core ethos of a legend that will outlive him.

SAM

La Mesilla, New Mexico Territory

November 1854

It seems like everyone in Doña Ana County has come to Mesilla's humble plaza to witness history. All eyes are turned upward as a pair of soldiers hoist an American flag above the plaza and a military band plays "Yankee Doodle Dandy."

Today, November 18, the first day of the New Mexico Territory's existence, Sam Bean stands alongside various officials at the head of the crowd. In the best family tradition, he's not only a businessman but a public servant. As an American who's been vested in Doña Ana County since 1849, Sam's perfectly positioned to help run this newly acquired land.

In Mesilla's public square, Sam can literally see his financial future. This will be the center of a prosperous American town, and he wants to be part of its foundation. He'll buy property right here on the square, where the stagecoaches stop and the saloons will rake in money by catering to teamsters and travelers. Permanency is on Sam's mind; he has a young family in Petra, five-year-old Celia, and a newborn daughter, Virginia. They live in a house around the corner from the plaza.

Crowded around a small platform, the vast majority in attendance are Mexican residents, who until now were citizens of that nation. Messila's population has steadily increased, to about one thousand people, and on November 16 they're being given a choice: become Americans or leave.

New Mexico governor David Meriwether listens patiently, waiting for his turn to speak. President Franklin Pierce appointed the Kentucky politician, a former Democratic senator, last year after Senator Solon Borland turned down the governorship.[150] He's a thick man with a fat forehead and double chin who would be bald if not for the prominent sweeps of long hair springing out the top and back of his head. General John Garland stands next to him, looking stern and proper for the audience. He and Meriwether just the day before met with Chihuahua governor Ángel Trías to formalize the military transfer.

The deal is called the Gadsden Purchase, named for the lead US negotiator and signed in the Double Eagle Hotel in Mesilla. It traded $10 million for twenty thousand square miles of disputed land.[151]

The situation here seemed destined for a different end—possibly a bloody one—just a few months ago. On April 3, troops under the command of Governor Trías occupied Mesilla, having done the same in El Paso days before. It was a benevolent occupation, but one that forbade trade with the United States. Sam Bean respects Trías but didn't appreciate this impediment to trade.

Then Antonio López de Santa Anna came back. He seized presidential power on April 30, after the Mexican government fell apart. Fearing war, he sealed the Gadsden Purchase, along the way managing to alienate the Mesilleros by ignoring the previous government's 1849 repatriation legislation. Those who were double-crossed described themselves as *los vendidos de Santa Anna*, "those whom Santa Anna sold."

---

150 In 1846 Borland challenged a rival newspaper editor to a duel, and during an 1850 debate over southern rights, Borland physically attacked Mississippi senator Henry Foote.

151 W. H. Timmons, "American El Paso," *Southwestern Historical Quarterly* 87 (July 1983–April 1984): 34.

When the music dies down, Meriweather speaks, pausing to allow his Spanish interpreter to recite his words to the assembled crowd. "By peaceful negotiations this disputed territory has been transferred to the United States," he says. "It is my hope that you all prove yourselves to be loyal and law-abiding citizens, but if you do not, it is my duty at all hazards to see the law is executed. Any citizen who prefers the Mexican to American government is free to sell their belongings and move to the other side of the line. But I hope you will give the American government an opportunity of showing its advantages."[152]

Seven weeks before, Sam won his first election, becoming sheriff of Doña Ana County. The position opened after the appointed predecessor, John Jones, skipped town in May, supposedly with purloined taxpayer money. (He did leave toward the end of his term, the time when officials account for the year's spending.)

Sam's commission won't start until the end of the month. The job will soon be a huge challenge. Thanks to the treaty, in two years Doña Ana County, his jurisdiction, will extend from the Texas border to the Colorado River, with settlements on both sides of the ninety-mile Jornada del Muerto.[153] At three hundred by eight hundred miles, it'll be larger than any state east of the Mississippi River.

A few weeks after the handover ceremony, on November 25, he takes the oath: "I, Samuel G. Bean, sheriff and collector of the county of Doña Ana and Territory of New Mexico do solemnly swear before Almighty God that I will discharge my duties as sheriff and collector of said county and that I will support the Constitution of the United States, so help me God."

It's a vow that will be tested.

---

152 Quoted in William Kiser, *Turmoil on the Rio Grande* (Texas A&M University Press, 2011): 94.

153 The area includes modern Arizona, and even in Sam Bean's time there were those in the region who agitated for it to become its own territory, and eventually its own state.

JAMES

Independence, Missouri
May 1854

James Bean watches silently as the remaining property of Samuel Owens is auctioned on the courthouse steps. The deceased trader's heirs and the Aull family have fallen out, between each other and within each clan, leading to a dissolution of Owens's assets under sheriff's order. The bidding today includes a fourteen-acre plot with a stately home on it. That property ends up with William McCoy, who has just completed his one-year term as mayor of the newly incorporated City of Independence.

James honors the spirit of Owens by rebuilding his life with trips to New Mexico, taking wagon trains there and bringing hard currency back to the United States. These days he's apt to travel by steamboat to St. Louis on the way home, a much safer way to carry thousands in specie. Even with Independence taking a back seat to Kansas City, there's opportunity; the eating house at the Wayne City landing caters to the traffic that still comes through there.

James is politically active, and he rubs shoulders with the current leading men of Jackson County. In the summer to come he'll be appointed by William Gilpin—a Mexican War veteran, Independence land speculator, and state politician—to cochair a Democratic Party County Committee. James also purchases land in the addition that Gilpin is developing in northern Independence.

Politics these days is fraught with peril. President Pierce has just signed the Kansas-Nebraska Act into law, setting into motion the seeds of civil war. Stephen A. Douglas introduced the bill in January, proposing to carve the Kansas Territory into two states: Nebraska, which would be a free state, and Kansas, where slavery would be legal, overruling a prohibition put in place as part of the Missouri Compromise.

No one was happy. The Whigs imploded over the issue, and northern Democrats fell on each other in division. The Republican Party formed in the ashes of this turmoil. Settlers from the North and the South are moving into the former Kansas Territory, dead set on championing their opposing views on slavery.

The rhetoric is heating up around Jackson County, just across the territory's line. Missouri's been a slave state since 1822, and the counties adjacent to Kansas are highly populated by southerners. The idea that abolitionist havens could be founded nearby is bad enough, but the rhetoric of radicals promises liberation raids on nearby slaveowners regardless of state lines.

The Kansas-Nebraska crisis prompts Abraham Lincoln to remain in politics. He sees trouble ahead. "The South flushed with triumph and tempted to excesses; the North, betrayed, as they believe, brooding on wrong and burning for revenge," he predicts. "One side will provoke; the other resent. The one will taunt, the other defy; one aggresses, the other retaliates."[154]

If James Bean likewise sees the storm clouds gathering, he's not letting it get in the way of reassembling his life in Independence. In 1855, William Moore dies, leaving behind his thirty-nine-year-old widow, Elizabeth, and his son, Charles. Elizabeth and James are close in age, mutually seeking a

154 Speech on the Kansas-Nebraska Act, October 16, 1854, *Speeches and Letters of Abraham Lincoln: 1832–1865* (New York: E. P. Dutton, 1907).

nuclear family, and comfortable with kids. Best of all, she's from Kentucky. She's a perfect wife.

James now has a family, an income, and property. It's time to bring his children home.

ROY

San Gabriel, California
February 1855

Roy Bean, half-drunk and maudlin, leans against the whitewashed wall outside Headquarters Saloon to watch the sun set. The sky provides the only easy gold California is offering these days. Panning no longer pays off since all the surface gold has been scraped away by earlier seekers.

Independent miners, Roy thinks bitterly, don't exist around here anymore. Gold has become just another wage job, and the only money goes to the companies large enough to invest in the heavy mining equipment that even now uses high-powered water drills. The lifeblood of Roy's business is a steady supply of rowdy boomtown workers. Without them, life at the saloon isn't just dull; it's financially kneecapped. His entire business model is based on getting the easy money from the pockets of those passing through.[155]

Amid this downturn, it's been a particularly tough month for Roy. He

---

155 Roy Bean didn't know that the California rush had peaked in 1852. That year, the same year his brother died, prospectors dragged $81 million in gold from the California ground, compared to just $45 million in 1855. Those statistics are not abstract for Roy Bean's bottom line.

has spent much of it in custody. It started innocently enough, with "Spanish Californians" in Los Angeles advertising the appearance of the great bullfighter Don Jesus, straight from the Plaza del Toros in Mexico City.[156] The Mexican and Anglo populations turned out in droves, Roy included.

To the crowd's annoyance, the bull introduced into the ring was "a mild ox, meek as a lamb." When the someone recognized the toreador as a waiter—or thought they did—the Americans in the crowd started to brawl, with Roy at the vanguard. It was a nice little riot, but it got Roy thinking about a more elaborate revenge.

He and a handful of accomplices took out ads in all the local Spanish papers touting the appearance of a race featuring a rare "Kanaka swimming horse," an island-hopping steed that Roy Bean himself said he would ride from San Pedro beach to Santa Catalina Island. He sold tickets for the event, as well as admissions to see the animal while it was stabled in Los Angeles. The animal was, naturally, only an old mustang; there's no such thing as a Kanaka horse.

The night before the race, Bean and a man he referred to only as "Ball" crept into the stable and stole their mustang. "The Spaniards too late found out that they had been done by hated gringo, whose only desire had been to get square with them for the deception practiced on Americans," Roy will say. But he also admits to turning a "handsome revenue" from the scheme.

The Kanaka episode was clearly a clumsy reprisal, a fleecing of more innocent victims instead of those who staged the bunk bullfight to begin with. Many of those who fell for the swimming horse also bought tickets to the bullfight and had been ripped off twice. But it was a perfect Roy Bean scenario: vigilante fraud for his own profit and devilish entertainment. Fairness was defined through his narrow prism: Americans getting wholesale revenge on highbrow "Spanish" Mexicans in Los Angeles.

The authorities were not amused, and it seems Roy was arrested for

---

156 *Pittsburgh Press*, September 25, 1893, which is also the source for all quotes from Roy Bean in this chapter, unless otherwise attributed.

the stunt. In mid-February he was placed in custody on charges including grand larceny, but the case was dismissed on February 22 "for want of witnesses," according to a newspaper brief. The article adds that he remained in custody "on another charge," but whatever it alleges also goes nowhere, and Roy is released.[157]

He's escaped the law (again), but these turns have put Roy in a dark, surly mood. This makes him volatile—and dangerous. With the sun now gone, Roy takes a last snort of whiskey, adjusts his Navy Pistols, and strides away from Headquarters to Frank Wahle's store to give him a piece of his mind.

The pair had words in town the previous night, an argument that was spiraling into a fight before being broken up. If Wahle thinks it's over, he has another thing coming. Tuesday's fistfight is on the path to becoming Wednesday's duel.

The appearance of the large, gruff man sets Frank Wahle on edge. The argument heats up to a boil, but before Roy can issue any kind of challenge, Wahle draws his pistol and shoots him in the chest.

Roy wheels and staggers from the store, visions of his brother's death crowding his brain. He makes it to the front door of Headquarters before collapsing. But his luck is better than Joshua's, and the bullet is removed without causing any infection. All he has to do is heal, savor the idea of Wahle languishing in that dirt-floor prison, and read the newspaper coverage of the shooting.

It's a rude surprise. The newspapers are not kind to the victim of this incident. "We learn that Roy Bean was shot through the chest Wednesday afternoon by some persons unknown," reads an item in the *Southern Californian*. "The event transpired at the store of Frank Wahle, where Bean was cutting up his rushes much to the inconvenience and disgust of the company. Although alive at last accounts it is hardly expected that he will recover."[158]

---

157 *Southern Californian* (Los Angeles), February 22, 1855.

158 "Affray at San Gabriel," *Southern Californian*, March 14, 1855.

The editor of the *Los Angeles Star* isn't much nicer, accusing Roy of dueling, which is in line with Roy's character but hardly fair and could lead to charges against him. "A free fight came off here on Tuesday evening last, in consequence of too free use of bad liquor," sums up the newspaper editor, named only as Felipe. "On Wednesday evening extensive preparations were made for a second act in the drama, and while the play was in full blast, Roy Bean—a notorious character and principal actor on the stage—received a pistol shot to the breast, which knocked him into a cocked hat, and put an end to the performance, to the great gratification of our peaceful citizens."[159] It's a good story, and a believable one, but no one was ever charged with dueling.

Instead, on July 13 Wahle is charged with assault with intent to kill. In August, Wahle's business associate Nathan Tuck parts ways with the man, including a very public notice announcing a "Dissolution of Partnership." But if Wahle did time in prison, there's no record of it in the California Prison and Correctional Records. Either his trial went quietly well for him, or else authorities just dropped the charges because he'd shot a belligerent jerk.

159 *Los Angeles Star San Gabriel*, March 15, 1855.

JAMES

Independence, Missouri
June 1856

The headline of the *Missouri Republican* reads, "Exciting News from Kansas," but James doesn't feel anything like excitement as he reads the front page. Abolitionists have murdered five proslavery settlers at Pottawatomie. It's a spark that might now consume Kansas and spread into his section of Missouri as well.

Everyone knows that Kansas's vote for a territorial legislature last March was a litmus test for the slavery issue. Thousands of Missourians, led by US senator David Atchison, crossed the border into Kansas to illegally cast votes. Free-staters sidestepped the results by electing their own delegates, adopting a constitution, and petitioning Congress for statehood. President Franklin Pierce denounced them as traitors.

That's when a proslavery posse, a good bulk of them Missourians, marched on Lawrence, Kansas. The city was a lightning rod, founded by abolitionists and home to a prominent movement newspaper. On May 21, the mob (led by Douglas County, Kansas, sheriff Samuel Jones) burned a house and destroyed several printing presses.

The proslavery militia then retreated, their point made. No one was killed.[160]

Three nights later, an abolitionist in Kansas named John Brown assembled six followers and stalked to a settlement on Pottawatomie Creek, in Franklin County. There, they butchered five proslavery settlers, including fathers and sons, within earshot of their shrieking families.

James reads the newspaper article and gets a flavor of the trouble the nation is now in. The *Missouri Republican* has been a stalwart Whig publication, but recent events have turned it toward proslavery Democrats. (In 1856, the *Republican* supported James Buchanan for president.) "What James reads is the same as what he's been hearing from his neighbors, business partners, and preteen boys. And while he's not a firebrand, the words rile his own slave-owning, southern heart: "The abolitionists are again under arms; so soon as the militia dispersed they began to murder in the dark. There is no open fight in them. For more than a year, the fanatics in Lawrence have been swearing that they would fight before surrendering. On the 21st they had a fair chance for a daylight fight, but they is not what they want. . . . Today we get authentic news of the murder of several citizens on Pottawatomie Creek in cold blood."[161]

What follows are details that James has already read in the "extra" spreadsheet published in Independence, some of which he suspects is exaggerated. Maybe the abolitionists cut the ears off that young man before hacking him to death. Maybe they didn't. In the end, the lad ended up a cadaver.

What James wants to see from the St. Louis-based *Republican* is a reaction from that city's Democrats, and he gets it: "What can be said of such things? They exceed the barbarities of savages. If the abolitionists are

---

160 "Exciting News from Kansas," *Missouri Republican* (St. Louis), June 3, 1856. Sam Jones would quit and leave Missouri for La Mesilla, New Mexico. There he found little opportunity. Sam Bean and others had beaten him to the turf.

161 Ibid.

men of blood, why not shed it as men? Because they are not men." After the rehash of the horror there's an update from St. Louis with more evidence of the panic spilling over into Missouri from Kansas. "Within a few days, many families have arrived from Hickory Point, in Kansas who were driven from their farms, and in some cases their negroes and horses stolen. The negroes were told that they could go to Missouri and be slaves or stay here and be free. Those that remained were armed. Some would not remain."

James Bean is reading the newspaper from his farm, worked by six slaves. The land sits just five miles outside Independence, along the river to the northeast of the city. It's out of the way of main roads, but also vulnerable. It's a ripe target for Kansas abolitionists if they take retaliatory aim at Jackson County for their involvement in the bloody events in Kansas.

The St. Louis newspaper confirms what he's hearing in town—the promise of more fighting ahead: "What is to be the end of these outrages? If they do not cease soon, they can only end in war and extermination of one side or the other party. . . . They ran with the very guns in their hands that they had sworn to fight with, and begged for quarter. It was granted, but as soon as the [proslavery] troops dispersed to their homes, Sharp's rifles are being flourished again. They will have one more time to use them."

ROY

San Gabriel, California
September 1857

Roy's antagonizing the locals, squandering his family's reputation, scrapping by at Headquarters, and stubbornly failing to craft a backup scheme. He's nearly been murdered, and even worse he was humiliated during the aftermath. Roy has got to change his image; as soon as he heals up, it'll be time for some public service. Hopefully one with a paycheck.

On September 5, he wins his first municipal election when he becomes a constable, doing the work for justices W. R. Heninger and Felipe Duarte. The job mixes courtroom security with court-approved property seizures, visits to people to serve court paperwork that they don't want, and public auctions.

As a moonlight job, it's a good fit for Roy. There's not a lot of flash to it, but it elevates him from a mere saloon and store operator into a public figure, albeit a minor one. The position bolsters his reputation; he wins reelection in 1858 and 1859.

In records "Showing the Expenditures of the County of Los Angeles from November 9th 1859, to November 13th, A. D. 1860," there is a line item for money paid to Roy Bean for constable's services in criminal cases tallying $45.45.

It'll be the last known record of Roy Bean in California.

SAM

La Mesilla, New Mexico
March 1860

Sam steps aside as the Butterfield Overland Stage rattles into downtown Mesilla, a pair of riders steering the sealed wagon past the town's new adobe church, which is just two years old. The mail route connects this small community to the world via direct routes to San Antonio and San Diego.[162]

As usual, the plaza is brimming with commerce. Vendors from Texas and Mexico sell fruit and vegetables from the backs of carts, butchers in stalls sell cuts of meat from freshly killed livestock, wood sellers push loaded burros to empty spots to unload. The town gets twenty-five cents per vendor per day. The open-air market brings citizens from the surrounding areas and soldiers on leave from Fort Fillmore.

Sam owns one of the best buildings on the block—a saloon formerly owned by the regional land commissioner Guadalupe Miranda. It's an adobe structure that was once a blacksmith shop, now a popular destination

162 Congress authorized a contract for an overland trail and letter-carrying service in 1857. The contract was won by John Butterfield and his associates, who proposed a southern route heading west from St. Louis, Missouri, and Memphis, Tennessee (converging at Little Rock, Arkansas), to California, and the Butterfield Stage Line was born.

for those coming in on the stage. The bar and gambling tables are filled with teamsters, gold-seekers, traders, tourists, and mail carriers. He also owns a hotel on the plaza—Petra complains that people trample the hotel's rooftop during bullfights in the plaza.[163]

The family lives with a twelve-year-old servant named Francisco Montoga.[164] Sam is now a public figure with growing personal wealth and a flourishing young family. The sheriff's job alone pays $2,000 a year, and he lists $6,000 in real estate on the 1860 census.

Sam, now forty, watched the traditional pueblo change into an American town. The jacales are gone from downtown, replaced by one-story houses, shops, and municipal buildings. Temporary thatch has been replaced with adobe walls and permanent log beams. The separate buildings along the plaza share contiguous facades, long porches that make full use of the prime frontage. During public proclamations, fiestas, and bullfights, crowds fill these areas like an amphitheater.

Sheriff Sam Bean's style as a lawman is not that of a gunslinger. Sam typically does his duties around town without a sidearm, as good a symbol as any of his preferred nonconfrontational style. Because he covers a beat that's bigger than most states, laissez-faire diplomacy is required to maintain any semblance of order. He won reelection to the position last year.

The sheriff's role is largely administrative anyway, more so than people realize. Sam does the usual procedural work for the probate and district courts—serving warrants and subpoenas. He also collects taxes, an onerous and thankless chore. These duties take him away from home more than he'd like; Petra dutifully loads his bullet belt before he leaves.

Aside from the dangers of travel, his duties also put him in harm's way. He observes that the Gadsden Purchase has "a charm about it" for ban-

---

163 Bloom, "Los Dos Frijoles Summary."

164 The US Census of 1860 lists Samuel Bean, forty; Petra Bean, twenty-six; Cecilia Bean, ten; Virginia Bean, six; Margaret Bean, four; and the twelve-year-old "servant" Francisco Montoga.

dits and outlaws. He can summon a posse of able-bodied men to pick up arms as needed. He develops sources among the population, informants who help him navigate the intricacies of the Mexican underworld. Sam also has contributed to the architectural evolution of Mesilla by commissioning the construction of an open-air stockade in the town, built attached to his home just off the plaza. Here he can house prisoners brought to the county seat to receive justice.[165]

After 1856, his responsibility as sheriff increased to encompass the western expanse that locals call Arizona. Sam appointed a deputy, George Matterson, to police the area, but the man is overwhelmed by the number of bandit gangs operating in the area. This does little to argue for the preservation of the current megacounty of New Mexico. But the US government in its infinite wisdom has denied their request for Arizona's independent territorial status.

Now the remote western section of Doña Ana County is practically seceding from the state. Orders from Santa Fe are routinely ignored. Sam appreciates their point: Tucson and Tubac, in the San Pedro Valley, are three hundred miles away from the county seat of Mesilla. He can't honestly pretend to have any control over the area. Besides his beleaguered deputy, a small reactive force at Fort Buchanan, and the dubious protection provided by a few mining companies, there's no real security there. Sam supports those agitating for the creation of a separate territory, and he actually is a signatory on an April 5, 1860, Arizona constitution created at a convention held in Tucson.

Things look better when it comes to Native American violence. When Sam tells people that he has "10,000 more Indians in my county than constituents," he's not exaggerating.[166] For this reason, relations with the

---

165 Larry Ball, *Desert Lawmen: The High Sheriffs of New Mexico and Arizona Territories, 1846–1912* (University of New Mexico Press, 1996): 11.

166 Maude McFie Bloom, "A History of Mesilla Valley," New Mexico College of Agriculture and Mechanic Arts (thesis with Sam Bean interviews), Mesilla, 1903.

Apache Mescalero are critical for keeping the peace, an effort that's complicated by tribal politics (an agreement with one doesn't guarantee others' compliance) and violations of any agreements by both sides.

But somehow Dr. Michael Steck, appointed the Apaches' agent in 1854, crafted an arrangement that seems to have soothed the situation. He's even induced some Apache to begin farming in La Luz Canyon at the base of the Sacramento Mountains. Things are far from perfect—murders and robbery persist on both sides—but the years of relative peace around Mesilla have increased the town's stability and prosperity.[167]

Life in Mesilla has been a series of personal and professional achievements for Sam Bean. In 1855 he served as territorial auditor, collecting taxes from the vast region. The next year, Sam and twenty-two-year-old Petra welcomed yet another daughter, Margaret. That year he faced re-election and warded off an attempt at the job by Jesús Romero, who may have won, only to have the results challenged and tossed out. (Details from available records are sadly thin, but Sam prevails to take office that year.)

Everything was looking up. And that's when Roy returned.

It was a hard road from California. Roy arrived wearing the tatters of a man who's spent too much time unsheltered in the wilds. Sam knows well the symptoms from his own long marches on too few provisions.

It took Roy years to ride Headquarters into the ground. The economy in California was in a recession, and plenty of folks closed businesses there besides Roy. But judging by his penniless arrival, he seems to have been run off in debt or chased off in a hurry. Maybe both.

The earlier quote about his area being charming for criminals comes from Bloom, who was also quoted in Ball, *Desert Lawmen: The High Sheriffs of New Mexico and Arizona Territories, 1846–1912*, 11.

167 On June 14, Governor Meriwether, who launched military campaigns against the Mescalero in 1853, signed a treaty with them. The Apache agreed to cede all their lands in New Mexico, 7.68 million acres, for 2.1 million acres for a reservation between the Sacramento Mountains and Pecos River and $72,000. The deal was never ratified.

And then there's the rope burn, a scarlet ring around Roy's throat, usually hidden by a neckerchief and high collar. Roy can't fully turn his head due to an injured neck. His story behind the damage is implausibly romantic and self-aggrandizing, even for him. The version he tells most often goes this way: Roy was a courting a beautiful Mexican lady who had been kidnapped and forced to marry a Mexican officer. The American, of course, challenged the groom to a duel and killed him. A half dozen men—the groomsmen—subdued the duel's victor, tied him to a horse, slipped a noose around his neck, and left him to die. The horse slowly started to wander off, stretching the rope tight, gradually strangling Roy. That's when his smitten love dashed from the shadows, cutting the rope and saving his life.

Sam has heard some whoppers, but this is a fine one. The real story seems to have indeed involved a lynching, but it was likely sent as a warning rather than a murder attempt. With Roy's predilection for bluster and scams, such backlash was pretty much inevitable. (He'd been shot and no one cared.) Roy also enjoyed targeting powerful people, using the rubric of being a Los Angeles Ranger. One way or another, Sam's brother crossed or antagonized the wrong people in California.

Shortly after Roy's arrival, Sam and Roy become partners in the saloon and freighting business. It's Sam's familial duty to give the young man a home and a job. However, keeping his volatile brother at the heart of his business in Mesilla seems inherently risky. What happened in California sounds awfully similar to what happened in Chihuahua. Sam is on guard against a repeat.

La Mesilla, New Mexico
June 1860

Sam Bean is constantly on alert against lynchings, which strike at the heart of the governmental authority he represents. He receives word of one brewing in Mesilla Valley, gathers a posse, and prepares to ride out.

The timing couldn't be worse. At moments like these, Sam has come to rely on Roy to watch over any prisoners held in the stockade connected to Sam's home. However, just yesterday Roy left for El Paso to fetch Petra's mother. With a healthy clutch of prisoners housed in the stockade—including an Apache and a Texan accused of a knife murder—Sam is loath to leave home but obligated to go.

Petra Bean goes through her usual routine of loading her husband's ammunition belt as she listens to his instructions. "I'll be back sometime tonight," Sam says. "No one will know I'm gone, and that's for the best. Pay no attention if they make a racket for dinner; I'll feed 'em extra tomorrow morning."

At dinnertime, the prisoners start to holler. They don't have much to look forward to except trials, tobacco, and routine meals. It's a long night for Petra and her young daughters, Cecilia, Virginia, and Margaret.

Sam doesn't appear the next morning, leaving her in a quandary. The din begins at dawn, until finally she breaks down and climbs the ladder placed outside the stockade. "Sam's not here," she says.

"Where's he at? What's the matter?" the sassy replies sail back at her.

Flustered, she decides to lie. "He's got a toothache is all. Just be patient."

"We got no dinner and no breakfast, this ain't right and you know it." The jeers get louder.

Fine, Petra thinks. She fetches the trays of food and steps to the large bolted door of the stockade. When she works the latch, the other side goes immediately quiet. She opens the gate, lifts the trays, and steps inside. The men have spread out inside the pen. There are locals and gamblers positioned behind the Apache and the Texan, and she realizes they're guarding her from a move by either.

After breakfast she allows the men to lounge in the open air, unguarded, outside the stockade. She hands out cigarette husks and tobacco plugs, and the prisoners blow smoke into the sunlight. They dutifully file back inside for dinner and a quiet night's rest.

Sam returns the next morning after riding all night, lynching prevented but in a panic over his family and the prisoners. He hears the story, his eyes taking in his wife with a newfound respect for her nerve. Once a Kirker, always a Kirker.[168]

La Mesilla, New Mexico
September 1860

Sam Bean's term as Doña Ana County sheriff expires this month, but the state needs him to take another tough job. The New Mexico assembly created "Arizona County" from western Doña Ana, and there's a job open for marshal.

He's a compromise candidate. The Arizona separatist movement by now has refused to recognize the authority of Santa Fe, saying they've already formed an independent territory. Sam Bean is one of the few that is trusted by both sides, and because of that he becomes US Marshal. He'll perform his duties from Mesilla and appear only when asked. Everyone seems to like it better this way.

When needed, Roy is there to back him up. "The Beans overpowered by force of character—personality," says one contemporary, Colonel Eugene Van Patten. "They knew no fear. They were notoriously slow to draw, both because they were slow of hand and because they didn't believe in killing. It wasn't law and order the American way, according to them."[169]

But the brothers aren't the seamless team that they appear to be. Roy's drinking and gambling grate on Sam. Roy embarrasses his brother at social functions with Mexican friends. One way to chill a room of Mesilleros is by defending slavery. New Mexico shouldn't be embroiled in the national

---

168 Booth, "Los Dos Frijoles Summary." Sam Bean relates this tale to Booth, who notes that when he returned, "Petra saw the love she yearned for dawn in her husband's eyes."

169 Bloom, "Shadows in Sam's Valley." Van Patten was a stage coach driver for the Butterfield Overland Mail Route, a Confederate officer, Doña Ana County sheriff, and cofounder of New Mexico State University.

struggle over slavery. This isn't a place for plantations, the Mexican population doesn't support slavery, and peons are cheaper workers than slaves. However, the issue of New Mexico's coveted statehood has been held for ransom by southern lawmakers.

The result is the 1859 New Mexico Slave Code—the state's first—which restricted enslaved people's travel, prevented blacks from giving court testimony, and limited owners' right to arm slaves.[170] The law allows incoming southerners to bring slaves, and a few appear in Mesilla. "It's all he can do to prevent bloodshed one day in the Plaza when a haughty southerner beats his slave," relates Maude McFie Bloom, relying on Sam as a source. "That night, the southerner was mysteriously stabbed and the negro spirited away, never to be seen again."[171]

The personal tragedy for Sam Bean is that the issue is driving a wedge between him and his brother.

Roy dreams aloud of importing slaves to create a lavish ranch, sparking fights. Sam laments the recognition of slavery in New Mexico, calling it a "shadow" that fell over Mesilla Valley and divided his family. He finds Roy's attitude about Mexicans even worse than when he left for California, a constant source of tension between the siblings. They argue heatedly, with Roy disgustedly comparing Sam's sermonizing to their father's.[172]

---

170 To learn more, see Shirley Ann Wilson Moore, *Sweet Freedom's Plains: African Americans on the Overland Trails 1841–1869,* University of Oklahoma Press, 2016, https://www.nps.gov/articles/000/chapter-1-race-slavery-and-freedom.htm. Mark J. Stegmaier, "A Law That Would Make Caligula Blush? New Mexico Territory's Unique Slave Code, 1859–1861," *New Mexico Historical Review* 87 (2012), https://digitalrepository.unm.edu/nmhr/vol87/iss2/3.

171 Bloom, "Shadows in Sam's Valley."

172 Ibid. Sam Bean recalled how he experienced "the bitterness of the slavery question rise up between the brothers." And their differing attitudes toward Mexican people were amply communicated and demonstrated during their lives.

Their business relationship endures; maybe a new venture can help mend the rift growing between them.

Sam's mind is on the gold that's been discovered in the forested mountains a hundred miles northeast of Mesilla. In May of that year a trio of disappointed miners drifting back from California stopped for a rest there, near Little Cherry Creek. One of the three, a dubious three-fingered character named Birch, was taking a drink when he spotted flakes of gold in the water. The men set to panning, and with that a new gold rush was on.

People from Texas, California, Sonora, Chihuahua, and Missouri are now arriving to New Mexico in droves. If Sam can't get rich panning gold or owning large mines, he can certainly sell miners goods and convert their earnings to whiskey and gambling thrills. Sam and Roy start running freight and passengers to the emerging town of Birchville.[173]

There, Sam sees a way to simultaneously expand his empire, gain a foothold in the mines opening inside the county, and shunt his brother somewhere far enough away that he can't cause any trouble. Sam knows exactly who can best tap this rowdy, emerging market with a storefront. The Bean brothers are opening a new boomtown business.

---

173 Birchville also goes by an older name: Pinos Altos.

JAMES

Jackson County, Missouri
September 1860

The Bean farm is not the biggest or most prosperous in Jackson County, but the location is lovely. It's a sparsely developed part of the countryside, inside the knuckle land where the Missouri river forms a dramatically tight loop, five miles northeast of Independence. James buys and sells real estate in town for profit, but this place isn't an investment. It's home.

It's a bustling household. The children from his first marriage live here: Aubrey, seventeen; Phantley (already going by his middle name, Roy) sixteen; Leon, fifteen; and Gordon, eleven. Elizabeth's son from her first marriage, Charles Moore, is also eleven.[174] The bond growing between the boys of this mixed family is a source of pride (and relief) for the married couple. The youngest ones are inseparable and all but idolize Aubrey and Roy.

On the 1860 census, James Bean lists his profession as "farmer," which in Missouri means growing a combination of crops (mostly tobacco and hemp) and keeping small herds of livestock. He employs a thirty-five-year-old farmhand named Charles Young, who lives on-site, to supervise the

174 Elizabeth H. Long was first married to William C. Moore, if y'all recall. The Bean family and ages are found in the 1860 Federal Census.

work. Also living on the property are six slaves; their homes are called "slave houses" on the census. They are not field hands: two enslaved women at the residence are forty-five and twenty-one years old; there are girls of nine and three, and two boys, aged eight and four. One of the slaves—the four-year-old—has another person's name listed under "ownership." The profile of most Missouri slaveholding households resembles family farms rather than plantations; this is even more the case for James's household.

It's tempting to envision James shouldering the expense of keeping enslaved families together, the most comfortable, charitable view of the situation. However, there's always the chance that these are "children of the plantation": the offspring of female slaves and their owners. With two teenage boys in the house, James is not the only candidate for perpetrator of the seduction or rape of slaves. There's also the possibility that the enslaved children are investments, to one day be rented as workers or sold, but their young ages make this the least likely option.

It's safe to assume that James, despite his self-identification as a farmer, depends on property deals and continual freighting to pay the bills. It's been a year of drought and famine, plagued by blazing hot winds. The lack of rain and steady gusts have made the plains a tinderbox, and the ashes of distant apocalyptic fires can carry to Independence. Even worse are the dust storms, billowing clouds of fine particle carried with the wind, descending without warning to blind and choke anyone or anything they catch. April and July suffered the worst dust storms, but the latest struck on August 26.

"Here it comes—in at the window, in at the door, over the furniture, over the floor; rolling and curling and whirling it flies, stopping your guzzle and closing your eyes," writes Kansas City's *Western Journal of Commerce* that year. "We breathe it, we drink it, we swallow it down, we 'gol-darn' the weather and 'gol-darn' the town; turning our noses in supreme disgust."[175]

---

175 Quoted in James Malin, "Dust Storms: Part One, 1850–1860," *Kansas History: A Journal of the Central Plains* 14, no. 2 (May 1946): 129–33, 141.

If 1860 had been an outlier, James's farm would be in better shape. Alas, since 1854 there has only been one good year—1859—for any kind of crops. The story for years has been no rain and little snow despite bitter cold snaps each winter. It's a good thing James's income is diversified with property deals, his restaurant at Wayne's Landing, and trade caravans along the Santa Fe Trail.

There's another looming threat, this one again blowing in from Kansas. Raiding parties of abolitionists have struck families along the Little Blue River, liberating slaves and stealing everything else while they're at it. James is a slave-owning farmer who lives in a fairly isolated section of the county—his house could be plundered by Jayhawkers without anyone knowing about it. Hopefully Abraham Lincoln will lose the presidential election and things will have a chance to settle down.

But this is hope speaking louder than reason. If the ugly times of Bloody Kansas truly have returned, this time James Bean has much more to lose.

SPECIAL DISPATCH TO THE *ST. LOUIS DAILY BULLETIN*

December 11, 1860

ANOTHER ABOLITION OUTRAGE! THE BORDER WAR

Independence—During last night a party of Abolitionists went to the residence of Morgan Walker, living ten miles southeast of this city—the owner of about forty negroes—and demanded them, saying that he, their proprietor, should not be hurt. Walker told them to take the negroes and commenced shooting. One of the gang fell dead on the steps; one was taken prisoner, and the messenger thought two others were killed.

Charleston Harbor, South Carolina
April 1861

The entire nation held its collective breath for the four months between Abraham Lincoln's election and his inauguration of March 4. As he took office, everyone knew the war was coming. The new President didn't want to fire the first shot, and until the southerners did, no one could exhale. Or scream.

The wait ends at 4:30 a.m. on April 12, when Confederate troops fire on Fort Sumter in South Carolina. The Civil War may have begun in this humble harbor, but no corner of the United States will escape it, even the frontier.

PART THREE

Plainly, the sheep and the wolf are not agreed upon a definition of liberty.

—ABRAHAM LINCOLN

ADDRESS AT SANITARY FAIR, BALTIMORE, APRIL 18, 1864[176]

176 *Collected Works of Abraham Lincoln*, vol. 7, 1809–1865, 302–03.

ROY

Birchville, New Mexico

May 1861

The twenty volunteer riders gather in front of Sam and Roy's store and saloon on Main Street. It's not the only saloon in this town, but it's the only one with a billiards table. The Bean brothers advertise this fact in the *Mesilla Times* and bill both brothers as "purveyors of liquors and cigars." It's a miner's heaven, the reward for hard days at the diggings, where a miner has to watch for Apache as much as gold or silver. And most meaningful, Roy and Sam operate a freight and passenger service line between their saloons here and in Mesilla.

On this day, Bean & Co. has ox-drawn wagons and teamsters on the road three days away from town. Roy's rightfully afraid they'll be ripe targets for an Apache raid. The situation is made even more dire by the cargo they're carrying: food desperately needed for the town and the hundreds of men working small mining operations in the nearby hills. The twenty men of Birchville are, at Roy's request, going to escort that train into town.

Roy appreciates the town's rawness, since larger towns have brought him nothing but restraint and trouble. Even now, in Mesilla, he and some friends are being sued by the prominent trader Anastacio Barela in a replevin suit, legalese for "an action seeking return of personal property wrongfully taken or held by the defendant."[177] But the professional gamesmen, independent miners, and entrepreneurs a hundred miles away in Birchville believe in the value of a duel, Anglo superiority, crony capitalism, and a community of men who don't shirk from direct confrontation.

A spirit of individuality defines the residents of any boomtown, both in their choosing to live on the edge and in the way they rely on each other, not outsiders, for the mutual good. With these moral notions and shared survival in common, it was easy for Roy to raise a posse of gunmen to ride out with him. Twenty men respond and set out for days of possibly dangerous trekking.

There may be a war on for the future of the United States, but today the fight is against Native Americans. Still, the next few days will help set into motion the fate of Mesilla and New Mexico during the Civil War.

After Roy thanks the boys and promises each a free drink at the mission's conclusion, he and the posse set off at a brisk gallop. The sunlight filtering though the towering pine trees flickers quickly as the men put spurs to their horses. It's obvious why the Mexicans called the place Pinos Altos. The town sits more than seven thousand feet above sea level, and the mighty pines sprouting thickly from the surrounding hills seem to touch the clouds. It's lovely scenery, to be sure, but those same trees could also be hiding mounted Apache warriors.

Mangas Coloradas, the chief of the Membreno Apache, has gone to war.[178] In December 1860, thirty miners launched a surprise attack on a group of Bedonkohes, a band of Apache, on the west bank of the Mimbres

---

177 There are no details extant except that it was dismissed in December 1861, when everyone had other things to worry about.

178 The name Mangas Coloradas (Red Sleeve) is the Spanish-language adaptation of his Apache nickname, Kan-da-zis Tlishishen (Pink Shirt).

River. They killed four men and captured thirteen women and children. A later enticement with a truce, and the subsequent betrayal of his son-in-law, Cochise, by the US Army at Apache Pass in early 1861, has rallied Mangas's cause. Now he and Cochise have vowed to destroy all Americans and Mexicans encroaching on their land.

The increasingly aggressive and organized Apache raids close roads. Birchville and its miners are cut off, held in a state of siege for months. Roy's supply train can help prevent looming starvation. But he needs men to ride out and escort the wagons into town, lest the Apache make off with the food and animals, and maybe the teamsters' scalps. (Abandoning freighter wagons is usually a way to escape a caravan raid unscathed, but it's also considered bad business and cowardly.)

It's not just the Apache threat that creates a civic feeling among Birchville's disparate population. The "sporting men" of the saloon and gambling worlds and the nonconformist miners share a similar, rough moral code. They are adherents of frontier justice, especially as it relates to hating Native Americans as an existential threat and an inferior race. And in Birchville, just as in Mesilla, southern secession is championed loudly, yet another shared cause that binds the rough community together.

The escort posse that Roy is riding with reflects the town. There are well-heeled volunteers, like Tom Helms, the co-owner of a large ranch outside town. At thirty-seven, the man has wandered across the West, living an existence that has left him hardened, steady, and calm in a crisis. Helms's ranching partner, the well-connected Tennessean Thomas Mastin, is also with them. The twenty-two-year-old is too much of a gentleman for Roy's taste—one contemporary, a Union man, calls him "bold, chivalrous and talented . . . and a pet of Jeff Davis"[179]—but he doesn't lack steel in his backbone. Just this May, Roy watched him trade six shots in a duel with the lawyer George Coldwell, putting his last bullet through his opponent's elbow even after having been winged by a previous shot. (The attorney eventually died from the injury.)

---

179 William Need to Hon. Simon Cameron, September 27, 1861.

Roy, Helms, and Mastin have become used to cooperating on big-picture efforts. The trio are all signatories of the Arizona Constitutional Convention that signaled the region's secession from New Mexico.[180]

Among the twenty are also veterans, like former army dragoon James Boyle and former infantry lieutenant Jack Swilling, a saloon operator and Overland Express rider whose military experience is devalued by his addiction to morphine. Henry Elam mounts a horse with them; the gambler and infamously violent drunk tells people he's never comfortable in a new town until he's killed someone there. Who's going to tell *him* not to come?[181]

The posse reaches the caravan at the head of Cook's Canyon, a four-mile stretch of road that passes through tall hills on either side and a popular spot for Mangas Coloradas to waylay wagon trains. And there on the hilltops appear the silhouettes of warriors on horseback. The wagon train, in a defensive circle, is pinned like a naturalist's beetle between mounted Apache forces on the heights. They must have been trapped for days—there are dead oxen strewn among the living inside the ring of wagons, tongues protruding from dry mouths.

The men in the Mesilla party begin to gather their courage for a charge when someone cries out that there's dust on the horizon from the south. The Apache see it, too, and by the way they're reacting they're not expecting reinforcements. It's a fifty-horseman-strong contingent of primarily Tejano militia from the Rio Grande Valley, moving north to hunt Apache and keep their northern trade routes open.

The teamsters cheer as the men from Mesilla charge to the wagons, watching the Apache melt away from the hills. The posse sends a rider to the approaching column; their combined numbers are enough to kill the

---

180 Sam Bean signed it as well, as mentioned.

181 Elam killed Francisco Ledesma in Mesilla later that year, and somehow beat the rap. Walter Earl Pittman, *Rebels in the Rockies* (Jefferson, NC: McFarland, 2014): 11, 19.

raiders before they get away. The teamsters tell a grim story of a three-day siege with no water, with the Apache launching regular attacks from their residence in nearby, abandoned Fort Mclane. A combined force of riders finds the fort empty, and they give up trying to catch the Apache after tracking members of the band for six miles.

Most of the men escorting Roy Bean's wagon train will soon go on to join a new militia unit called the Arizona Guards that Union officers created to protect the area. Too bad for them: the effort is run by southern rebels from the start.

New Mexico, already torn by Apache unrest, is about to become a front line of the Civil War. And with all the double crosses and spy games being played here, Roy can't help but get involved.

Birchville, New Mexico
June 1861

Reading the *Mesilla Times* has become akin to getting a briefing from a junior military intelligence officer. Roy turns to its pages for details of troop movements at Fort Fillmore, reports on the morale of the men inside, applause for officers who left the Union, and, he now reads, the date when a dispatch for Union reinforcements was sent. It's a Confederate guerilla must-read.[182]

News of Union reinforcements catches his eye. Word of an impending invasion has been floating for a while, and Roy's been hearing about it from his Confederate contacts in town. It seems to be true, since the Federals

---

182 Charles S. Walker Jr., "Confederate Government in Doña Ana County: As Shown in the Records of the Probate Court, 1861–1862," *New Mexico Historical Review* 6 (1931), https://digitalrepository.unm.edu/cgi/viewcontent.cgi?article=1459&context=nmhr. Walker notes, "There is no doubt that the *Mesilla Times* was pro-Confederate. The writer remembers a copy in the possession of Mr. George Griggs, of Mesilla, published before the Confederate occupation, on the front page of which is a description of the Confederate flag, a copy of the poem Dixie, and another poem glorifying the land south of the Mason and Dixon Line."

are digging in with a purpose. And since Fort Fillmore is just six miles from Mesilla, this isolated mining town could become a battleground.

Thanks to the newspaper coverage and the rumor mill, the larger strategic situation in New Mexico was well-known to the public. Colonel E. R. S. Canby, in charge of the military effort from Santa Fe, was frustrated by his superiors' withdrawal of regular troops for service in the east, on top of having most of his officers flat out resign to join the Confederates. The idea to protect New Mexico from both a Confederate invasion and an Apache uprising was to replace the departed troops with local volunteers like the Arizona Guards, who were to be recruited by the territorial authorities.

The military man holding the bag by then was Major Isaac Lynde, commander of the Seventh Infantry. In mid-June, Canby ordered Lynde to take over the command of Fort Fillmore, where he was to run his effort to control the area. Easier said than done: the entire Mesilla valley was alive with rebel activity, if you knew where to find it. And Roy did.

The first source was the Arizona Guards themselves. Formed by the Union, its mandate to thwart Apache raids remained the top priority, but locals knew that every member from Birchville was a Confederate just waiting to switch sides. That included the two prominent businessmen of town, Helms and Mastin.[183]

An even more clandestine group called the Brigands, which reported to the Union, was also active in the area. This shadowy bunch was formed in Santa Fe in summer 1861 under John Phillips, a gambler and saloon owner who volunteered to organize the group. But Phillips was a double agent who'd been surveying the Union defenses in the territory and feeding information to the Confederates in Texas.

And then there was the San Elizario Spy Company. Formed in El Paso by Commander Bethel Coopwood, these ardent Confederates were the first around Birchville to launch actual operations against the Federals at Fort Fillmore. Guided by locals, many from the Arizona Guards, they

---

183 Donald Frazier, *Blood and Treasure: Confederate Empire in the Southwest* (College Station: Texas A&M University Press, 1995): 109.

stalked the fort like Apache and likewise stole horses. Without mounts, the cavalrymen inside the fort were reduced to mere infantry.

A reckless young saloon operator like Roy would have been valuable to any rebel guerilla ring paving the way for an invasion. And indeed, one report cites the involvement of local merchants in a major caper. According to one of Coopwood's men, First Lieutenant Enrique B. D'Hamel, on June 15, Captain Coopwood, "with a half dozen rich men" (and aided by a turncoat first sergeant inside Fort Fillmore named Coulter), drove off two hundred horses and mules, delivering them forty miles south to a Confederate quartermaster in El Paso, in return for a Confederate government receipt, of course.[184]

Roy Bean doesn't appear on the limited surviving rosters of any of these groups, but he was anecdotally associated with both the Arizona Guards and the spy ring.[185] He was in a prime position to meet contacts in this subrosa world and indulge in some morally defensible horse theft. And rolling the purloined stock down to El Paso would have been old hat for him, given his teamster experience. Indeed, one of the nicknames connected with his band that did guerilla work at the time is the Forty Thieves.[186]

When Major Lynde reaches Fort Fillmore in July, he's dismayed to find that local secessionists have already run off with most of his cavalry horses. The battles here haven't started, but local partisans have already begun fighting the Civil War.

---

184 Enrique D'Hamel, *The Adventures of a Tenderfoot* (Waco, Texas: W. M. Morrison, 1914): 8.

185 Coopwood and Roy Bean even did business together in Texas much later, as we'll see. I mention it here because the future relationship supports claims of Roy's wartime service.

186 Horace Bell describes Roy's prewar service: "He assisted in organizing a company of Confederate sympathizers that called themselves the Free Rovers. Others called them the 40 Thieves." Horace Bell, *On the Old West Coast* (New York: William Morrow, 1930): 228.

SAM

La Mesilla, New Mexico
July 1861

Overnight on July 24, 250 troops of the Second Texas Mounted Rifles cross the Rio Grande and enter Mesilla. The population turns out to greet them, taking in the ragged and desperate condition of the conquering Confederate army. They cheer anyway, an atypical reaction from New Mexicans to their traditional rivals from Texas.

This battalion, under Confederate lieutenant colonel John R. Baylor, has been ordered to occupy a handful of forts along the western Texas frontier, most of which are abandoned. Instead, Baylor has decided to declare the entire New Mexico (and Arizona) Territory part of the Confederacy. With himself as supreme territorial governor.

Baylor was born in Kentucky but was reared while traveling with an army; his father was a military surgeon. He settled in Fayette County, Texas, at age eighteen to make his way there. He served as a Jack County Indian Agent until he was fired by Governor Sam Houston. It turned out that Baylor was a blatant Indian hater. Starting in 1860, his weekly publication, the *White Man*, advocated for the forceful removal of all Native

Americans from North Texas. It reached a thousand subscribers via the Butterfield Coach.[187]

Baylor's current dream is a slave-holding Confederacy that stretches coast to coast, with enough people, land, and ports to stand up to the northern states. But dealing with Indians is never far from his mind, or from the minds of the residents in the New Mexico and Arizona Territories.

Sam Bean is dumbfounded by the invasion. As a native Kentuckian, he's naturally sympathetic to the southern viewpoint. But his aversion to slavery puts a firm limit on how much he can support the invading Confederates. He's not someone who helped bring the Texans across the border, as Roy did. But he will be painted with that same brush.

Sam's more of a partisan for Doña Ana County, and as such he views the war as a disruption. All Sam can do now is watch to see which side comes out ahead.

And he gets a front-row seat to the struggle on July 25, when Major Lynde and his 380 men arrive in the cornfields outside town with a couple of "mountain howitzers" in tow.[188] The Union commander approaches Mesilla, flanked by his command staff, to demand Baylor's surrender. After the refusal, the federal troops fan out into a line, and the howitzers start to arc cannonballs into Baylor's now massed men. Most zip over their heads, but Sam sees dusty impacts close enough to the rebels to knock some over. Several seem unable to get back up.

---

187 Adlai Feather, "The Territories of Arizona," *New Mexico Historical Review* 39 (1964): 30. Donald Frazier, *Blood & Treasure: Confederate Empire in the Southwest* (Texas A&M Press, 1995): 18–19. Jerry Thompson, "Baylor, John Robert," Handbook of Texas Online, https://www.tshaonline.org/handbook/entries/baylor-john-robert.

188 A. F. H. Armstrong, "The Case of Major Isaac Lynde," *New Mexico Historical Review* 36 (1961), https://digitalrepository.unm.edu/cgi/viewcontent.cgi?article=2069&context=nmhr.

The Union troops then surge forward, but to Sam's experienced eye the attack falters well before anyone shoots at them. The cornstalks push back against the infantry's advance, slowing them and breaking formations. The Texans and the local militia open fire on the stumbling men with a chorus of Sharps rifles, peppering the troops with balls and driving the Federals into a general retreat. Baylor's riflemen then turn their guns on the three companies of charging Union cavalry; horses and men tumble, and this attack also fails entirely.

Lynde limps back to Fort Fillmore, leaving about a dozen dead, not including two officers. The cheering Confederates lose only two men and a handful of wounded. Although most of the artillery shells passed over the dismounted troops' heads, the balls struck their horses that were tied in the rear, killing more than twenty animals.

The Battle of Mesilla is over. If Sam wants to know who runs his town and territory, he now has his answer.

ROY

Outside San Augustin Springs, disputed New Mexico Territory
August 1861

Roy Bean has seen thirsty men before, and as a survivor of the Jornada del Muerto and other deserts, he has certainly been one. But there's something pathetic about the Union troops he's encountering as part of the vanguard chasing Lynde's shattered command.

Baylor left Mesilla to double back and secure Fort Fillmore, which he bypassed in favor of taking the city. At nearby Birchville he met up with the partisans of the Arizona Guard and other paramilitary groups, who would serve as guides during the hunt for Major Isaac Lynde. Roy Bean and his Free Rovers were among the local volunteers involved.

Everyone's disappointed to find Fort Fillmore abandoned. The place is a vulnerable death trap for defenders, if for no other reason than there's no water close by. A siege there would mean waiting for dehydration to wear down the defenders, or setting up a firing squad to cut them down as they sallied from the fort.

It doesn't take a master tracker to see which way the Federals went. There's a trail of litter on the road to Fort Stanton—blankets, exhausted animals, books, weapons, cookware, musical instruments, all the detritus of soldiers on the run. Roy smells blood: his quarry is on a desert march that can destroy even the well equipped. No matter how many of them are left, if the hollowed federal force can be caught, they can be captured or destroyed.

As Roy rides with the advance scouts, he sees that the road trash is being joined by enemy soldiers. They're collapsed in bony heaps under any available shade, begging for water, arms waving for help. Many Union men seem to be half-drunk; word filters through the ranks that they filled their canteens with whiskey instead of water, an idiotic mistake.

The number of the surrendered Union stragglers rises into the hundreds. Roy realizes they are closing in on the most popular pass through the Organ Mountains, but any local knows it isn't the quickest. By taking another pass instead, the Confederates catch Lynde near San Augustin Springs.

With Baylor's men numbering just 250, it might seem absurd to ask Lynde for a surrender since there were more than twice as many Union troops present at Fort Fillmore. But only 200 federal troops remain after the dry march, and those who are left are in no shape to fight. Lynde surrenders his entire command unconditionally. The prisoners get water from the nearby spring and start the embarrassing march back to Mesilla, where they will swear to never again serve the Union once released.[189]

Roy reaches Mesilla with the triumphant Confederates, who hold an all-night party to celebrate—and to entice Arizona Guardsmen to join the regular army. Many do, but Roy resists. He's seen too much irregular warfare to submit to being a foot soldier. Taking orders has never really been Roy's forte, anyway. He doesn't mind participating in this war, as long as it's on his own terms.

---

189 In the future, Roy Bean's Confederate States Army service marker will say, "In a narrow canyon, took part in capture of 800 Federals by 250 Confederates." It's not a lie, just slightly exaggerated and lacking context.

La Mesilla, Confederate Territory of Arizona
August 1861

On the first of August, Baylor midwives the creation of the Confederate Territory of Arizona, which includes all of Doña Ana County to the Colorado River. Baylor divides the new territory into four counties and grants Arizona a separate judicial district, a popular move: "The social and political condition of Arizona being little short of general anarchy, and the people being literally destitute of law, order, and protection, the said Territory, from the date hereof, is hereby declared temporarily organized as a military government until such time as Congress may otherwise provide. The judicial power of this Territory shall be vested in a supreme court, two district courts, two probate courts, and justices of the peace."[190]

On August 2, Baylor appoints officials. The Doña Ana County clerk, Charles A. Hoppin, and the sheriff, John A. Roberts, will continue in office. The probate court will resume work just a week after Baylor arrives. Baylor names Samuel Bean marshal for the Confederated Arizona Territory, a new title for his old job.

The position is responsible for some baseline local federal tasks, like conducting censuses, informing citizens of changes to the legal system, and collecting the occasional fugitive for federal trial. Sam also serves as a Spanish translator in court cases and as a justice of the peace, jobs for a local administrator who's devoted to running New Mexico smoothly.

It'll be hard to do. The Texan invasion is causing a mass migration and inflaming unrest. "The Indians seeing that the whites were at war, increased in boldness . . . while fear of Texans and war induced nearly half the Mexican population of the Mesilla Valley to flee to Mexico," reports William Frederick Milton Arny, a government Indian agent, in the *Santa Fe New Mexican*.[191]

---

190 Frazier, *Blood & Treasure: Confederate Empire in the Southwest,* 61.

191 Quoted in Donald Howard Couchman, *Cooke's Peak—Pasaron por Aqui: A Focus*

Sam was seemingly uninvolved in actual wartime activities. But he was a Confederate public official, and as such an acknowledged rebel. And that kind of news spreads across the nation.

"I have just seen a copy of the *Mesilla Times*, a secession newspaper," reads one column in the *Illinois State Journal* that manages to capture both the tone coming from the New Mexico and Arizona Territories and the northern reaction. "From this it appears that a complete succession government has been organized there, from the governor down to the justice of the peace. . . . *The Times* calls for troops in order to enable the traitors to hold the territory, and apprehends an attack by way of Southern California." The column also notes that the newspaper "demands the extermination of the whole Indian race."[192]

The Arizona Guard is absorbed into the Confederate army, with many new volunteers unwittingly signing up for battlefield sacrifices as far away as Louisiana and Arkansas, but Roy heads back to Birchville. He can now reap the rewards of life under the new Confederate government, with his reputation enhanced as one who helped change the direction of the territory.

His war prize is a six-pound cannon, donated by the Confederate States Army (CSA) for the defense of the mining town. Roy gives it a home outside the Beans' saloon to draw in customers. It's a militarily defensible choice because the walls of the town square enable it to double as a fort, and the saloon sits on one corner with a good field of fire. But with no cannonballs provided, it'll be better as a conversation piece than an artillery piece anyway.

---

on United States History in Southwestern New Mexico (Santa Fe: New Mexico Bureau of Land Management, 1990): 64–65.

192 *Illinois State Journal* (Springfield), October 18, 1861. The *Mesilla Times* quoted is the August 10 edition.

Birchville, Confederate Territory of Arizona
September 1861

The town of Birchville is slowly waking on September 27. Listless, hungover miners wander the streets, some doggedly resupplying for forays into the mountains. Roy Bean is at the store, feeling every bit of their sluggishness but needing to be on hand to keep the operation running after the drama of armies, generals, and military spies.

That's when Mangas Coloradas's warriors, hundreds of Apache on horseback, storm the town. The miners dash into Roy's store, panicked and angry. He orders them to close the window shutters, stick their weapons out the firing ports, and shoot anyone riding past. The sounds of gunfire, war whoops, and all manner of terrified shouts float to them from nearby buildings.

Peering out a narrow slat, Roy sees big groups of Apache tear past on horseback, shooting rifles into the buildings and lofting arrows over them to land in the protected square within. There must be hundreds of them. The return gunfire drops warriors and their horses in bone-breaking tangles, but the numbers are too high to make a dent. When an Indian is wounded or even killed, other Apache risk gunfire to collect them.[193] (At the same time, Apache warriors are attacking mining camps outside Birchville, killing three men and driving many potential defenders deep into their shafts for safety.)

Roy shoots at them in fearful anger. The assault is a total surprise—where the hell are the Arizona Guardsmen who are supposed to be on patrol? Two small forces are nearby, but apparently neither saw this coming.

Now there's a fresh hell brewing—Apache warriors tossing torches on the wooden roof beams and at the base of the log walls. This is a disturbing sign that Coloradas's intention is not livestock theft, but eradication of the intrusive mining town and return of the land to the Apache. If the flames

193 Edwin R. Sweeney, *Cochise: Chiricahua Apache Chief* (Norman: University of Oklahoma Press, 1995).

catch, the settlers and miners will lose their only refuge and can be cut down by the horsemen. This is looking like the first act of an epic massacre.

But now there's a new smattering of gunfire from an unexpected direction. One of the Arizona Guard patrols is riding back in the nick of time, and at its head is no other than young Major Mastin. He has just fifteen men, but he also has an idea of how to put them to good use.

The buildings fail to catch fire, so the Apache have retreated to a distance, which is actually bad news because it means they're collecting for a dismounted charge that could sweep into the buildings and dig out the defenders with force of numbers. They intend to end this siege right away, before any more possible reinforcements arrive.

Mastin enters the store, one blood-smeared arm hanging crooked, with some of his militiamen trailing behind. (The others are fighting elsewhere.) The Arizona Guardsmen snatch the supply of fuses and gunpowder shot—kept in a dry, windowless storeroom—and demand that Roy fetch all the nails, silverware, and buckshot he has in stock. Roy helps move boxes of this improvised ammunition outside, where he sees several soldiers pushing the cannon away from the building to get an optimal angle on the Apache's expected approach. Then he takes a position with the Arizona Guardsmen who are protecting the battery, ready to put his rifle aside to pass the gun crew handfuls of makeshift ammunition as needed.

He's expecting the wave of dismounted warriors, but when they appear, Roy is still shocked and terrified. The Apache are wearing leather headbands, breechclouts, and knee-high moccasins, and they're loaded down with bows, shields, clubs, lances, and the occasional rifle. All of these weapons and clothes have been blacked, one of the camouflage techniques used by skilled Apache veterans. They are coming fast and screaming purposefully, showing no fear or respect for the guns aimed at them.

The rifle fire rattles bloodily through their ranks but doesn't thin them enough. But when the six-pounder roars, the battle changes. Through the mushroom of gun smoke lies a carpet of dead and wounded warriors, shredded by a hail of shotgun pellets and whirling nails, while those behind them stumble in surprise.[194]

A six-pound smoothbore field gun can be fired twice a minute. The second blast of shrapnel cuts down the attackers after they drag away the dead and wounded, just as they reform for another charge. And yet again the cannon blasts, at near point-blank range. Meanwhile, defenders inside the buildings concentrate on shooting where the cannon can't touch, picking off riders and dismounted warriors as they see them. After each cannon spray, the Apache dash back in to collect the stricken. It's part of their religion to bury the dead with honor, Roy knows, but this custom certainly plays havoc for them during a coordinated attack.

The Apache give up after an hour of aborted attacks. The quiet is surreal, but at least Roy's ears are deafened to the cries of wounded men and horses.

Word filters in from the mining camps of simultaneous attacks and killings. Five Arizona Guardsmen and seven settlers have been killed. Mastin and his men retreat to Mesilla, and they take most of Birchville and the miners with them.

Roy Bean is among them—only a madman would stay during an uprising. It'll break Sam's heart to hear it, but the saloon-store in Birchville is as dead as those Indians who charged the cannon. For Roy, it's back to tending bar in Mesilla for the time being, alongside his brother the Confederate marshal. It's a sad ending, but it could have been worse. He's better off than poor young Mastin, dead from an infected arm.[195]

The citizens of Birchville have won the battle, but when they abandon the town they lose the war to Coloradas. The raid has all but depopulated the once-thriving mining community. The mines are silent, the

---

194 Frazier, *Blood & Treasure*, 109.

195 Martin Hardwick Hall, "Captain Thomas J. Mastin's Arizona Guards, C.S.A.," *New Mexico Historical Review* 49 (2021).

hills and trees spared for a brief moment. In time, the town will rebuild with a new crop of fortune seekers. While it sits abandoned, its settler name is also abandoned: people refer to it by its traditional moniker, Pinos Altos. Even a century later, decades after all the magnificent pines have been cut down or burned, the name will remain.[196]

196 Chief Mangas Coloradas will be lured to an army camp and executed in 1863. The trees will be lost in the decades ahead, cut down to fuel massive steam-powered silver- and copper-mining equipment.

JAMES

COLONEL CHARLES R. JENNISON'S PROCLAMATION TO THE PEOPLE OF EASTERN MISSOURI

November 26, 1861

To the People of Jackson, Lafayette, Cass, Johnson, and Pettit Counties, Missouri:

I have come among you with my command, under the authority of the General Government, for the purpose of protecting the supply trains, and all other property of the United States Government, and for the purpose of throwing a shield of protection and defence around all men who are loyal to that Government.

No excesses will be committed by any soldier in my command.

We march to enforce the laws and sustain the Government. Every loyal citizen is expected to give evidence of his loyalty by active efforts for the protection of the flag. For four months our armies have marched through your country; your professed friendship has been a fraud; your oaths of allegiance have been shams and perjuries. You feed the rebel army, you act as spies, while claiming to be true to the Union. We do not care about your past political opinions; no man will be persecuted because he differs from us. But neutrality is ended. If you are patriots you must fight; if you are traitors you will be punished.

The time for fighting has come. Every man who feeds, harbors, protects, or in any way gives aid and comfort to the enemies of the Union, will be held responsible for his treason with his life and property. While all the property of Union men and all their rights will be religiously respected, traitors will everywhere be treated as outlaws—enemies of God and man, too base to hold any description of property, and having no rights which loyal men are bound to respect. The last dollar and the last slave of rebels will be taken and turned over to the General Government.

Playing war is played out, and whenever Union troops are fired upon the answer will boom from cannon, and desolation will follow treason. Loyal citizens will be fully remunerated for all property taken from them for the use of the army.

All the land between Fort Leavenworth and the headquarters of the army of the West is under the jurisdiction of the United States, and we propose to have a regular road over it and safe communication through it, no matter at what cost of rebel treasure and blood.

It is hoped that you will see the necessity of abiding by the laws and actively sustaining them. But if you raise an arm against the Government we have sworn to protect, the course I have briefly marked out I will follow to the letter.

C. R. Jennison

Col. First Kansas Cavalry
Kansas City, MO[197]

---

197 "Colonel Charles R. Jennison, Proclamation to the People of Eastern Missouri, November 26, 1861," House Divided: The Civil War Research Engine at Dickinson College, https://hd.housedivided.dickinson.edu/node/38487.

Jackson County, Missouri
December 1861

The sound of hoofbeats brings James Bean to his window, where he peers out, rifle in hand. The sudden relief of seeing seventeen-year-old Aubrey returning home makes his knees tremble. Only now, with the boy in sight, can he admit how nervous he's been.

The news spills from Aubrey's mouth even as he comes through the door: the Jayhawkers are gone, marching back west toward their headquarters in Kansas City. They've been looting and burning homes along the way, and James has never been happier that his farm is northwest of their line of march. This time, he's avoided the scythe.

His eldest son has been to town, at first scouting for safety and then to gather details from the still-stunned residents. The sad tale started three days before, when volunteer Kansas troops arrived at night on the sixteenth and turned Independence's public square into an armed camp of nearly three hundred men, without tents. And they aren't just any Union troops; the men came from the Seventh Kansas Cavalry.

James's face falls when he hears this. The Seventh is led by "Doc" Jennison, and there is no greater demon's name to invoke in Jackson County.

Charles Rainsford Jennison was a physician, a soldier, and the plague of Jackson County's citizens for his infamous history during the Bloody Kansas years. He was among the harshest of the antislavery guerillas who wandered Missouri in the mid-1850s, torching farms, freeing slaves, and stealing horses. As the war drums beat, he started up again; in the preceding year, he'd visited the county several times, stealing from and burning remote farms exactly like James's. State authorities indicted him for some of the outrages, but there was no appetite to pursue charges against the Jayhawkers once the war seemed inevitable.

In fact, the Union ultimately gave Jennison his own regiment, the Seventh Kansas Cavalry, mustered on October 28, 1861. He became Colonel Jennison, tasked with organizing a volunteer unit to patrol Kansas City.

It was the perfect position from which he could torment civilians across western Missouri.[198]

It is true that almost no one in Jackson County voted for Lincoln in the 1860 election, and Confederate sympathies in the area ran deep because so many people had migrated there from southern states. But in Missouri there was a big difference between disagreeing with the government and seceding. The state's politicians voted against leaving the Union but also refused a demand to raise troops to put down the rebellion. The response from Washington, DC, was an attempted arrest of the governor, his cabinet's flight from the state capital, and federal occupation of the state's key cities.

Even in Jackson County, at the start of the war there was a prevailing sentiment of neutrality despite the residents' strong southern roots. People like James Bean had more immediate priorities than fighting other Americans. His world wouldn't collapse if he lost his six slaves, but he had everything at stake if war were to tear the state apart.

But for many in Missouri, the war was more personal. The violence of the mid 1850s had infected too many in Kansas and Missouri, setting the stage for vicious guerilla campaigns in both states. Even the larger, set-piece battles there had personal grudges attached.

Sterling Price, a Mexican War veteran, former Missouri governor, and the state's bank commissioner, had become the most dangerous Confederate in Missouri. He was very vocally antisuccession until Union captain Nathaniel Lyon seized a state militia camp in St. Louis. Price considered the move an outrageous declaration of war against the state, and he switched sides with a vengeance. As the head of the Missouri State Guard, he was ready to attack Lyon, who by then had maneuvered the state politicians to

---

198 Ralph Monaco, *Scattered to the Four Winds: General Order No. 11 and Martial Law in Jackson County, Missouri* (Independence, MO: Jackson County Historical Society, 1863, 2013): 35–48.

oust Governor Claiborne Fox Jackson out of office and replace him with an unelected Union supporter.[199]

The opposing forces met at Wilson's Creek, 170 miles south of Independence, on August 10. There, Price's guardsmen and regular troops, led by Brigadier General Benjamin McCulloch, whipped Lyon's army, which retreated and left his corpse behind. He'd been recently promoted to general, making him the first Union general to die on the battlefield in the Civil War.

Victory is a dangerous intoxicant. Price must have thought he could claim the whole state for the Confederacy, so he led the Missouri State Guard north to ultimately besiege Lexington, Missouri, in September. They took the city, and the surrendered Union soldiers were compelled to listen to a speech by none other than deposed Governor Jackson, who used the opportunity to harangue them with a lecture about waging illegal war.

Battles had taken place in Jackson County. On November 10, Lieutenant Colonel Daniel R. Anthony took three companies of the Seventh Kansas Volunteer Cavalry east of Independence along the Little Blue River, picking a fight with a force of Confederates who had been recently recruited by a Captain Upton Hays. Outnumbered four to one, Anthony's forces attacked anyway and then limped back to Kansas City as the battle's clear loser. The defeat left his boss, Colonel Jennison, eager to teach the Missourians a lesson.

When acting Jackson County sheriff William Miles asked Jennison to quell rebel sympathies in Independence, the colonel was all too happy to overreach his orders and march his men east on a raid. William Moorehouse was one of Jennison's Jayhawkers in Independence that night, and he penned a letter about the events that ran in the *Freedom's Champion* weekly newspaper in Atchison Kansas. "We went down from Kansas City on the double quick and once more surprised the natives of Independence.

---

199 Ralph Monaco, *Blood on the Streets* (Independence, MO: Jackson County Historical Society, 2012): 8–9.

We found the city all quiet." He called Jackson County by the derisive nickname "Secessia."[200]

Jennison could have destroyed the town and killed whomever he wanted. That's what happened to Osceola on September 23, when Union militia leader James Lane capped a victorious skirmish with Price's troops by looting and burning every building in town. It ended with two thousand civilians homeless, two hundred slaves freed, and nine locals executed after show trials.

It sure looked like Independence was going to face a similar fate. The arrests started the night the Jayhawkers arrived and continued into the next day. Every adult male was taken into custody. Sheriff Miles helped Jennison separate and free the Unionists. Those not released based on Miles's opinion were forced to sign deeds of forfeiture turning over their possessions to the US government. Anyone who didn't sign would be considered a traitor subject to detainment, trial, and possible execution.[201]

James can feel the outrage radiating from his son as he relates these details. By now, Roy, Leon, and even young Gordon and Charles have gathered to listen. This is where guerillas come from, James thinks sadly.

The Kansas raiders were going to burn the town, witnesses were sure of it. But William McCoy, the purchaser of Samuel Owens's house downtown, approached Jennison, arguing for some sort of mercy. The negotiations must have gone well, because the cavalrymen were content to simply loot every store and house in sight. Women were also likely assaulted, unless this was the one combat zone immune to opportunistic sexual violence. (Reports from the era are anecdotal, wrapped in propaganda and stymied by social stigma.) The looting of food and clothes is often a staple of a soldier's life, but these cavalrymen stole everything they could and burned the rest. These were punishment raids with an additional profit

200 *Freedom's Champion* (Atchison, KS), January 4, 1862. His letter was written on December 23, 1861.

201 Monaco, *Blood in the Streets,* 11–13.

motive, or maybe it was the other way around, given the neutral and even pro-Union homes that were routinely looted by the Seventh Cavalry. The Union troops stayed in Independence, even sleeping in the cold with no tents. Their base in Kansas City, Fort Merriman, was "no place at all, no forage, no chickens, no nothing. There is not a house to be seen any place within five miles of camp, and cold is no name for the weather," wrote Moorehouse. Compare that to the days of looting, eating, drinking, and bullying to be done in Independence, and the choice was clear.

Poor John Duke's shoe store was cleaned out. After stealing all the adult-sized boots, the Seventh Cavalry grabbed the raw material in the shoemaker's inventory. This included some fine red leather he had ordered from St. Louis. (James's merchant's brain no doubt cringed in sympathy.) Nearly 150 pairs of shoes were made from those scraps during the raid.

On day three of the occupation came a report of guerilla movements nearby, and the Seventh Cavalry men marched out, many with legs wrapped in red leather.[202] They never found any guerillas, but Jennison's men did leave a swath of burned houses and stolen livestock along the route back to their fort, just as they did on the way to Independence. They also rounded up those deemed disloyal.

"If you had been there you could have seen a splendid specimen of Jayhawking," gushed Moorehouse. "When we arrived at Camp Merriweather, we had 100 head of secesh horses and mules and about 50 contrabands."

Not everyone was thrilled. Pretty soon, Union major general Henry Halleck wrote a letter to General-in-Chief George McClellan: "The conduct of the forces under Lane and Jennison has done more for the enemy in this State than could have been accomplished by 20,000 of his own army. I receive almost daily complaints of outrages committed by these

---

202 The nickname "Red Legs" originally referred to this specific paramilitary outfit because of this incident, but it became conflated with "Jayhawkers" to describe all Kansas guerillas who ravaged in Missouri during the Civil War. John Duke gave his statement to the *Illinois State Journal*, and it was reprinted in the *Wyandott Herald* (Kansas City, MO) on July 25, 1889.

men in the name of the United States, and the evidence is so conclusive as to leave no doubt of their correctness."[203]

Given this aggression toward civilians, it's no surprise that the already volatile residents of Jackson County became bloodthirsty guerillas, including members of the Quantrill, Maddox (to whom James had sold property), and Younger families. Lane's raid and the brute occupation of Independence inspired William Quantrill's plan to burn Lawrence, Kansas, in revenge.

James Bean's home was unscathed, and he wasn't bound by an official investigation or even a loyalty oath. But that didn't mean anything in anarchic Jackson County, where reavers were set free to do their indiscriminate worst under the color of authority. James fears he'll lose his property with either a signature, a torch, or a bayonet.

The events of the last three days have proven one thing to him: life in this county has become unbearable. Where is he to go? His father-in-law lives in Platte County, which is only safer than Jackson County by comparison. He can hunker down here or do the same there. It's not a solution. He could head to Texas, but he'd be a starting over as a virtual stranger.

The best option seems to be Confederate-controlled Memphis. An increasing tide of Missouri refugees are washing up there, a community that knows James well enough to allow him to do business. It's on the river, making it a reliable trading town, and can offer cargo and contacts James is familiar with. And if things improve, he could take a steamboat to quickly return to Independence to check on things. Like whether his farm and store have been burned.

He moves his entire family to Tennessee, but without the slaves. If they followed the path of those owned by James's cousin-in-law Nick Asbury in Platte County, they migrated to Kansas with their owners' permission to

---

203 *The War of the Rebellion: A Compilation of the Official Records of the Union and Confederate Armies,* United States War Department/University of Virginia, 1902, https://www.loc.gov/resource/g3701sm.gcw0099000/?st=gallery.

become free.[204] The men and women may have taken the children and fled, using the local extension of Underground Railroad safe houses called the "Lane Trail." Even if the enslaved children were illegitimate children of the Bean family, that doesn't mean they'd be taken with the Beans. Children of the plantation were still slaves, and they were usually sold when they were older, often after having been trained in a skilled trade to help make their lives better. There's no record of sale or emancipation for the six humans who lived with the Bean family that would permit us to know what happened to them.

James Bean, after leaving a yearslong reliable trail, also vanishes amid the wreckage of the Civil War in Missouri. After making a name for himself in Independence, he became a piece of human flotsam swept into a vast tragedy. It's as though Jackson County was erased, and James along with it. No newspaper articles, property purchases, or public records prove his existence for years after he left Missouri. If not for his son's military records—they became Confederates—his flight to Tennessee wouldn't have left a trace.

---

204 *Oskaloosa (KS) Independent*, February 23, 1884, quotes Asbury's former slave Harry Nichols, at age one hundred, from a letter handed to a newspaper reporter: "I lived there 'til the war, then I come to Kansas."

SAM

ORDER FROM COMMANDER, SECOND TEXAS MOUNTED RIFLES

March 20, 1862

To: Captain [Thomas] Helm
Commanding Arizona Guards

SIR: I learn from Lieut. J. J. Jackson that the Indians have been into your post for the purpose of making a treaty. The Congress of the Confederate States has passed a law declaring extermination to all hostile Indians. You will therefore use all means to persuade the Apaches or any tribe to come in for the purpose of making peace, and when you get them together kill all the grown Indians and take the children prisoners and sell them to defray the expense of killing the Indians. Buy whisky and such other goods as may be necessary for the Indians and I will order vouchers given to cover the amount expended. Leave nothing undone to insure [sic] *success and have a sufficient number of men around to allow no Indian to escape. Say nothing of your orders until the time arrives and be cautious how you let the*

Mexicans know it. If you can't trust them, send to Captain Aycock, at this place, and he will send thirty men from his company—but use the Mexicans if they can be trusted, as bringing troops from here might excite suspicion with the Indians. To your judgment I entrust this important matter and look to you for success against these cursed pests who have already murdered over 100 men in this Territory.

I am, yours, with great respect,
JOHN R. BAYLOR
Colonel
Commanding 2nd Regiment Texas Mounted Rifles [205]

This memo to the Arizona Guard gets Baylor fired. There was no truth to his claim of the Confederate Congress's order to exterminate Native Americans, not to mention the barbarity of the order itself. When news of his excesses reaches Confederate president Jefferson Davis, he relieves Baylor as governor and revokes his commission as colonel.

By then, General Henry Hopkins Sibley had arrived in the Arizona Territory with three regiments of Texas Mounted Volunteers to inherit Baylor's forces and secure the territory for the Confederacy. But things for the rebels will only get worse when the Union army from California finally reaches Arizona.

La Mesilla, Confederate Territory of Arizona
July 1862

Sam Bean returns to Mesilla from Santa Fe with something like disappointment. Four days on the road was a peaceful break from the nightmare here. It was somehow comforting to get the dispassionate perspective on the travails of men that is afforded by mountains and deserts. He's in the midst of losing his home, his business, and his stature, but those sorrows seemed smaller on the trail.

---

205 *War of the Rebellion: Serial 105*, Chapter LXII, 942.

As he rides into the plaza, the worries return in a flood. These could be the last days he spends in Mesilla, his home for ten years. Sam has watched the tide of war rise and recede, and in its wake his life is in ruins. He's now a Confederate official in reconquered land. That makes him a traitor. Even now, Petra is packing up the valuables for a trek to San Antonio. (Because she grew up the child of James Kirker, such flights are unpleasantly familiar to her.) Sam has no idea if he'll be able to return.

Sam remembers a lifetime ago, in February, when he watched two thousand Confederate troops under Sibley march away to conquer Santa Fe. In Mesilla there was great relief—that was a lot of undisciplined men for a small town to host. That month, Sam took advantage of the chaos and planned for the future by investing $1,000 in half of Nestor Varela's dramshop and gambling hall in Mesilla's square, located right next to the coach stops. On March 6, Sam and Roy bought Varela out entirely for another $2,000.[206]

Hopes for stability faded shortly after the ink dried. After taking Santa Fe, the Confederate army was ensnared by Union forces that traveled from California. The ensuing fight included a pyrrhic southern victory at Val Verde and on March 28 the loss of all their supplies during the otherwise good Confederate showing at the battle of Glorieta Pass.

Drained of supplies, Sibley was forced into a long retreat along the west bank of the Rio Grande. The men had no food or water, and soldiers started falling away as stragglers and corpses. Gangs of desperate, looting Confederates met armed resistance from civilians. The same army Sam watched march out of Mesilla came back in pieces, half its size.

Glorieta Pass was the end of the Confederate invasion of New Mexico, but it was not a quick death. Confederate troops remained in Mesilla until July, swelling with the arrival of stragglers, when Sibley finally took off for San Antonio with his army.

---

206 David Thomas, *La Posta*, vol.1, Mesilla Valley History Series Las Cruces (Doc45 Publishing, 2013): 43.

Sam reckons he had just enough days before the Federals arrived to go to Santa Fe and finalize his accounts there, a major node of his freighting network. He'd beat the advance of the Union detachment under Colonel Edward Eyre. Those Union troops would be in Las Cruces by the end of July, and Sam needs to flee New Mexico quickly. Staying in Mesilla would mean arrest or even execution. He doesn't want to stick around to find out if the Union is in a forgiving mood.[207]

The war has claimed another casualty: Sam and Roy Bean's business relationship. On May 6, Sam made it official by buying out his brother's stake in their businesses.[208] The cash should have given his brother a chance to buy a wagon and some animals. And for Sam, owning property would preserve a sliver of hope that he'd one day return.

Now that he's home, Sam hopes to see Roy back at the store and hear how his big idea is coming along. Lately his younger brother has been talking about buying a wagon team and becoming a Confederate teamster, otherwise known as a cotton smuggler. When it comes to misbehavior for a cause, you can't beat a civil war. Sam Bean has no such aspirations. Southern independence has cost him enough already; now he just wants to wait out the war somewhere he and his family can be safe.

But when Sam returns to the saloon, Roy's not there. Other men are waiting for Sam—locals who want to get their cash from the saloon's safe. Gamblers, visitors, and even locals stash their money at the saloon, where it is secure from lurking thieves. With the entire territory falling apart, their urgency to retrieve the money is understandable.

Sam opens the safe, only to find it empty. He is now on the hook to cover the men's losses before he leaves for Texas, which means cutting into cash he needs to fund his family's flight. "Those gamblers were about ready

---

207 On August 15, 1862, ten companies of the First California Infantry, under the command of General James H. Carleton, arrived in the Mesilla Valley.

208 Thomas, *La Posta*, 61.

to slit Roy's throat, and mine too," Sam says.[209] There's only one suspect. Now that the war is moving on, Sam figures Roy has moved on with it. "There was a good horse and saddle missing, too," he says.

Sam has no time to lament this bitter turn of events. He will have to be content to leave with his family, any hard currency he still owns, and any sellable goods as will fit in his wagon. The only reasonable destination is Confederate-controlled Texas. A river of displaced settlers, Apache-spooked miners, and broken soldiers are heading east, and he and Petra are set to become part of it.

Sam Bean has worked for a decade to become a top public servant and businessman in New Mexico, but it took less than a year for him to lose it all and leave as a homeless rebel.

---

209 Sonnichsen, *Judge Roy Bean*, 47–48.

JAMES

Memphis, Tennessee
April 1862

The riverfront tells this city's wartime story better than the men in the saloons on Beale Street. James Bean wanders the wharves, watching the action with a professional trader's eye. The commerce being conducted here happens in a frenzy—goods for the Confederacy unloaded from ships and onto eastbound trains (or westbound steamers), and cotton smuggled across the South heading to Memphis for export to Europe. It's easy to understand but amazing to see happening at scale: hundreds of steamships lashed to the docks, swarming with black and white laborers.

All the steamers in the South had been commandeered by the CSA to haul goods for the rebel government, but a select few sidewheelers were turned into gunboats. James had never seen anything like them. Engineers had cut off the Texas (upper) deck and installed a structure made of five-hundred-pound cotton bales stacked three high, with another row of bales serving as platforms for a hundred sharpshooters. The bales were secured with iron straps. One threatening-looking thirty-two-pound cannon was mounted to each of the bows.[210]

---

210 Information about the fleet from Kati Engel, Civil War Naval Operations and

These were "cottonclads," the unlikely heroes of the Battle of Galveston. Other versions had no cannon, but instead were armed with a ram and gangplanks for boarding parties. In this configuration, river fighting in the 1800s was similar to ancient Greek naval combat.

Turning his back on the river, James crosses Beale Street. The stores here are still stocked with goods from the northern and southern states alike. Barkers on the street lure him with descriptions of world-class saloons and jaw-dropping bordellos. Restaurants and hotels remain busy, and even the theaters offer shows.

It doesn't take much poking around to find signs of the rampant smuggling going on in Memphis—and not between the Confederacy and foreign merchants, but between American merchants in the North and the South. There were those in Union territory eager to sell wares to the desperate southerners, and Memphis was their most popular port of call.

Memphis was also a destination for wounded soldiers. The city contained twelve hundred military hospital beds, which filled to capacity after any major battle in Tennessee. The grim presence of the ambulatory wounded on the streets was a reminder of the chaos raging outside the city, if the urban bustle allowed someone to forget.

Memphis was not immune to the war, but compared to Missouri and many other places, it was an oasis of normalcy and basic humanity. That's why the governor and state officials fled from Nashville to Memphis when the Union approached, making it the final holdout of the state's Confederate government. There was nowhere else to run to, for them and for James Bean and his family.

There are jobs in Memphis for refugees, but they require performing manual labor in warehouses, hospitals, and wharves, not the kind of work James is prepared to do. Maybe he could manage a depot or open a store.

Engagements, Naval History Command, https://www.history.navy.mil/browse-by-topic/wars-conflicts-and-operations/civil-war/cw-operations-and-engagements/1862-civil-war/memphis-1.html.

But who would lend him the hard currency? And how long would it be before the Union arrived to tear it all apart?

His sons Aubrey and Roy are not interested in normalcy. They're nineteen and eighteen years old, eager and able to join the Cause. Word among the refugees spreads that Overton Barrett is raising an artillery company, bringing displaced Missourians into the war from Tennessee. When Barrett's Tenth Missouri Battery musters in Memphis on April 1, privates Aubrey and Roy Bean are among them.[211] The Union has victimized the brothers' family and community, and they're motivated to respond.

The men still don't have cannons when the unit marches out on May 19, traveling to Corinth, Mississippi. Weaponless, James's boys are heading toward combat.

Memphis, Tennessee
June 1862

It seems like the entire population of Memphis has turned out this morning to witness the last charge of the cottonclads.

James Bean stands among thousands gathered on the cliffs just south of the city, eyes fixed on the drama unfolding on the river below. The eight steamship gunboats of the "Confederate River Defense Fleet" are heading into battle, black smoke belching from their stacks and silhouettes of small, scrambling figures etched against their white bales.

The cottonclads are charging a force of eleven Union ships. Through his field glasses, James sees that the five Union ships in the lead are city-class ironclads, containing thirteen guns on each.[212] Six federal ironclad ram ships chug behind them.[213]

---

211 "Aubrey Bean" and "Roy Bean," Civil War Soldiers database, National Park Service, https://www.nps.gov/civilwar/search-soldiers.htm.

212 The ships were the *Benton*, *St. Louis*, *Cairo*, *Louisville*, and *Carondelet*.

213 Engel, Civil War Naval Operations and Engagements.

The situation seems hopeless. Still, the citizens of Memphis give a rousing cheer from the riverbank. The River Defense Fleet could have surrendered; no one in town would have blamed them. The Union has cut off the rail lines to the north and east, the main army has fled, and it has left a token rearguard that's ready to retreat to the south. Everyone here knows Memphis is lost.

But the Confederate River Defense Fleet's commander, James Montgomery, is making a final stand. This wasn't his first choice; he wanted to take the eight cottonclads south to Vicksburg, but there's no coal to make the trip. Now he can only sink the ships, surrender them, or lead them onto the river in a blaze of glory. He chooses to fight.[214]

James and the rest of Memphis have a front-row view of one of the last and oddest naval battles on the Mississippi. Montgomery is approaching from upriver, so the first guns to boom are three mounted on the sterns of the Union ironclads. Return fire from the eight cottonclads seems paltry.

The cottonclads' strategy is to riddle their targets with rifle fire while quickly closing in, using their speed to ram the enemy ship or table it with boarding hooks. When close enough, the crews cut lines and drop gangplanks from the top Texas deck. The "horse marines" use the planks to dash across and take the enemy ship in hand-to-hand combat with sabers and pistols.[215] They can't win in a ranged shootout; the River Defense Fleet must get close to do any real damage.

The Union cuts the distance for them—well, two vessels do—as a pair of rams burst past their line of friendly gunboats and charge into the Confederate ships. James hears the excited chatter of the crowd at this seeming error; other Union rams are veering away, apparently confused.

The sharpshooters on the decks of the cottonclads open fire, peppering the oncoming ships. Undeterred, one of the federal rams (the *Queen of the*

214 John V. Quarstein, "Battle of Memphis," Mariners' Museum and Park, May 20, 2021, www.marinersmuseum.org/2021/05/battle-of-memphis/.

215 As the weapons and nickname indicate, these were usually cavalrymen.

West) impacts the cottonclad *Colonel Lovell*. The Confederate ship bends crookedly, nearly splits in half, and sinks quickly. Soldiers leap into the river, but James sees some tumble bonelessly into the water. The Union ship slowly disengages, badly damaged, then limps toward shore to sink in the shallows.

Two Confederate ships aim at the other approaching Union vessel but manage to only hit each other head to head, and one impacted cottonclad's sidewheel splashes into the water. Montgomery is a riverboat captain, and he picked fellow captains to command the flotilla. None have military training, and now it shows.

The Union ironclads catch up with the charging rams, divvy up their targets, and fire broadsides into the Confederate fleet. The pair of damaged steamers are picked apart on the banks of the Arkansas shoreline, blasted into pieces of flaming cotton and kindling. In the center of the river, two cottonclads sink; one (the *General Sumpter*) bursts open when a shell detonates a boiler. Another manages to get cornered on the riverbank and surrenders.

In less than an hour and a half, the Battle of Memphis is over. The river is now strewn with broken-back steamers, some in flames, some still belching their last, black breaths from smokestacks. Men swim like rats for the shore. James can see the burned cotton bales and corpses floating downstream. Nearly two hundred Confederates die on the river that morning.

The crowd on the bluffs is in a panic. The Union is on the way, unhindered, and will own the Mississippi once Memphis is taken. The predominant talk is that the Union will burn the city, idle discussions that James would rather shield his frightened children from. Thinking like a logistician, which is what being a trader is all about, he knows this is too vital a port town to destroy. Furthermore, there are large hospitals here that the Union will need as the war grinds on. No, the logical thing is to preserve Memphis.

It makes sense that James and his exhausted refugee family would stay to see what happens. There's nowhere to hide from this war; the prospects in Memphis look better than nearly anywhere else. At least here, the fighting has stopped, and the regular army, not some local militia, will be in charge. It's too important a place to hand over to undisciplined, grudge-holding locals.

Indeed, the occupying soldiers under Colonel Thomas Fitch take a hands-off approach after removing the Confederate flag. There's little looting or abuse, something that the skeptical and unfriendly citizenry nonetheless appreciates. "The Yankees thus far have behaved themselves," writes one woman in an anonymous letter to the *Memphis Daily Appeal*, a passionately Confederate newspaper. "Col. Fitch it is hoped is not such a beast as Baylor."[216]

When Major General Ulysses Grant arrives in Memphis on June 23, he finds "successionists governing much in their own way. . . . In a few days I expect to have everything in good order."[217] He posts guards around Memphis, orders clergy to omit prayers for the Confederacy, and appoints a provost marshal with three regiments to keep order. Even wandering about, not to mention looting, are forbidden to his men. Grant wants the soldiers to stay in camp, and so they do.

Memphis will soon become a nodal point for all sorts of traffic: soldiers arriving whole and later returning to the city's growing hospitals wounded, supplies for the frontline troops, even commercial exports bound for Europe. More refugees with allegiances on both sides continue to gather. This includes escaped or freed slaves, who find construction work with the military and hostile stares from both residents and refugees.[218]

Most of all, there is peace in Memphis. The emphasis on keeping mil-

---

216 *Memphis Daily Appeal,* June 12, 1862, https://chroniclingamerica.loc.gov/lccn/sn83045160/1862-06-12/ed-1/seq-2.

217 John Y. Simon, "The Papers of Ulysses S. Grant, Volume 05: April 1–August 31, 1862," *Volumes of the Papers of Ulysses S. Grant*, vol. 14 (1973) https://scholarsjunction.msstate.edu/usg-volumes/14.

218 In time, this racial tension boiled over into riots. However, the seeds of a diverse city were being planted, as some postwar African American community leaders came to town during the war.

itary posts quiet and safe is a priority of the Union army authorities, and controlling this port and hospital town is crucial to strangling the Confederacy. Thus, Memphis is graced with police officers, fire departments, health services, and functioning courts. The army also provides food and clothes for the needy, and allows local operation of schools, churches, and markets.

What prospects exist for a Missourian with two sons in the Confederate army is yet to be seen. But here, under a more benign occupation, James Bean's family has a chance of surviving the war. That is, if Aubrey and Roy can somehow stay safe.

He can't shake the vision of the cottonclad crews, leaping terrified into the water from wrecked ships and drifting lifelessly along the river's current. James has witnessed hundreds of lives thrown away cheaply in a lopsided battle that meant nothing. The carnage, while awful, is but a tiny portion of the larger maelstrom that has swallowed his boys.

ROY

Eagle Pass, Texas
December 1863

The lights of Eagle Pass are a welcome sight for a weary Roy Bean. The 350-mile journey westward across central Texas is blissfully ending today, December 28, at this small border town on the Rio Grande. Roy's an old hand at long-haul desert travel, but any trip through the Texas Badlands is a grind on man and beast.

It was a lonely Christmas on the road, spent with roughneck teamsters and dozens of lowing oxen. But there's no taking a break for holidays in the cotton-hauling business, the lifeblood of the Confederate economy. Roy is ferrying forty bales of cotton—eighteen thousand pounds of contraband if you ask folks in Washington, DC—in ten wood-wheeled wagons.[219]

The Confederate government and military took over the shipping and selling of cotton in 1862, opening a perfect chance for a freelance hauler like Roy to find work. He had a fine time that year operating as one of the

219 "Ox-drawn wagon train hauling cotton to Brownsville/Matamoros during U," Yturria Family Photographs Collections, UTRGV Digital Library, University of Texas, Rio Grande Valley, 1860, https://scholarworks.utrgv.edu/yturriaphoto.

flood of mercenary traders streaming toward Matamoros carrying cotton gathered from all parts of the state.

There, he could watch Mexican laborers load the contraband cotton onto barges to float downstream on the Rio Grande from Matamoros to the coastal port of Bagdad, where foreign ships flocked to load the cotton and sail it across the ocean for resale. On his way back north, Roy loaded the wagons with Enfield rifles, ammunition, medicine, percussion caps, cloth, shoes, and food. These he delivered to the Confederate quartermasters at the military depot near the remains of the Alamo Mission in San Antonio.

But now the route to Matamoros is closed. Last month six thousand Union troops landed at the mouth of the Rio Grande, taking the ports of Brownsville and Corpus Christi. Now Eagle Pass, located due west from San Antonio where the Rio Grande makes its way south, is the only way through to get cotton to Mexico. From there, the cotton can still be floated on barges or carried by Mexican-flagged steamships to the European ships waiting at Bagdad.

Roy's overland trip is three hundred dangerous miles longer, through Apache and Kickapoo lands. Bandits on both sides of the border routinely raid wagon trains loaded with cotton and then retreat to the other side of the Rio Grande. Roy and the crew keep their rifles close. The duration of a trip to Eagle Pass increases, and so does the price per trip. The Confederacy is being strangled, but until it dies there's money to be made.

Journeys to Eagle Pass don't start in San Antonio but in Harrisburg (which will eventually be made a part of Houston). Roy rendezvouses with the cotton there, supervises its loading onto wagons, and hires a squad of well-armed crew to serve as drivers and escorts. He shoulders costs up-front, and he isn't paid until he offloads the shipment at the border. The entire party is anxious to offload, get paid, and head back to San Antonio.

Roy hopes for a quick turnaround at Eagle Pass, but the place is as hectic a port and customs town as he's ever seen. His deal goes sour when he reaches the designated cotton exchange and finds no one there. Bean and his crew (each member of which costs nine dollars a week out of Roy's pocket) must now waste time settling the deal—an oversight in planning that he blames squarely on his client, Pat Milmo.

Pat Milmo, born in Ireland, is a banker and storeowner in San Antonio who goes by "Patricio" in deference to his adopted land. Milmo is often getting rich off the war, as many others are, by hiring teamsters to move large amounts of cotton for the Confederate government.[220]

Indeed, opportunists like Milmo help San Antonio boom during the war. Even as Confederate scrip becomes worthless, the traders help keep hard currency circulating in the city. "The streets of San Antonio are always crowded, the stores full of goods," resident Mary Maverick writes to one of her CSA-serving sons. "The place is actually flourishing and silver abounds. Strangers from the east who visit here tell us we know nothing of the war."[221]

It takes thirteen days for a disgruntled Roy to finally sell Milmo's cotton to the right buyers at Eagle Pass. While at the exchange warehouse, he snoops around for other inbound shipments that belong to Milmo. Befitting a wealthy storeowner and cotton smuggler who owns a bank, there are plenty. Roy brazenly loads everything of Milmo's that he can carry into his wagons (guns, shoes, and supplies for the Confederate army, mostly) and leaves Eagle Pass for home. As he leapfrogs from trading post to trading post, he sells the stolen goods.

Jefferson Davis and the troops in the field will miss the purloined items the most, but for Roy it's just payback against Milmo. The best revenge ends with money in his pocket—and with someone who perceives slights as easily as Roy Bean, there's plenty of opportunity to enrich himself.

---

220 Jack Becker and Matthew K. Hamilton, "Wartime Cotton Trade," Handbook of Texas Online, the Texas State Historical Association. The handbook lists him in august company: "Steamship owners Mifflin Kenedy and Richard King, along with cotton broker Charles Stillman, merchant and banker Patricio Milmo, and others, greatly profited from the trade." By 1863, cotton from Texas (and parts of Louisiana and Arkansas) paid for $4 million in war supplies.

221 Ronnie C. Tyler, "Cotton on the Border, 1861–1865," *Southwestern Historical Quarterly* 73, no. 4 (April 1970): 456–477.

JAMES

Kentucky/Tennessee/Missouri
August 1862–July 1864

It's a big civil war, but James is really only preoccupied with two parts of it: the movements of the Tenth Missouri Battery and the condition of Independence.

His sons are finally seeing where the Bean family comes from, albeit in a most unlikely way. Their unit has been tasked with supporting General Braxton Bragg's August 1862 invasion of the Kentucky heartland. The scheme depends on the native sons there rising to join the rebellion; Bragg brings twenty thousand rifles to arm them.

That month Independence experiences a downtown battle between 350 Union troops and 800 mounted Confederate recruits from Jackson County. The Union soldiers surrender on August 11, and a local guerilla named George Todd executes two men held prisoner. The Confederates hold Jackson County for the moment.

Aubrey and Roy enter their first real battle at Perryville on October 8, when they take frontline positions with Barrett's battery in a brigade commanded by Colonel Samuel Powell. At four p.m., they receive orders from Bragg to advance west on Springfield Pike. Ahead is a Union battery that's hammering Bragg's left flank as he attempts an assault. No one knows that this isolated battery is actually an entire corps of federal troops.

The attack is repulsed, and even worse the attackers are now themselves being pursued by an entire brigade, which has appeared on their right.[222] The Confederates race toward Perryville, enemy close behind. The Tenth Missouri Battery unlimbers its guns at a cemetery on the western outskirts of town, covering the frantic retreat. The Union responds by setting up its own artillery, and a proper duel develops.

Being in range of enemy cannons is a test of discipline more than anything else, challenging any man's ability to focus on reloading and aiming even as enemy balls furrow the earth around him or burst overhead. And with the all-too-common habit of Confederate cannons exploding when fired, having steely nerves comes with the artillery job.

Amazingly and over objections from frontline commanders, the Union forces are ordered to withdraw. The number of casualties is making them cautious, with 894 killed, 2,911 wounded, and 471 captured or missing. Confederate casualties are just as bad: 532 killed, 2,641 wounded, and 228 captured or missing. Doing the math, that means one-fifth of the men involved are now casualties. Aubrey has been hit by splinters of whirling shrapnel, the start of a ghoulish tradition of his being lightly wounded by opposition cannon fire. No one knows if he's unlucky to be hit so often, or very lucky not to be injured worse.

By October 1862, it's clear to Bragg and his men that the Bluegrass rebel uprising is a dream. "Our only hope was in Kentucky," Bragg writes his wife. "We were assured she would be with us to a man, yet in seven weeks occupation, with twenty thousand guns and ammunition burden-

---

222 This would be the Thirty-First Brigade of Colonel William P. Carlin (Mitchell's division).

ing our train, we only succeeded in getting about two thousand men to join us and at least half of them have now deserted."[223]

Bragg leaves the state through the Cumberland Gap and winds his way to Murfreesboro, Tennessee, on November 20. There the men join with Kentucky troops to become the Army of Tennessee. Their first assignment is to defend Stones River, outside Murfreesboro. On New Year's Eve, the Union attacks, Bragg again fumbles, and the Confederates withdraw three days later. Stones River had the highest percentage of casualties on both sides of any battle in the war, and Aubrey again catches a small piece of shrapnel.

Aubrey and Roy don't see much action during the 1863 Chickamauga campaign, even when they take the field at Missionary Ridge, where the southern troops are soundly routed. During the chaotic retreat, Barrett's battery again is tasked with protecting the Confederates as General Grant and his subordinate, General Joseph Hooker, chase them down.

On November 27, the Bean boys help Major General Patrick Cleburne slaughter Hooker's troops as they try to force their way through the Ringgold Gap without any artillery. The cannons had been disguised under brush and branches, which aren't flung aside until the advancing federal troops are within 150 yards. Cleburne says, "Now, Lieutenant, give it to 'em!" Six shots from two twelve-pound guns sweep the Union troops, who are Missourians under Brigadier General Charles Woods. "Five or six rapid discharges broke the right of this line to pieces and caused them to run for shelter under the railroad embankment," Cleburne writes in his report.[224]

The two guns then turn on Union troops who are climbing an incline

223 Frank van Der Linden, "General Bragg's Impossible Dream: Take Kentucky," American Battlefield Trust, April 17, 2009, https://www.battlefields.org/learn/articles/general-braggs-impossible-dream-take-kentucky.

224 General P. R. Cleburne's report of battle of Ringgold Gap., December 9, 1863. Found in J. William Jones, ed., *Southern Historical Society Papers,* vol. 9, 2.

to dislodge defenders there. The battle unfolds over five hours of steady firing, until a rider from Bragg tells Cleburne that the rest of the army is safely through the gap and they can retreat as well. Cleburne tallies 20 killed and 201 wounded; official Union casualties number about 509 killed or wounded, but most people think Hooker plays down the actual figures.

Were Aubrey and Roy with Cleburne at this pivotal time? Maybe. Two of the battery's four guns were used, so it's basically a fifty-fifty proposition. Cleburne himself especially praised a Tenth Missouri Battery lieutenant named Brown for his actions that day. But no one in the line of fire of a lesser rank was cited.[225]

James Bean's sons are imperiled but alive. His home of Independence is faring much worse.

There was a time not too long before when the name Quantrill wasn't known outside Jackson County. But after August 21, 1863, it's being damned by Unionists coast to coast. William Quantrill has been fighting a guerilla campaign against the Union, building a gang from former James Bean business associates and neighbors. Ever since the Jayhawker massacre at Osceola, he's been plotting retaliation. His target is the most popular target for Missourians during the Bleeding Kansas era: Lawrence. The Missourians destroy the town and kill approximately 150 men and boys.

Afterward, Union general Thomas Ewing takes swift action to drain northern Missouri of people to dry up the guerilla threat. He issues General Order No. 11 on August 25. It requires that "all persons" living in Jackson, Cass, Bates, and northern Vernon counties "remove from their present places of residence."[226] Now several hundred thousand Missourians—Unionists and Confederate sympathizers alike—must go

225 Cleburne is considered one of the best Confederate leaders of the war. Example: At Cumberland Gap, when the men had to cross a river, he solicited volunteers to go first and build fires so the soldiers could dry off after crossing.

226 Kathy Alexander, Legends of America, July 2023, accessed https://www.legendsofamerica.com/mo-generalorder11/.

into exile. They stream out of the counties in pathetic columns, mothers leading ox-drawn wagons, children herding livestock, enfeebled refugees taking turns riding malnourished mules.

Union Lieutenant Colonel Bazel Lazear of the Missouri State Militia, on the hunt for Quantrill, is shocked by the scene. "There is hundreds of people leaving their homes from this country and God knows what will become of them. It is heart sickening to see what I have seen since I have been back here," he writes his wife on September 10. "A desolated country and women & children, some of them almost naked. Some on foot and some in old wagons. Oh God, what a sight to see in this once happy and peaceable county."[227]

Jayhawkers and criminals loot every empty building and farmhouse. It's systematic destruction, and James harbors no illusions about his farm surviving the purge. One day the fighting will stop—it must—but now it seems there will be nothing left to go home to. However, the news is also a validation of his decision to leave. Elizabeth and the boys could even now be huddling against the cold in a roadside refugee camp, with nowhere to go. Instead, they can welcome 1864 from a place of relative safety.

Aubrey and Roy spend their winter in Tennessee. The unit's been absorbed into the Confederate's reserve artillery and is now under General Joe Johnston. (No tears are shed for Bragg's departure from their chain of command.) Johnston has built an enormous defensive line of earthworks and redoubts across the state, but the Union won't attack it. Somewhere along the way, both Bean privates are promoted to corporal.

On May 5, 1864, Johnston orders Brigadier General James Cantey's infantry brigade to Resaca, Georgia, a hamlet along the Western & Atlantic Railroad on the north bank of the Oostanaula River. The Tenth Missouri Battery, now rearmed with four twelve-pounder howitzers, is ordered to help defend the crossing there. At the Battle of Resaca the next week, the battery showers cannon fire on Union troops attacking across Camp

---

227 "The Civil War Letters of Colonel Bazel F. Lazear," *Missouri Historical Review* 92 (July 1997): 254.

Creek. A cannonball burst again dings Aubrey, who laughs off this new minor injury as the Federals flee. But elsewhere Johnston's been flanked, and the rebel army retreats on the fifteenth.

The Federals are heading to Atlanta, but the Confederates won't give up the city without a fight. Aubrey and Roy are among four gun crews perched atop a steep cliff in the northwest section of the city's defenses. It affords a great line of sight over an exposed approach into Atlanta, so when the Union surrounds the city, the Confederates can see the enemy arrive and form their own lines across from their position.

On July 17, the Confederate government replaces Johnston with General John Bell Hood—a move that is taken as a sign of panic from Virginia. Three days later, Union cannons reach a position where shells can hit downtown Atlanta. And they do, for the next thirty-six days. Hood finally orders a retreat on September 1, and by midnight the last of his infantry units are marching.

They leave Corporal Aubrey Bean behind. This time, a bombshell has done more than its usual damage. Roy stands over the prone body of his brother, killed at age twenty-one. "Be it said to the everlasting fame of Capt. Barrett, he never buried his men in the trenches," a newspaper will memorialize. "Aubrey lies in the cemetery at Atlanta."[228]

---

228 *St. Louis Post-Dispatch,* January 27, 1875.

PART FOUR

Nations reel and stagger on their way;
they make hideous mistakes; they commit frightful wrongs;
they do great and beautiful things.

—W. E. B. DU BOIS, 1935[229]

229 W. E. B. Du Bois, *Black Reconstruction in America,* 1935. I like the next part, too: "And shall we not best guide humanity by telling the truth about all this, so far as the truth is ascertainable?"

JAMES

Independence, Missouri
July 1865

James Bean has seen corpses before, victims of violence left abandoned to the elements. They're stripped of more than just life; they're robbed of dignity. It's the nature of rot to expose what's normally hidden—networks of browned tendons, the structures of bones, the hollow recesses of empty eye sockets. People always want to put a blanket over a dead body, hiding the forced immodesty and restoring at least some respect to the soul that once inhabited its shell.

Independence is a corpse, and no blanket is big enough to cover it. The town square, where James once saw hundreds of wagons clustered, is dirty and deserted. The once-busy streets are desolate and lined with dark, empty homes. Every window and door is knocked out, except those that have been boarded. And James sees that local hooligans have pried apart some of those slats, either to squat or to loot.

General Order No. 11 was repealed in January 1864, but no one was quick to return while the fighting was ongoing. On October 22, 1864, two Union brigades chased the Confederates through Independence, capturing two cannons and three hundred men. The Confederates regrouped southwest of town, while the Federals received reinforcements. After a daylong battle, almost all the rebel forces fell back across the Big Blue River. Local guerilla (and murderer of prisoners) George Todd died in this, the second Battle of Independence. The next day, the Confederates were defeated in the Battle of Westport, the first of many defeats they suffered on their way to Texas.

The two downtown battles left galaxies of bullet wounds and ragged cannonball holes across the walls of the buildings. "The marks of the Civil War showed on every house and on every face," visitor Ferdinand Helff writes in 1865.[230]

The north and west sides of Courthouse Square are now entirely uninhabited. But like a seed sprouting in a burned field, signs of life prevail. A lonely number of stores on the south and east sides of the square seem to be operating. Nearby, the Jones Hotel is open for sluggish business, and the town's doctor (Doc Stark) and dentist (Doc Henry) are seeing patients. And the Owens-McCoy house is still standing and occupied. William McCoy has stayed in Independence this entire time, although he had the sense to send his family away. The house saw fierce fighting and even served as a position for troops in the urban battle; James can see a cannonball still embedded in its face.

The ride to town through Jackson County has shown James the extent of the devastation, and it makes the ruin of Independence look healthy. In every direction lie the broken remains of burned farms, lonely brick chimneys standing forlornly on the blackened earth. No structure outside the city has been spared. The fields are empty of livestock, hillsides of wild growth poking up through the old ashes of scorched crops. The roads are also empty since the river trade has shifted entirely to Fort Leavenworth and Kansas City. This landscape has been scourged by war, transformed into a wasteland.

It's no wonder that James's twenty-one-year-old veteran son, Roy, has decided to settle in St. Louis to rebuild his life. He stayed with Barrett's

---

230 Quoted in Sally Schwenk, "Cultural Resource Survey of Independence Square," Historic Preservation Services, Missouri State Parks, 1999, 43.

Tenth Missouri Battery until its dissolution on April 16, 1865, when the unit was captured during the Battle of Columbus, Georgia. They almost made it to the end: on May 9, Robert E. Lee surrendered at Appomattox.[231]

James's other boys—Leon, Gordon, and Charles Moore—are teenagers ready to explore adulthood. This shattered land can't offer much for them but bad memories. James suspects they'll soon leave, and he can't blame them.[232]

But James isn't going anywhere. He still has land here, a good reputation, resilient Democratic political allies, and surviving business contacts. James helped build this town once; he can do it again. He'll start by reviving his restaurant: 1865 federal rolls show James C. Bean paying taxes on July 1 for an "eating house" at the sluggish but reestablished steamboat landing at Wayne City.

Like Jackson County and much of the nation, James Bean is ready to start over.

---

231 Legally, the war did not end until President Andrew Johnson made a proclamation saying so on August 20, 1866.

232 Leon David Bean vanishes from records at this point.

ROY

San Antonio, Texas

August 1865

An army occupies Military Plaza tonight, but it's not made up of infantry soldiers or cavalry troopers. Instead, an encampment of cooks and hungry patrons gathers around the public square. To Roy it looks and smells like a congregation of chuck wagons on the trail, with mesquite fires flickering under tall open-air cauldrons, each heralded by a slender column of fragrant smoke.

Instead of covered wagons, these vendors arrive in the early evening with elaborate handcarts and set up makeshift, unsanctioned restaurants—braziers, tables, lanterns, silverware, coffee cups, and all. The tables form a square, with several unaffiliated vendors working in the center. All of the operations vanish by dawn.

Luckily for Roy, they serve customers well past midnight. He's seated at a table, scooping cumin- and cayenne pepper–seasoned beef-and-bean stew into a tortilla. He's half drunk and hungry but puts the food aside for a moment to chat up the young woman who sold him the food. Young and unmarried women run these operations, a true attraction for men in need of both a late-night meal and some friendly company. A conversation with these fetching Mexican cooks is part of the dining ritual here, but there's a limit to the flirting. Roy has never seen a "chili queen" working a plaza without an elderly relative lurking nearby.[233] She soon leaves him to scarf the food down.

The plazas of San Antonio are hubs of late-night action, staying busy as late as two a.m. There's more than just chili, coffee, and tamales on offer. Mariachis, dancers, and troubadours perform, the truly talented ones ringed by tip-tossing gawkers. People-watching here is a form of entertainment—soldiers, cattle hands, merchants, gamblers, and family men mingling together, eating at the long tables, and rubbing elbows watching the street performers. This is the one place in San Antonio where the lives of Anglos, Tejanos, and Germans (who outnumber both groups) intersect.

It's a crowd that attracts Roy on several levels. As an independent freighter, he's always looking for another job. As a single man, he's always keen to find women. As an alcoholic, he's always in search of a drinking partner. As a prankster, he's always hunting for accomplices and victims. And as a showoff, he needs an audience. He's dressed to impress all these people, wearing caudillo finery that shows off his large frame and signals his seemingly good financial condition.

Military Plaza's east side is dominated by the back of San Fernando Cathedral, its dome and bell tower standing out against the dark sky well above the squat buildings that surround it. That's why Santa Anna hoisted a flag of "no quarter" from the tower during the Alamo siege—everyone nearby could see it. If there's a spiritual heart to this city, the cathedral is it.

It's been a long night of carousing, and Roy bids farewell to his chili queen and stands, watching her lean over to quickly grab the empty plate and silverware. It's about two miles to his home from Military Square. Like a Californio, he of course rode into the heart of town. His horse is

---

233 The origin of chili con carne is hotly debated (ha ha), but there's no doubt that the chili queens of San Antonio were the springboard that made it a nationally known dish and were early masters of American street food.

at the Lexington Stables on nearby Market Street; he's got the cash to pay for such luxuries.

It's a good time to be a teamster. Sure, things were dicey after the fall of Memphis, when the Union closed the Mississippi River and cut Texas off from the rest of the Confederacy. Stockpiles of cotton amassed inside warehouses, and the teamsters were grounded. And there was rioting in April when unpaid rebel soldiers took what they felt was owed to them—by looting from government storehouses and civilian merchants alike.

But after the war ended in May, the town recovered quickly and is now prospering as a transshipment point for commercial and military traffic that serves the entire Southwest. It's a hub of the cattle trade, as well as a market for wool from imported merino sheep, which are grown in numbers in South Texas and now the Hill Country. Wagons and cowboys are needed because all but two Texas railroads fell victim to the war, and the surviving lines (the Houston and Texas Central, and the Galveston, Houston, and Henderson) are famously unreliable.

And so mule-pulled freighters still roll. (Oxen are out of style now that massive cotton loads aren't the norm.) It's a boom time for freelance teamsters like Roy Bean who can fill the demand with their own wagon teams. It pays and it keeps him on the road, where he gets in less trouble. It's a pattern that has developed: when he's in town too long, his schemes and ego create turmoil. When he's traveling, the troubles seem to quiet.

He doesn't have a boss, but he is answerable to investors. Roy's cut a deal with local businessmen Julien Romain and Rafael Quintana, who have paid for eight wagons and their teams of animals in exchange for being paid off, with interest, from the profits they'll earn.[234]

Roy rides south on South Flores Street, passing houses with nice flat lawns and well-tended trees. The darkness of an orchard extends to his right, and a block after that he's greeted by the stern limestone faces of the US arsenal buildings. The most prominent is a rectangular block topped

234 Bexar County District Court, Rafael Quintana vs. Roy Bean, Civil Case 3303, February 6, 1872.

with a corbelled gable roof. Next to it stand the commanding officer's quarters facing west, toward Roy on Flores Street. He can see lamplight inside. He also can see the swell of a barrel vault, a building clearly designed to hold explosives.[235]

The density of buildings continues to thin as he rides south, homes becoming more sporadic and larger fields holding sheep and cows. He's on the outskirts of town, where he's made his home. When South Flores crosses San Pedro Creek, he eases off the road to follow the waterway.

Roy soon reaches his home, an open-air campsite centered around a large canvas tent. His eight wagons are here, along with more than a dozen mules separately staked to serenely graze the grass inside a handmade wooden fence. He stores his equipment and sellable goods here when they're not at the city's wagonyard being readied for an excursion.

One secret to Roy's seeming prosperity is to pay nothing while he's in San Antonio, in between his frequent trips. He doesn't own this land and has no idea who might. He started squatting on San Pedro Creek just after a terrible flood in March, when the Olmos Basin five miles north of town overflowed into the San Antonio River system and caused a fourteen-foot rise in four hours. These days the creek-side land is pleasantly empty, shaded by trees and healthy for the mules.

Roy Bean is in a city with a lot of hustle, and he's capitalizing on the good times. Despite a rough aspect and squatter digs, he comes off as a successful figure in recovering, postwar America. Of all people, he one day runs into Horace Bell while the lawman is in San Antonio on assignment. Roy projects this image on the Old West chronicler: "When I was in the service at San Antonio in 1865, Roy was there with his wagon train. He was still freighting to Mexico, in business for himself. He's making a lot of money doing it, too."[236]

---

235 "Arsenal," City of San Antonio website, accessed November 6, 2023, www.sanantonio.gov/historic/scoutsa/HistoricDistricts/Arsenal.

236 Bell, *On the Old West Coast*, 228.

SAM

La Mesilla, New Mexico
October 1865

Samuel Bean stands in downtown Mesilla, taking in the familiar corner of Avenida de Mesilla and Calle de Parian. It would feel good to be home, if he had one.

When Samuel and Petra Bean went to ground during the last years of the Civil War, they all but vanished. The only sign they left, beyond anecdotes, was the birth of Samuel Fermin Bean, born in Bexar County, Texas, on September 15, 1865.

One intriguing yarn relates a legal standoff between the Bean brothers in San Antonio over the missing contents of the safe in Mesilla. "Sam insists the money was stolen, Roy denies," writes Maude McFie Bloom, who interviewed Sam. "Sam vows not to speak again, not til Roy has made up the money." It's his brother's refusal to admit the wrongdoing that offends Sam so deeply—"to refund without explanation would be humiliation."[237]

---

237 Bloom, "Los Dos Frijoles Summary." Bloom puts the safe theft in 1858, but no one else does. This conflicts with the dates of Roy and Sam's joint operation of the store in Birchville/Pinos Altos; it's doubtful Sam would have entrusted that satellite venture to the man who'd stolen from him.

With war over and son safely born, it was time to go back to New Mexico. But it's not been a pleasant homecoming. The saloon, hotel, and store in Mesilla are all under new management.

In August 1862, Abraham Cutler became US marshal—Sam's old job—and immediately started seizing the property of rebel sympathizers for resale. Among those targeted was Samuel G. Bean, for having participated "in armed rebellion against the government of the United States."[238]

The cases depended on testimony, although Cutler didn't really seek more than one piece of it before acting. He paid people to come in from out of town to damn a Confederate so that he could present the documents to Judge Joab Houghton for rubber-stamp court approval.

In Sam's case, the man on record is Cristobal Ascarate, a member of one of the most prominent Mexican families in the territory. He had extensive cattle ranches and silver mines in Mexico and owned a palatial estate in Las Cruces. There wasn't much for him to say beyond what a casual newspaper reader could recall: Samuel G. Bean served as a civilian Confederate official.[239] But Ascarate's participation can also be seen as the reassertion of traditional Mexican power during the region's transition back to the United States.

William Fredrick Milton Arny, the government Indian Agent, describes in the *Santa Fe New Mexican* the common viewpoint of the invasion and the locals who enabled it. "The destruction caused by the Texan invasion in 1861 and '62 has had a most disastrous effect upon this country," he writes. "They consumed its substance, caused the loss of almost its entire mercantile and mining capital, and much injured the agricultural interests; it impoverished the whole country." He cites the exodus of Mesilleros as a most crippling factor in the collapse. During the Texans' brief

238 Thomas, *La Posta*, 43.

239 Ibid.

reign during the war, nearly half the Mexican population of the Mesilla Valley fled to Mexico. Now "they are slowly returning," Arny notes.[240]

Sam Bean was here well before the Confederate Army arrived. He helped build Mesilla during its early, formative years. But local Mexican power players like Ascarate have shouldered him out of its future just the same. There's justifiable frustration that goes back decades before the Mesilleros were kicked out by invading Texans, bitterness over their status as *los vendidos de Santa Anna*.

On April 13, 1863, the Bean house and businesses, property of the US military, were sold at auction. Only Cutler didn't put *all* Sam's property on the block. He bought a half interest in one of Sam's businesses for just one hundred dollars.[241] It was a sweetheart, insider deal, and it was not Cutler's only one. His behavior in Mesilla eventually gets him indicted.

The saloon's new owner is Leopoldo Carillo, who won the public auction. Operations at the building are up and running. An army officer bought Sam's house and corral, east of the plaza, but the man hasn't been able to move in, and the property remains locked by sheriff's order.[242]

It's time to unleash the family's secret weapon: Petra Kirker Bean.

Mesilla was her home longer than anywhere else in her life, and she's loath to part with the town. She tells as much to the local deputies, who understandably feel sorry for this former, fallen leading citizen. They even allow her to walk through the house one last time, gathering memories, as

---

240 Quoted in Couchman, *Cooke's Peak*, 164.

241 Doña Ana County Court House Deed Records, box 3, file 24, April 3, 1863; and Edward Tittmann, "The Exploitation of Treason," *New Mexico Historical Review* 4, no. 2 (1929), https://digitalrepository.unm.edu/cgi/viewcontent.cgi?article=1430&context=nmhr.

242 Thomas, *La Posta*, 61–62. The address of the house is 1910 Calle de Parian, La Mesilla. "Ver'nada Art Studio & Gallery in the Historical Old Tortilla Factory on Calle de Parian," *Las Cruces Bulletin*, July 15, 2011.

women often want to. With her are Anna, age six, and the newborn infant, Samuel G. Bean Jr. Who could say no?

The deputies don't know they've been had until Petra steps inside and locks the door. She refuses to leave, crying injustice and inhumanity. With this, the Bean family moves back in, waiting to see if the authorities are brazen enough to evict them. Instead, the army officer reaches out and offers to sell the property to them. Sam buys back his own house and animal yard.[243] He is supposed to be grateful for the gallantry, but he just can't feel it.

As for the dramshop, hotel, and saloon on the plaza, they're gone. The odds of Sam getting his property returned are slim, and that any attempt to do so would spotlight his treasonable public service is guaranteed. Lawsuits have been filed by other victims of Cutler, but none of them served in Confederate public office. It'll be easier to start a new freight operation and store in Mesilla and move forward.[244]

Sam Bean, forty-five years old, after a lifetime of struggle and risk, once again needs to rebuild his life in New Mexico. Given this homecoming, he wonders if there's still a place for his family in Mesilla.

243 Thomas K. Todsen, "Territorial Postmasters of New Mexico—Sam Bean of Mesilla," *La Posta: Postal History Journal (Mountain and Desert West)* 6 (October 1974): 38 and 43; and Sonnichsen, *Judge Roy Bean*, 49.

244 Sam did provide accounting testimony for two Unionist Santa Fe traders who set up a shipping operation in Mesilla and had their property seized by the US military. The firm lost its suit.

ROY

San Antonio, Texas
May 1866

San Antonio, like all of Texas, is thick with Confederate veterans, but there aren't too many who are aware of the shadowy role Roy (or any civilians) played during the invasion of New Mexico and Arizona. So it's with great interest that he sees that the San Antonio-El Paso Mail Route has finally been reopened by none other than Bethel Coopwood, former commander of the Arizona (aka San Elizario) Spy Company.[245] He'll have to look up Coopwood and talk war stories. As he gets older, Roy cultivates and enjoys more friendships. Living alone in his creek-side shack, he's nevertheless a social creature.

Roy's getting ready for yet another trip to San Antonio, eight wagons even now being loaded at the San Antonio yard. But other eyes are watching him.

When he's ready to leave, he finds that the wagons and animals are gone. He quickly learns the unwelcome reason: the sheriff came by and seized them on behalf of Roy's creditors, Julien Romain and Rafael Quin-

245 In November 1866, Coopwood turned the service over to the firm of Sawyer, Risher, and Hall. But he did business in San Antonio—including eventually with Roy Bean.

tana. They spotted Roy loading goods, traced him back to his lair, and are using the law to get the money that Roy owes them for the wagons. Now the whole train is stuck in a city impound lot.

This bad news soon has company. Roy's lounging at his home, mulling how to respond to the seizure, when a man who calls himself Mr. Lively arrives. He's the landowner, and he's shocked to discovered a large, bearded teamster living here. Roy has an idea of how tangled the real estate records are after numerous wars and regime changes and decides to just bluff. He claims the land belongs to him, and the fight soon goes to Justice of the Peace Alexander Nordhaus.[246] A July hearing goes against Roy, who must vacate the land and pay sixty-four dollars on top of it.

Roy seeks a new trial and somehow receives one, but by now he's annoyed Judge Nordhaus. The judge and the plaintiffs hold the next hearing without informing Roy of the date, and on August 4 that judgment also goes against him. Nordhaus sends word to the sheriff to deliver a writ of execution to squatter to make Roy leave or face arrest.

But Roy's guerilla strategy to delay and frustrate has prompted his foes to make a mistake. Now he can go to the district court and raise a stink about the unfair process, which he promptly does. After he's granted an injunction, Roy knows he's in a good position to bargain.

The fight has drained his coffers, and his solution to being broke has always been to rent his wagon service for a long-haul trip. This he does—by walking into the unguarded impound lot and out with four of his former wagons in tow. (Quintana has already sold the other four.) Then it's off to El Paso, his enemies left behind to bubble and stew like pots of chili.

When he returns to San Antonio, wagons and animals stowed on the San Pedro property, he finds Lively and his partner eager to bargain. The pair comes by Roy's encampment with a deal designed to buy him out—

246 Nordhaus was born in Germany, came to America in 1854, and lived in South Carolina before taking a boat to Galveston with his American wife, Hannah. He was a lieutenant in the Confederate army and a lawyer. He died in 1871; his son Eugene became a prominent state politician.

and make him go away. They'll pay him to leave, but he wants expenses covered. The two up the ante by offering to buy Roy forty mules and six wagons as well, a $3,000 windfall for the squatter.

It's an amazing solution, seeing how it kills two lawsuits with one stone. But Roy adds another condition anyway, one that will enshrine the incident in San Antonio's collective memory. He stipulates that he receive "a jug of his favorite whiskey" to seal the deal.[247]

Roy doesn't see any need to leave town. He's armed with an uncommon amount of money, and the place is still growing. If he's going to settle down, this is the time and place to do it. He will do what his brothers have done: find an underdeveloped plot of land, lay claim to it by opening a saloon, and extend roots from there. He needs a Headquarters for San Antonio.

The question is, where? Roy sees how the city is spreading into once-empty parts of South Flores Street, like weeds multiplying along a wagon trail. He's been evicted from his squat because of this growth. Now he can open a place in its path and grow in prominence as the neighborhood does.

The place he picks is called Dogtown, located on South Flores where the San Pedro Creek meets the San Antonio River, far enough on the outskirts to lack municipal services.[248] It's named after its reputation for being overrun with packs of stray mutts. For the time being, only poor Mexican families live there.

This will be the epicenter of Roy Bean's new life. He blows into the area like a low-rent don, establishing his forceful personality while buying property and hiring staff. The saloon is going to shake up the quiet neighborhood.

Part of establishing a saloon is doing some neighborly outreach. So he sets out to meet the locals worth meeting, namely the monied ranch families

---

247 R. Franklin Hall preserved this oft-told San Antonio tale in a *San Antonio Express* article in 1907, and it's quoted again in the newspaper on June 18, 1977.

248 Currently the 400 block of E. Glenn Ave.

living in these outskirts. Roy's soon paying special attention to ranchero Leandro Chavez, who lives on Corpus Christi Road. Part of Roy's intention in settling down in Dogtown is to find a wife, and Chavez's eighteen-year-old daughter, Virginia, has caught his eye.

The Chavez family is not wealthy, but the name goes back to the first Spanish settlements here and, even farther, to an aristocratic European bloodline. Roy's hostility toward Mexicans makes this an odd match, considering Virginia's dark hair and complexion. But he's following the social lead of the Tejanos, who care more about separating elites from commoners than about strict racial screening. Lineage and social status can redefine race, especially when convenient. In this way, a good Mexican family with an attractive daughter can be regarded as fellow European descendants, albeit ones from hated Spain.[249]

From Chavez's perspective, the newly arrived Anglo is a rich man on the verge of becoming richer by settling down, and he's well armed with charisma and dashing adventure stories. His brothers have been sheriffs and mayors; his friends include well-known local figures like mail carrier Bethel Coopwood and freight operator James Hickman, who often hires Roy.

He's a forty-year-old, lawsuit-plagued saloon owner with a sketchy background. She's an eighteen-year-old innocent from a deeply rooted, traditional San Antonio family. Two humans couldn't be farther from each other in experience and expectations. But to Roy, she's perfect. Now all his considerable energy is directed at one thing: the courtship of Virginia Chavez.

---

249 "Understanding race in this context not as a biological trait, but as a tool of social stratification, makes it easier to understand why Anglos might look fondly upon Tejano elites as fellow European descendants despite the fact that Spaniards were not a class of people Anglo-Americans are known to have admired." Roque Planas, "Between Black and White: Race and Status Among the Tejano Elite in 19th-Century San Antonio," *Journal of the Life and Culture of San Antonio*, accessed November 7, 2023, www.uiw.edu/sanantonio/blackandwhite.html.

San Antonio, Texas
October 1866

When Roy was a boy, weddings were intimate gatherings held inside family homes. These days the couple is treated like royalty, dressed in finery and standing in front of everyone they know inside a church. There are engraved invitations to ceremonies and receptions. Marital events have become status symbols.

Roy rather likes the new way, since all the attention is fixed on him and his young bride.

It's October 28 and he's standing with Virginia Chavez inside the San Fernando Cathedral.[250] She's wearing an off-white dress that won't show dust, and a short but very wide train fans out behind her like an albino beaver tail. She wears no veil, but a long ribbon of lace circles her hair and flows down to the small of her back. She holds a bouquet of wildflowers—fans are passé—but she does carry a rosary. Her dark eyes gleam with nerves and excitement whenever they meet Roy's.

If ever there is a face to make an honest man, that's the one, Roy thinks. And maybe he even believes it.

Roy's life seems to be heading in a steadier direction, but his past seems eager to catch up with him. Clouding his courtship and his colonization of Dogtown was unwelcome news from the courthouse when Pat Milmo finally sought revenge for Roy's wartime theft of his property. His suit asked for $350 in losses. Roy responded with vigor, countersuing for his losses accrued during the thirteen-day delay at Eagle Pass. That amount, he tallied, was worth exactly $2,028.[251] The banker wasn't expecting this brazen turnabout. Roy had the habit of bluffing men who challenged him by escalating the situation—like threatening to go to pistols for trivial

---

250 Virginia Chaves, "Texas, County Marriage Records, 1837–1965," FamilySearch, accessed November 7, 2023, https://familysearch.org/ark:/61903/1:1:K61K-JWS.

251 Sonnichsen, *Judge Roy Bean*, 53–54.

affronts—and this was the legal version of that instinct. And it worked: when Milmo stopped pursuing his case, so did Roy.

So far in his life, Roy has seen the law at work from many vantage points, and he's not impressed with any of them. There's nothing to inspire respect after watching men warp the justice system for their own ends, including Roy Bean himself. All he knows is that it's meted out equally badly from saloons and brick courthouses. It's the same crooked game, no matter the parlor.

In any event, the lawsuits have been defeated, and Roy feels the exhilaration of starting anew. (He's unaware that a vengeful Quintana will again sue, and again lose.) He has a home in San Antonio, a business to support his family, and a section of city to develop in his own image. And he has many long nights with Virginia to look forward to.

For Roy the best part of the ceremony isn't the vows or the first chaste kiss. It's the whoops and applause heaped on him as the married couple walks down the aisle. He likely knows that plenty of people in the audience are confused at what's happening, and the age difference isn't as shocking as the disparity in their reputations. For as long as he lives, and well beyond, people will wonder how Roy Bean managed to get such a good woman to marry him.

Pretty soon, she's wondering the same thing.

San Antonio, Texas
June 1867

A lot of traits overlap between narcissism and alcoholism—self-absorption, shamelessness, an overdeveloped sense of entitlement, a lack of empathy. But Freud is only eleven years old, and his essay "On Narcissism: An Introduction" is more than thirty years away, so these terms aren't available.

Which is fine, because anyone who knows Roy Bean for any length of time can quickly diagnose him. He's a mean bastard when he's drunk.

Roy reels into his home's front door on the evening of June 19, full of expectations of what he deserves to find. Marriage requires that he support the family, a great labor he's bearing manfully, and in return he gets servitude and gratitude. That's the deal. And where's his bride now? Sleeping, he fumes. He's home from the saloon but comes plagued by the kinds of dismal troubles that plague a grogshop operator. Is a hot meal and a greeting too much to ask? She's a lazy Mexican who needs a lesson.

Roy stokes the fire and fetches a hot stick. The tip trails signatures in smoke as he stalks into the bedroom, stealthy as an Apache. He lifts the covers, aims the stick at Virginia's ass, and pokes.[252]

The reaction is immediate as the burned and screaming woman struggles to her feet. It's an awkward movement: Virginia is seven months pregnant with their first child. The mutual shouting only stops when she flees the house, seeking shelter with neighbors and leaving for her parents' ranch as soon as possible.

Even at a time when spousal abuse was accepted, if often frowned on by polite society, such an attack on a pregnant woman was outside acceptable norms.[253] Even more importantly, Virginia and her mother are ready to press official charges, and Roy is charged with an assault that they said threatened the life of his wife.

This language was subtle but important. Texas law defined assault as a criminal act without reference to the circumstances surrounding it. The definition of abuse, on the other hand, incorporated surrounding circumstances. Roy's attack was being treated as a dangerous, unmitigated assault.

Word of Roy's actions must have spread, because his lawyers claim that he can't have an impartial jury in San Antonio. They seek a change of

---

252 Sonnichsen, *Judge Roy Bean*, 60.

253 For example, in 1867 a North Carolina jury acquitted a husband for hitting his wife with a switch because it was smaller around than his thumb. An appellate court agreed, saying courts shouldn't "interfere with family government in trifling cases." Cited and summarized in State v. Rhodes, Supreme Court of North Carolina, January 1, 1868.

venue and win a move to nearby Boerne. Now he can work on Virginia to drop the charges, with the delay pushing the trial past her due date.

The boy is born on July 12, 1867, at the Chavez family ranch. The joy of the birth of Roy's first child is clouded by the fact that he's been kicked out of the house and the new parents are opponents in an ongoing court case. Roy Jr. is baptized on August 20 at San Fernando Cathedral in an all-Spanish ceremony.[254] Before too long, the family is reunited, and Virginia is no longer pursuing the charges. (The case will be unceremoniously dismissed late the following year.) Her shame, the hassle, pressure from family and religion all work to reunify the Bean family.

Still, things between them are undoubtably rocky. Roy lives with his in-laws during the fallout of the court case, but he'll soon be back to living full-time in Dogtown, and so will Virginia and Roy Jr.

Virginia at age twenty is essentially trapped in a partnership with a volatile, egotistical scoundrel. And now her assumed name is being attached to an unsavory neighborhood in San Antonio. People no longer call Roy's stretch of South Flores street Dogtown. After the saloon has been up and running long enough to earn a bad reputation, they start referring to the neighborhood as Beanville.

254 Roman Catholic Archdiocese of San Antonio Sacramental Records, 1700–1996.

SAM

La Mesilla, New Mexico
March 1870

Sam Bean scowls as he watches the wagon teams unloading armfuls of dry goods into the new store on the town square's southern side. He knows the building's been acquired by out-of-towners J. Edgar Griggs and Joseph Reynolds, and their ambition can be measured in the large floor space of their new mercantile operation in Mesilla.

The shop is located next to the adobe store of the Barela family, who have been stiff competition to Sam but at least are from New Mexico. There are other new faces, including doctors, lawyers, and carpenters, all presenting new opportunities but also new competition for Sam's small store and freight business.

Mesilla, now with a population of fifteen hundred, is prospering as a center of commerce and nearby mining. It seems to be a good place to raise a family, and Sam's is growing around him. He's fifty-one, Petra is thirty-six, Anna Bean is ten, and Sam Jr. is five. Manuela Buola, a forty-eight-year-old "domestic servant," lives with them. For a family once thrown into exile, they've reclaimed their home.[255]

---

255 Petra Bean, Federal Census, Mesilla, Doña Ana County, New Mexico Territory, 1870.

But Mesilla is hardly a postwar utopia. The factions of the Civil War are still at it, now under the flags of the Republican Party, which is stocked with former Union officers, and the Democratic Party, which has southern sympathizers at its core. The fight has devolved into a political power struggle, fought not over principles but for control over property. Democrats carry the torch of the idea to carve off the independent territory of Arizona from New Mexico, a movement that inflames passions on both sides. The rhetoric is becoming violent.

This political tension is growing at a time when Mesilla is sliding into disorder. As commerce increases, it draws scoundrels and outlaws. The city and county are not ready for the influx; Mesilla is a county seat but the last judge to reside here left in 1867. "Law and justice have fallen into contempt, and some of the vilest scoundrels that ever infested a community have enjoyed complete immunity," noted the *Santa Fe Daily New Mexican*, blaming the lack of a judge.[256]

In these challenging times, Sam Bean keeps a low profile. He's been evicted from Mesilla once, and his family is only now getting back on its feet. Public service in today's atmosphere means political fighting or battling gunmen—or both. Sam tries to content himself with business and family, instead of being any sort of commanding figure in Doña Ana County.

Sam lives in the shadow of his former life, and people know he's sensitive about it. "Sam never did get over being called an old rebel," recounts one short biography, which included an interview with Sam's grandson. "Though it is told that many a youngster had his britches warmed for saying it aloud where Sam could hear."[257]

---

256 *Santa Fe Daily New Mexican*, September 1, 1871.

257 Richard W. Helbock and Ruth Dolezal, "New Mexico Post Offices," *Postal History Journal* 6 (October 1974), 13–16. The write-up is notable for having obtained information from an interview with Roy Bean, grandson of Sam Bean.

La Mesilla, New Mexico
August 1871

Even by New Mexico standards, the summer has been a hot one. The rains of August have come and gone, leaving only a cloying heat that seeps into people's bodies and warms their blood to a boil. It would be convenient to blame the weather for driving the citizenry of Doña Ana County into a frenzy, shifting the responsibility from human behavior to animal reaction.

It's election season, with candidates for sheriff, probate judge, and a territorial delegate leading the contested races. Republican sheriff Fabián Gonzales is being challenged by Mariano Barela, a 240-pound behemoth and local Democratic Party leader who comes from a deeply rooted family and owns fourteen thousand acres of local land. It's a nasty campaign, with Democratic and Republican newspapers slinging stinging charges of criminal doings and intimidation. In June an unknown attacker tried to shoot Manuel Barela, brother of the candidate for sheriff. The Democratic newspaper *The Borderer* declares that the Republicans are ready to assassinate their political foes.[258]

A date is coming that promises trouble: August 27, when Mesilla will host rival political rallies. Hundreds of Democrats will gather in the town plaza to hear José Manuel Gallegos, their nominee for territorial delegate to Congress, stump for the crowd.[259] Republicans have decided to gather at the home of local party leader John Lemon, who's also a candidate for probate judge. The two locations are just blocks apart.

Lemon and his wife, Luciana Pope, moved to Mesilla around 1860, and he opened a mercantile store and a freighting business serving area forts. He refused to support Baylor and found himself imprisoned and

---

258 Darlis Miller, "William Logan Rynerson in New Mexico, 1862–1893," *New Mexico Historical Review* 48, 2021, https://digitalrepository.unm.edu/nmhr/vol48/iss2/2.

259 Gallegos ran against Republican J. Francisco Chaves, a veteran of the Civil War in New Mexico.

threatened with hanging until the Confederates were pushed out. Now he's Mesilla's leading Republican, and a firebrand. Lemon is also the current owner of Sam Bean's confiscated property on the southern edge of Mesilla Plaza, that coveted dramshop real estate where the stagecoaches operate.

The threat of the rallies becoming violent spurs troops from Fort Selden to spend the day in Mesilla. The men of the Eighth Cavalry mill around the plaza as the speeches bluster and crowds applaud. The two camps seem happy to keep to themselves, enjoying a whiskey-filled morning, and in early afternoon the soldiers start the march north, back to their fort.

In the plaza, the Democratic rally ends with a ceremonial march that isn't meant to head anywhere but the downtown square. But at Lemon's home, the Republicans have decided to march around the plaza themselves. Lemon leads the way.

The timing couldn't be worse. The Republicans reach the plaza and start their march in a direction going opposite to the Democrats, allowing each side to heap abuse on the other as they circle. The two columns meet in front of the Reynolds-Griggs store, Lemon at the head of one side and I. N. Kelly, printer of *The Borderer*, at the other. Kelly is holding an axe handle.

The two men yell for a bit before shoving each other. Mariano Barela tries to push his bulk through the wall of human bodies to defuse the situation, as a prospective sheriff should. But Deputy US Marshal Apolonio Barela—a probable relative—pulls a pistol and fires it into the air. No matter what his intention, the reaction to the gunshot is immediate.

Kelly swings the axe handle, cratering Lemon's head. Before the probate judge candidate's body hits the ground, Lemon's friend Felicito Arroyas y Lueras pulls his own pistol and shoots Kelly dead. A moment later, Arroyas y Lueras's chest explodes as a bullet tears into his heart.

A full riot erupts as the sides charge, makeshift clubs swinging. More gunshots blast from both sides, and noncombatants stream from the plaza in terror. As the battle is joined, a third force arrives—the congregation of

San Albino has emerged from mass into a wild melee. The panicked parishioners crush and trample each other in their flight from Mesilla Plaza, pressing together as they try to access the narrow streets.[260]

Mariano Barela is among the surging combatants when a bullet streaks past him and smacks into a young man standing nearby, killing him.[261] Gunmen from both sides blaze away from the neighboring buildings, and no one wants to bring an axe handle to a gunfight. The battle peters out, with fear of being shot overriding the desire to break the bones of a political rival.

Federal employees in town dispatch a messenger on the road to Fort Selden to get the US troops back. The gunmen infesting the plaza stay there all afternoon, trading shots. But by the time sixty cavalrymen ride into town in early evening, even the last holdouts have gone home. The troops find a bloodstained plaza: nine people dead and about forty injured.

There is an investigation, of sorts. Second District Judge Hezekiah Johnson spends two days in Mesilla and leaves without indicting anyone. No one is ever arrested; too many are guilty. Soldiers remain in Mesilla during the election and a few weeks afterward for good measure. But the violence has receded back into the homes and minds of the citizens who formed the opposing mobs.

The September election is a Democratic sweep across the New Mexico Territory, including Gallegos winning as New Mexico delegate to Congress and Barela as Doña Ana County sheriff. Disgusted Republicans flee New Mexico en masse. Most notably, locals Ignacio Orrantía, former

---

260 *Weekly Democratic Statesman* (Austin, TX), September 21, 1871.

261 S. M. Ashenfelter filed a story for the *Silver City (NM) Independent* that listed the dead: "Sotello Lopez, Francisco Rodrigues, Felicito Arroyas y Luera, Fabian Cortez, the Chihuahua bully, and an idiot boy who was shot down while standing beside Mariano Barela." Quoted in *History of New Mexico, Its Resources and People*, vol. 2 (New York, Chicago, and Los Angeles: Pacific Coast Publishing, 1907): 567.

sheriff Fabián Gonzales, and ninety-six families from the Mesilla area leave to settle the city of La Ascensión, Chihuahua.

Sam Bean watches all this drama unfold from the sidelines. He's not politically active, doesn't appear in newspapers, or run for any office. Not being a public man has its advantages, given the political and social atmosphere, but there is no ignoring the blood spilled outside his door.

The fracas only strengthens the allure of the emptier parts of New Mexico, and there's plenty of wilderness yet to tame. The mountains hold untold treasures, not only in the silver and copper found there, but in the mining boomtowns that continue to rise and fall. He's older and has more responsibilities, and he should be grateful for the opportunities Mesilla offers, but Sam Bean's heart is still that of a frontier entrepreneur.

ROY

San Antonio, Texas
February 1872

Daytime at the Beanville Exchange is usually reserved for sluggish drunks or restless gamblers who may have nothing else to do. This gives Roy plenty of time to scrutinize the day's delivery—a sack of several hundred brass coins. Each is about an inch wide, and the saloon's name is stamped on one side along the outer ring. The words in the center say, "Good for 5 Cents at the Bar."[262] That's enough to buy a cheap cigar.

Token salesmen have just started wandering the Texas cattle trails, filling orders for a promotional idea that Roy Bean understands implicitly. Customers order a drink or a cigar, or pay for a game of pool in cash, and are given tokens instead of change. A shortage of coins makes this an understandable practice. In reality the tokens ensure that a customer spends the entire amount, during this visit or the next. The marketing appeal of a saloon token gives rise to the hiring of "drummers" to travel the Chisholm and other trails, handing out tokens and talking up the saloon.

Roy tosses the bags of coins in a safe and mulls the rest of his day. Even

---

262 Jerry Adams, "Judge Roy Bean," *Trade Token Tales,* 2001, https://tokenguy.tripod.com/tokentales/page49.htm.

the usual collection of daytime riffraff is missing. So he closes the bar, harnesses a mule to a wagon, and heads southwest into the nearby groves. This is the land of James Hickman, the Santa Fe Trail trader who posted Roy's bail in Mexico years ago. He's only gotten more prosperous and has accrued many tracts of undeveloped land in the suburbs of San Antonio. Hickman once asked Roy to keep an eye out for tree poachers and other trespassers. Unwittingly, he invited the saloon operator to raid his land.

Roy sets his axe to a spindly piece of deadfall, his large body making a small stack of firewood. The cart is not filled and Roy needs cash, so he eyes a dead tree standing nearby. Hickman won't miss this one.

But the sound of voices in Spanish stays his hand; another crew is arriving to work the trees. They are charcoal burners, who lease lands from owners to harvest and burn wood. Sometimes they reside on the leases. Roy waits for the team to disassemble some wood, and then moves in, pistol at the ready. He treats all charcoal burners the same way, whether they are allowed by Hickman or not. He bluffs the men, seizes their wood, and hauls it into town. Last Christmas he pulled the same stunt but distributed the stolen wood to poor people in Beanville.

It takes the rest of the day to deliver the cart to the plaza and sell the load of purloined wood. Cash in pocket, he heads back home to reopen the Exchange and settle into some whiskey. The neighborhood remains a curiosity for downtown citizens and soldiers on the way to the arsenal. Anywhere west of San Pedro Creek, including Beanville, is considered a Mexican neighborhood. Anything east—for example, downtown—is dominated by Anglo-German influence.[263]

The city is steadily growing, with new two-story buildings, cathedrals, and waterworks being constructed. But for Roy, the streets seem

263 San Pedro Creek was "a significant social barrier," notes Professor Laura Hernández-Ehrisman author of *Inventing the Fiesta City: Heritage and Carnival in San Antonio* (Albuquerque: University of New Mexico Press, 2016) in an interview with Texas Public Radio (Bri Kirkham, April 1, 2022), https://www.tpr.org/history/2022-04-01/no-boundaries-how-san-antonios-red-light-district-grew.

narrower, darker, and less exciting than when he first arrived. Civilization has taken hold in San Antonio, with its rules, laws, and regulations. It chafes against Roy, who clings to his frontier mentality in defiance of the progress around him.

His family just adds to his pressures. Roy Jr. is five years old and already looks as dark and dusky as his mother. Another boy, Santiago, was born in late 1870 but died young, casting a grim pall over the household.[264]

Without the saloon paying off as needed, Roy sometimes takes his battered wagon and debilitated team of mules to perform contract deliveries to Chihuahua. These business trips double as drinking benders, opportunities to show off his considerable billiards skills, and long nights betting at cockfights.

On the road, he's a free agent. At home, he's a sitting target. On February 6, Rafael Quintana files another lawsuit against Roy to reclaim those eight wagons.[265] It's destined to go nowhere, like the earlier suits, but for the successful trader the ill will clearly lingers.

Roy tends to alienate his business partners. Hickman will soon catch him poaching trees and intimidating his charcoal men, and the two will fall out. Roy's reputation is being steadily degraded in San Antonio.

San Antonio, Texas
November 1875

The Bexar County District Court opens its session as it always does: with the bailiff using a long, T-shaped pole to poke the whitewashed canvas ceiling. Doing this creates a brief chorus of squeals and squeaks from the awakened bats roosting between the upper floor ceiling and the roof. Roy can still smell the acrid stench of guano as he watches the process from

---

264 Santiago Bean, "Texas Births and Christenings, 1840–1981," FamilySearch, accessed November 7, 2023, https://familysearch.org/ark:/61903/1:1:F65X-WLQ.

265 Bexar County District Court, Rafael Quintana vs. Roy Bean, Civil Case 3303, February 6, 1872.

the defendant's chair, but after the bats are chased off, the courtroom is at least free of their high-pitched distractions. Everyone in town calls the courthouse, built in 1851, the Old Bat House.[266]

Seated next to Roy is Bethel Coopwood, the forty-eight-year-old former Confederate spymaster. He spent several years in Mexico and California before returning to Texas to make a good living as a lawyer, postmaster, and owner of a long-haul delivery service. In June, Coopwood signed a contract with the Texas California Stage Line Company to run a mail route between Austin and a no-account railroad stop on the Galveston, Harrisburg, and San Antonio line called Harwood. (It's twelve miles from the town of Luling.)[267] He's also won some head-shaking fame for his attempt to introduce camels to the western United States. By now, he's given up on the beasts being accepted for widespread usage and is focusing on sales to circuses.[268]

The third and final defendant, Jesse H. Holden, is another Spy Company veteran, one of the first volunteers to join in 1861. He and his brother Andrew enlisted on the same day (July 11), just as Coopwood was forming the company in El Paso. The Holdens are cattlemen in Mason County, Texas.[269]

Reunions with Confederate veterans of the New Mexico invasion

---

266 Sylvia Ann Santos, "The History of the Bexar County Courthouse," Bexar County Historical Commission, accessed November 7, 2023, www.bexar.org/DocumentCenter/View/4102/The-History-of-the-Bexar-County-Courthouse-by-Sylvia-Ann-Santos?bidId=.

267 *Denison (TX) Daily News*, June 17, 1875.

268 *Galveston (TX) Daily News*, October 28, 1875. After the war, Coopwood was nearly killed (and his brother David was shot and drowned) when troops of Juan Cortina shot at them while they were traveling on the steamboat *Bell* on the Rio Grande.

269 Civil War soldiers database, National Park Service, https://www.nps.gov/civilwar/search-soldiers.htm.

should be a point of pride for Roy, whose exploits during the era—with all the horse theft and contraband smuggling—were more shadowy and less heroic than those of a typical soldier. Association with Coopwood in particular should firm up his connection to the Lost Cause, which is a valuable commodity in Texas society and politics.

Instead, the three men are in the Old Bat House as codefendants, charged with "Preventing the Execution of Civil Process." It's a misdemeanor offense that applies to a wide array of possible petty crimes. This time, it covers resisting arrest, which is fairly common. After all, this is the first year that city cops in San Antonio have been issued uniforms, part of a wider law-and-order push in the city. Police also enforce firearms laws that now prohibit the open carrying of pistols.

Roy suspected trouble that night as soon as the policeman[270] strode up to him, but Coopwood was undaunted, damn him. For once, Roy was not the leader of the mischief; Coopwood and Holden were the ones who resisted and ended up arrested, while Roy remained free but named as a lesser accomplice.

The trio faced a joint two-day trial, which started Friday and extended into late Saturday. Coopwood, a lawyer, put up a spirited defense, claiming he was illegally restrained. He also claims he's authorized to carry a weapon (he's not) and complains that the jury was comprised of six men instead of twelve.[271]

Now it's Monday morning—time to hear the verdict. All three are found guilty. Coopwood and Holden are fined $250 each, Roy just five dollars.[272] The men part company outside the Old Bat House, their latest reunion sullied by the outcome. Coopwood is enraged and vows to appeal to the Texas Supreme Court, which he does the next year, only to lose.

---

270 Identified as P. Fox in court documents.

271 Ex Parte Coopwood, 44 Tex. 467 (1876), Supreme Court of Texas.

272 San Antonio Express, November 22, 1875.

The Bexar County Courthouse and its jail, which sits in the rear of the courthouse and is surrounded by a wall studded with broken glass, are on the northwest corner of Military Plaza. The area showcases the way downtown San Antonio is transforming. Where jacales once stood there are now small masonry buildings, and the long, squat adobe buildings rest in the shadows of taller peak-roof structures. The building boom is happening across downtown and in nearly every neighborhood east of San Pedro Creek.

Roy Bean is watching a new city emerge all around him, but he's not growing with it. This latest brush with law enforcement is another sign that his life here is heading for a dead end. He's been in San Antonio for more than a decade, but it's feeling farther than ever from being his home.

JAMES

Independence, Missouri

January 1875

James and Elizabeth Bean wait outside their house in downtown Independence on January 15, dressed in their finest. Inside, their home is loud with guests, clinking silverware, and cooking meat, a wedding reception that's waiting for the arrival of the newlyweds. All four of them.

Not only are his sons visiting Independence, but they're also arriving as newly married men. Gordon and Phantley Roy Bean gave up on Jackson County to build their postwar lives in St. Joseph, Missouri. P. R., after a stint in St. Louis, now works as a bookkeeper at Waterman and Bernard, while Gordon is a traveling clothes salesman with Schuster, Ketchum & Co.[273]

This has been a banner week for the boys. On January 13, Gordon married Mittie Porter at her aunt's home in St. Joe. He and P. R. then boarded a train for Lexington, Missouri, where P.R. married Tillie Chan-

273 The primary owner of this outfit was Adam Schuster (b. 1837), an immigrant from Prussia, an early Missouri pioneer, a banker, and a cattleman. As a salesman for the company, Gordon traveled store to store as a "Knight of the Handshake." The following year, Gordon left Missouri after signing with Charles P. Kellogg, owner of a large clothing manufacturer in Chicago.

cellor, whose family lives there. Today, the rolling double-wedding party arrives at James's home in Independence, "within 100 yards of the place where these men were born," the *Independence Herald* states. "Here, many of their old friends who had known them in childhood, as well as old schoolmates, called upon them."[274]

The party continues the next day, when John and Bettie Smarr host yet another reception. The young men have a lot of gratitude for their foster mother and father. The *Independence Herald* calls them "brothers of the same opinion," gives their wartime biographies, and prominently mentions the ghost hovering over these proceedings: Aubry Bean, "who fell in the 'lost cause.'" Their late mother, Mary, isn't mentioned.

The day ends and the celebration is over. "Both young gents and their beautiful and interesting wives have left for their home in St. Joseph to enter into their new role of existence." The prominent mention of Independence's traditional municipal rival is not lost on James, Jackson County's steady partisan.

James at age sixty is rebuilding his store business, but he's also got his eye on public office. This year, he reemerges as the city's most prominent justice of the peace. James is a public man again. The newspapers call him by his former moniker. Squire Bean is back.

Serving as a JP often involves banal work, like arranging property sales and hearing small claims cases. Farmers arguing over hogs make their way to his court. But he also organizes jury trials and processes prisoners accused of violent crimes. In one case, his ruling was appealed and upheld by a higher court.[275] And of course, he's still the man to go to for an easy wedding.

---

274 "Two Brothers of the Same Opinion," *St. Louis Post-Dispatch*, January 27, 1875. According to the article, the item was first run in the *Independence Herald*.

275 "In the Doughterty-Schmidt suit before Squire Bean yesterday, the jury hung and were discharged. The case will be heard next Saturday." *Kansas City Times*, December 3, 1875. On December 9, the *Kansas City Times* reported that James Bean's ruling in Overfelt vs. Hinters had been upheld by the Law and Equity Court.

For James, his personal recovery remains tied to the rebirth of Reconstruction-era Independence and Jackson County. It's a time of prosperity, of new homes and churches on Rock and Delaware Streets, but also one of dubious land deals and enrichment schemes by lawyers turned real estate agents.

The trauma of war hadn't fully left Jackson County. The most visible example of this was in the support given to the James-Younger gang, Confederate guerillas turned outlaws. The year before, the Adams Express Company had hired the Pinkerton National Detective Agency to find the band after it robbed one of company's train safes at Gads Hill, Missouri. An agent named John Whicher came to Jackson County to look for the outlaws; on March 11, 1874, travelers found him shot to death along a lonely rural road.

Revenge comes this winter. On January 25 (ten days after the Bean family wedding reception), Pinkerton agents surround the James family's farm in Kearney, Missouri. Frank and Jesse James aren't there anymore, but their mother and their half brother's family are. The Pinkertons throw an incendiary device into the house to start a fire, which it does (and then some) when it rolls into a lit fireplace and explodes. The woman loses an arm, and nine-year-old Archie Samuel is killed.

Undaunted, the gang strikes again, this time in their native Missouri. On January 31, they rob a southbound train on the Iron Mountain Railway. When they steal from the passengers, they examine their hands to avoid targeting working men. More importantly, they hit the express company's safe in the baggage area. When newspapers attribute the crime to the Arthur McCoy gang, the James-Younger gang telegraphs the *St. Louis Dispatch*[276] to claim it for themselves.

One bit of business remains before they leave Missouri. On April 12, 1875, an unknown gunman kills Daniel Askew, a former Union militiaman suspected of providing the Pinkertons with a staging area for their

276 Merged with the *St. Louis Evening Post* in 1878.

raid in Kearney. After that, the Pinkertons give up the chase, and the James-Younger gang moves on from Missouri to Minnesota.[277]

That month, April, James Bean hears a case of assault with intent to kill. It's filed against James Green, a storeowner on Main Street who "severely chastised an impertinent negro who was trespassing on his property," according to an account in the *Kansas City Times*.[278]

On paper, the preceding years contained watershed moments for equal rights. In 1868, the Fourteenth Amendment to the US Constitution granted African Americans citizenship and equal protection under the law, and in 1870 the Fifteenth gave black men the right to vote.[279] But Missouri was still roiled by racial attacks, including school and church burnings, and an African American exodus. By 1870, there were fewer African Americans in Missouri than before the war. Those who remained clustered in cities for safety.[280]

Given this environment, it's notable that Green's victim is brave enough to pursue charges against him in Jackson County. He's testing the concept of equal justice in America, and Judge James Bean is the arbiter. If a crime has been committed, its severity warrants referral to a higher court.

---

277 Their crime saga will continue there and in Tennessee into the early 1880s.

278 "In Kansas City Forty Years Ago," *Kansas City Times*, April 4, 1916, a rerun of an article filed from Independence on April 4, 1876.

279 In fact, the Ordinance to Abolish Slavery in Missouri became law in January 1865, eleven months before passage of the Thirteenth Amendment to the US Constitution, which abolished slavery nationwide.

280 "Progress Amidst Prejudice: Portraits of African Americans in Missouri, 1880–1920, Introduction to the Collection," Missouri State Archives, accessed November 7, 2023, www.sos.mo.gov/archives/education/aapc/intro. These were the days before southern states passed Jim Crow laws, which the Supreme Court upheld in Plessy v. Ferguson (1896). After that, racial segregation was considered legal, and more states passed segregation laws. The court reversed the *Plessy* decision in 1954.

To be sure, it's an obscure event, a ruling predestined to be lost to posterity. But it's nevertheless a moment when James can rise above his personal history and any ambition he may still harbor for a future in local politics.

Perhaps there are mitigating circumstances to consider. Maybe the victim was drunk, or truly was trespassing in a legal sense. (Hard to imagine him pressing charges if that were the case.) Perhaps James recognizes that the tenet of frontier justice—"he deserved it"—somehow applies here, if the man was rude or challenging. But James is a former slaveowner from a family of Kentucky slaveowners. The biggest mitigating factor in the case, no matter the other circumstances, is the victim's race.

James rules that no crime was committed, and Green is discharged. Ugly as it is, the popular will of the people of Jackson County has been enforced. The name of the man who Green beat is never published or recorded.

It can at least be said that Judge Bean offers his services regardless of race. One article describes a case brought to his court by a black laborer named Ben Williams who was stiffed by an employer.[281] But it's Sam's liberal, no-question style of marrying people that draws white and black couples alike from across Jackson County and Kansas City. Newspapers even start covering his unorthodox weddings.

One afternoon in August 1876, Andy Richardson and Susie Letcher make headlines when they arrive from Kansas City to be married in Independence. "He had paid her constant attention for over a year, but Susie's parents objected to her marrying Andy, and frequently ordered him out of their house," records the *Kansas City Times*, which dutifully notes they are "(both colored)."

James could ask her age—she looks younger than the mandated eighteen years—or simply refuse the out-of-towners. He also could just marry them at his office or conducted a street-side ceremony. But when it comes to weddings, he's still sentimental. James arranges a snap location and

281 The jury ended hung and a retrial was scheduled, but it wasn't covered. *Daily Journal of Commerce* (Kansas City, MO), March 1, 1877.

finds cheery witnesses at Monroe's grocery store, where the young couple "were joined in holy matrimony. . . . The loving couple left on the 5 o'clock Narrow Gauge train for Kansas City. It is not known whether the bride was eighteen or not, and perhaps the end is not yet."[282]

Reckless or romantic, Squire Bean's reputation for easy weddings has returned, along with his public image. Time has entirely exorcised the ghost of the tragic, trailside service James rendered to Fannie Owens in 1845.

Independence, Missouri
February 1877

James and Elizabeth Bean are spending another quiet night at home on February 10 until they're roused by an urgent banging on the door at eleven p.m. It's a breathless and rattled William Fisher, a farmer who lives six miles outside town. He witnessed a murder.

At eight p.m. that night, Deputy County Marshal Henry Hughes had approached Fisher with a warrant to arrest two woodcutters who were working on Fisher's land, Frank Miller and Dick Green.[283] The preceding week, the two men and another man called George Tarwater spotted a handful of teens sitting on a fence and chased them off for sport by riddling the fence with gunfire. When the kids ran, the men snapped shots over their heads, laughing uproariously. No one was hurt, but the writs were signed.

The arrest went bad when Green pulled a revolver and shot Hughes, who died within minutes, gasping the names of his wife and children.[284]

Now the city's official response is in the hands of James Bean, acting coroner. The first thing he does is keep calm. There's no point racing out in the middle of the cold winter night while murderers are skulking about.

---

282 *Kansas City Times,* August 20, 1876.

283 No relation to James Green the storeowner.

284 "The Murder," *Daily Journal of Commerce*, February 14, 1877.

Instead, he sends Fisher to call on a downtown doctor, J. T. Brown, and let him know that Squire Bean will need his company at first light.

The pair set out in the doctor's horse-drawn wagon on a grim Sunday-morning ride to Green's farm. They can see the deputy's body just outside the door of a small shack, whose chimney shows there's an unlit stove inside. The men approach the corpse at a steady but slow pace. Poor Hughes is stiff with rigor mortis. But the chill has kept the insects and bloating at bay. There's not a lot of blood, either.

James takes a moment to use the woodcutter's abandoned supply to restart the fire. By the time he turns back to the body, the doctor has stripped the man's shirt and jacket. There are two bullet wounds, "Navy sized," as Dr. Brown puts it, one punched above the nipple and another burrowing into the shoulder.

He probes the wounds with a metal rod to determine trajectories but can remove only one of the balls embedded in the body. Brown says the one he recovered, which tore through a lung, was the fatal shot. With the witness testimony collected by James and the forensic evidence documented by the doctor, the inquest is finished. It reaches two simple conclusions: there's been a murder here, and Miller and Green are the suspects. And legally, that's all it has to determine.

The doctor redresses Hughes and wraps him in a blanket, and the pair hoist the corpse into the wagon. The deputy is buried on Tuesday, the same day Marshal Leggitt rounds up Miller and Green in a bloodless surrender. On Wednesday, the results of the Bean and Brown inquest are printed in Kansas City's *Daily Journal of Commerce*.[285]

Now justice must wait for a grand jury to meet in five days. Residents are in a panic that the men, whether in jail or released on bail, are vulnerable to vigilantes. "A very low murmur of lynching was heard, and it was apprehended that an attempt might be made to force the jail," reports the *Daily Journal of Commerce*. "The marshal however made every preparation to protect his prisoners."

---

285 "The Murder."

Quick frontier justice has been denied, and the wheels of actual justice move slowly. It takes until mid-March for the inquest's results to even be submitted to the court.[286]

FROM *DAILY JOURNAL OF COMMERCE*

April 29, 1877

We understand that Mr. Harmon Smith of Rush Bottom is to enter suit against Squire Bean for performing the wedding ceremony of his daughter, Sarah Smith, and Mr. George Miller on Sunday last. As he (Mr. Smith) alleges that the marriage was against his wishes and without his consent, and that his daughter has not yet reached her majority. How it will terminate is not known.[287]

FROM *DAILY JOURNAL OF COMMERCE*

December 15, 1877

About ten o'clock yesterday morning, his honor Squire Bean was seen making his way to Larkins' livery stable, where he hired a horse and buggy and started out on the Gilpin Town Road. As this was something unusual for the Squire to do, it of course creates quite a number of comments and inquiries. His destination, as acknowledged by himself, was Gilpin Town and the object of his visit was ostensibly to take acknowledgement of a deed. This tale was rather thin, however, and did not entirely satisfy the curiosity excited by his unusual actions and some parties . . . made up their mind to find out what the Squire was up to. Their investigation brought to light

286 *Kansas City Times*, March 14, 1877.

287 Indeed, no record exists showing how the case was resolved.

the true status of affairs, which was the joining together in the bonds of matrimony Major Robert Rickmond, aged 86 years, and Mrs. Mary Fayha, aged 84. The affair was intended to be kept very secret but on the Squire's return he found the old but true saying goes, "The best laid plans of mice and men oft go astray." The JOURNAL wishes the happy couple much joy in their new phase of life.

Independence, Missouri
December 1877

The rest of Independence will remember Peter Hinter as a portly, good-natured barber. Closer acquaintances know him as a sad widower, left with children and a weakness for strong drink. Still others will recall his service as the president of the insurance board of Independence and as a justice of the peace.

But James Bean, thanks to his position as coroner, will always remember him sprawled on his back on his barbershop floor, head flung backward at an impossible angle, the red crescent of his slit throat stretched open and yawning. The man killed himself on December 18, and a wide, still-wet pool of blood spills across the floor.[288]

There is a job to do, which will save James from giving in to the horror of the scene. His inquest must determine the facts of this violent death. It's an obvious suicide. Not only is a barber's straight-edge razor lying by his side; Hinter removed his jacket and used it as a pillow to better expose his neck to the blade. The man apparently tucked his long beard aside for the same reason.

Broken glass from an empty store window litters the floor. This is odd—Hinter broke into his own establishment. But Hinter is an irresponsible drunk, and this doesn't surprise James nearly as much as the man's grisly suicide. There must have been more than just whiskey at work here.

James leaves the store, where a doctor can examine and remove the

---

288 *Kansas City Times,* December 19, 1877.

body without him, and gathers statements from witnesses. He starts with the man who reported finding the corpse, Bean family friend John Smarr Sr. He was walking past the barbershop when he noticed the broken window, poked his head inside, and saw the body.

W. J. Bailey was the last to see Hinter alive from his position guarding the city jail. Around two a.m., the man wandered over, asked for some water, and struck up an odd conversation. "They're going to hang me," Hinter said. "I know you're building gallows back there to string me up." He stayed for about two hours before blundering off toward his barbershop.

This talk of hanging makes James fear that the deranged man has hurt his family, but they're unharmed. Hinter's eldest son, Julius, arrives with frightening details. Hinter wasn't even drinking, he says, but just snapped during the night. In a frenzy, he dashed to a neighbor's house to borrow a pistol, claiming a burglar was trying to break in. But when he got back home, he pointed the gun at Julius, who collected the young children and fled. Now Squire Bean empanels a jury of whoever is around to hear this testimony on the record and make his official ruling of a suicide.[289]

It's been a long, depressing day of work. As exhausting as it is, James never flinches from public service, and last spring he took on more. In June, the new city council appointed him city assessor, another duty that builds his résumé as a servant of Independence—and an aspiring Democratic politician.

At six p.m. he's leaving Monroe's store, where he's been unpacking the traumatic events of the barber's surprising suicide with neighbors, when a well-dressed young man sidles up to him and shyly asks if he's a justice of the peace. He's from a good but stern family in Lee's Summit. Equally stern are the parents of his prospective fiancée, who just happens to be waiting for them on the south sidewalk of the town square. James "made the happy couple one flesh in his usual genial manner, and they departed on their way rejoicing," reports the *Daily Journal of Commerce*, which calls

289 *Kansas City Times.*

it "one of the most romantic affairs that has transpired in the 'Orchard City' for some time."[290]

The next day, one regional newspaper covers the suicide, while another covers the wedding. As this single day in December demonstrates, in good times or bad, Squire Bean is in a position to see the best and worst of his beloved community.

Independence, Missouri
March 1878

I'll be damned, thinks James Bean, old Hinter is finally right. They've built a scaffold in the downtown plaza. It's tucked in an alley at the back of the courthouse, where spectators can't gawk at the upcoming hanging of Dick Green. Today, March 1, he'll finally swing for the death of Deputy Marshal H. H. Hughes.

It turns out that Green's real name is Edward McFarren, and he's the son of a well-to-do Iowa farmer. He's wanted in Fremont, Iowa, for assaulting a sheriff, horse theft, and jailbreaking. He goes to trial under his assumed name, and "Richard Green" is found guilty of first-degree murder by a jury after just thirty minutes of deliberation. The sentence is delayed by a failed appeal to the Missouri Supreme Court.

James is a sanctioned execution witness, but many hundreds have turned out for the hanging. There are crowds along the heights north of town, staring down into the alley. A company from the Kansas City Guard is sealing off the scaffold area. Marshal Leggitt (Hughes's boss) presides over the hanging and grants the condemned his last words. "I die for my crime in the faith of my Lord and Saviour," he says, and then they affix the hood and noose, and drop him to a neck-snapping death.

Frank Miller may have it easier since he didn't shoot Hughes. He's granted a change of venue and will be tried in Lexington, Missouri, in May. (He'll be found guilty of first-degree murder and sentenced to hang,

---

290 *Daily Journal of Commerce*, December 19, 1877.

but Governor John Phelps commutes it to ten years of imprisonment later in the year.)

James leaves the hanging feeling weak. The execution itself doesn't upset him—he's seen worse endings to human life—but he's feeling weary. James's growing fatigue and weight loss are punctuated with bouts of peripheral edema, when his hands and feet swell with fluid. On occasion, the urine streaming into a chamber pot or outhouse has been oddly frothy. But today, after struggling home from the hanging his inquest set in motion more than a year ago, he spots a new worry when he relieves himself: the diminished stream is stained pink.

The moment he's been dreading is here—admitting that he's sick. It's time to consult a doctor. With his symptoms and a urine test, the diagnosis comes quickly. James is afflicted with Bright's disease.[291]

It was named after Richard Bright, who was the first to describe the symptoms in 1827 and link them to kidney disease. Following this observation, Bright and other physicians soon built a case that connected the condition to heart issues. This knowledge does not mean that doctors knew how to treat the stricken. Patients seemed unable to remove water from their systems, so doctors prescribed diuretics. This might have been a fine idea, if the diuretics had been in the form of concoctions made from ginger, dandelion, or birch bark. But all too often doctors dosed patients with mercury compounds that purged their systems in every direction. Mercurial treatments like calomel were commonly used when the kidneys sputtered, even though many physicians suspected that they further weakened sick people.[292]

---

291 These days the condition is broadly called chronic nephritis with hypertension.

292 In 1863 the US attorney general banned calomel's use in the army and lost his job for it; it was used well into the 1890s. See Israel Dana, "The Treatment of Chronic Bright's Disease," *Boston Medical and Surgical Journal*, September 24, 1885; Theodore Pappas, "Bright's Disease, Malaria and Machine Politics: The Story of the Illness of President Chester Arthur," *Surgery Journal*, December 19, 2017; Garabed Eknoyan, "On the Etymology of Nephritis: A Historical Appraisal of its Origins,"

James knows that the disease probably isn't going to kill him this year or even next. But he has a debilitating condition that could cripple him long before he dies from it. His life's latest upswing is being interrupted by events beyond his control, only this time it's not a plague or a civil war. This time, the tragedy is purely personal.

St. Joseph, Missouri
November 1880

The news is out: Gordon Bean's back in Missouri to make his mark. After nine years of peddling wares for Chicago firms as a traveling salesman, he's opened a wholesale clothing operation in St. Joseph with local business associates. "This is a strong team and is bound to succeed," reads the *St. Joseph Gazette*, announcing the store's planned January opening more than a month in advance. "It will add much life of trade to this city, for the competition it will bring to bear is one if the elements that make trade lively."[293]

St. Joseph has been a hub of trade since before the Hannibal and St. Joseph Railroad became the first to cross Missouri in 1860. Now the rail network has nearly reached the entire nation. Factories send products here—dry goods, groceries, hardware, saddles, drugs, clothes, and liquor—for shipment to retailers out west. Selling to immigrants who were traveling west was the last generation's game; now the rails have enabled the rise of middlemen, often called "jobbers."[294]

One of Gordon Bean's partners is Milton Tootle, a rising success in

---

American Society of Nephrology, 2020; and Steven Peltzman, "From Dropsy to Bright's Disease to End-stage Renal Disease," *Milbank Quarterly*, 1989.

293 *St. Joseph Gazette*, November 24, 1880.

294 "Historic Resources of St. Joseph, Buchanan County of Missouri," US Department of the Interior, National Park Service, June 26, 1989, section E, 7. The National Register of Historic Places property documentation form also notes, "By 1879, over fifty businesses were wholesale houses. New firms were continually founded by junior members of the established houses, who found trade promising enough to warrant

the wholesale dry-goods business. The reputation of the men behind the new firm—Gordon is described as "one of St. Joseph's most energetic and efficient commercial tourists"—supports the newspaper's prediction of success.[295]

Thirty-two-year-old Gordon is growing in business stature, and he needs money to support a growing family. At home on 120 Nineteenth Street are his twenty-five-year-old wife, Mary, daughter Sadie, age four, and son Edward, age two.

And his invalid father, James Bean.[296]

Things have gone downhill quickly for James, now sixty-five. Bright's disease steadily rendered him housebound, and he's becoming increasingly thin and frail. Living on his own is impossible, so he's abandoned his cherished Independence to live with his son in the rival city of St. Joseph.

He and wife, Elizabeth, have split up. She's living with her son Charles Moore in St. Louis. James and Elizabeth left Independence knowing they would never see each other again. From then on, both of them listed their marital status on federal forms as "widower."

Still, there are joys in St. Joseph. The presence of his grandchildren is a solace, to be sure, but what James really enjoys is watching Gordon carry the mantle as a notable man of Missouri commerce. The booming city has given the ailing James hope for the future of his state, his nation, and his family.

This atmosphere invigorates him. On the federal census form, he lists his occupation as "capitalist." It's a defiant if unheard declaration against the creeping disease that has sidelined him from commerce and society.

---

starting opposition houses." See: https://mostateparks.com/sites/mostateparks/files/HistoricResources-StJoseph.pdf.

295 *St. Joseph Gazette*, November 24, 1880. Tootle was an outfitter turned jobber who would go on to become one of "the most prominent leaders in the wholesale dry goods business" in St. Joseph, according to the National Park Service.

296 Federal Census, 1880.

SAM

Georgetown, New Mexico Territory
June 1880

There's no hiding the glee Sam Bean feels as the stagecoach comes into view, rattling down the muddy street. The sixty-one-year-old is standing at Georgetown's center, where its two streets meet to make a V and where the stage from Silver City stops. It's not quite a downtown yet, but Georgetown is quickly growing. There's a newly opened hotel and butcher shop here, signs of growth that Sam hopes the passengers on the stage will notice and appreciate.

The vehicle is drawn by four horses, with four men seated, exposed but armed with rifles and shotguns, on the front. Another gunman stands on the rear of the coach, armed with a pistol. They are on guard for robbers and Native American "renegades," both of which groups infest the mountains here.

As the coach gets closer, Sam recognizes one of the riders seated outside—his fifteen-year-old son, Samuel Jr. He looks like a boy among the men, but Sam can't help but feel a surge of pride to see him riding shotgun on the trail, even if just for a ten-mile jaunt. This is an essential part of being a Bean: rolling through the wilderness on guard against attack, with nothing but wits and weapons to see you through. It makes Sam Sr. feel old and young at the same time.

Stagecoaches are rarer than they used to be. Railroads now form webs across the territory, leaving the coaches to feed the rail connections.[297] Sam hired one, laden with trunks carrying their most personal belongings, to bring his family from Silver City, where he relocated the family from Mesilla to chase some low-yielding mining ventures there.[298] Now he's uprooting them again, for an even less developed hamlet.

The stagecoach comes to a halt, Sam Jr. waving at his father. The boy hands the shotgun to one of his fellow riders, shakes his hand, and climbs down from the carriage. The door opens and Petra emerges, already looking skeptical. She's forty-seven years old and entirely unimpressed by a primitive boomtown. But even she smiles as the Garcia children, Leandra and Porfilia, tumble out of the carriage to reach their adopted father. Annie Bean, Sam's eighteen-year-old daughter, follows close behind.[299]

"Not enough room inside, so I asked to ride on top," Sam Jr. announces, hand outstretched. "I borrowed the shotgun; mine's packed away. We was looking for Indians."

It's not what Sam Sr. wants Petra and the girls to hear, but Junior's keen

---

297 "Until the railroads penetrated various parts of the Territory from 1879 on, the stagecoach lines represented the only means of regular commercial transportation. After 1879, the stagecoach lines became feeder operations used entirely to supplement rail transportation." William Wallace, "Stagecoaching in Territorial New Mexico," *New Mexico Historical Review* 32 (1957): 205.

298 Thomas K. Todsen, "Territorial Postmasters of New Mexico—Sam Bean of Mesilla," *Postal History Journal: Mountain and Desert West* 6 (October 1974): 13–16.

299 The historical record documents an oddly narrow window when the Bean family traveled to meet their father. On June 7, census records list Petra and the children in Silver City. Three days later, Sam and the rest are listed in another census record in Georgetown.

to focus on firearms. There are a lot of guns on display around Georgetown; the community is on constant alert against Apache raids. When things get especially tense, small posses gather for communal defense. There are not many men to form a militia—about fifty people live here. The surrounding Grant County only has a population of forty-five hundred, just more than one person for each square mile.

But people keep coming here, and this is where Sam Bean wants to devote his attention. He's bought land in this budding community, seeing a boom and loath to pass it up. But he's not eager to repeat the family's usual pattern of opening a store or a saloon. On the 1880 federal census, he calls himself a "farmer."

"The town wasn't even here until the Magruder family's mine opened," Sam tells his family. "That was just three years ago. It grew outward from the claim's water supply, see, in a big V. We're in the commercial area, where the streets meet. Up that one going north has the new school, and soon a church."

"What's along the southern street, father?" asks Anna, with a mock innocence that earns a stern look from her mother.

"Saloons and bawdy houses," he says, refusing to take the bait by sugar-coating it. "That's where the miners live, so it'll be best to leave that street well enough alone. Now get back inside the carriage and let me mount up. I have a horse for Sam; we'll lead the team home."

Sam meets Petra's eye. "You'll love it."

The doubts in his wife's returned gaze are as obvious as a Congreve signal rocket. He can hear her just as clearly as if she were speaking: Silver City was bad enough; now you're bringing the family *here*?

ROY

San Antonio, Texas

October 1881

Roy Bean takes in the oddly long, oval face of W. N. Monroe, railroad builder and recently elected city councilman of Los Angeles. He's clean-shaven, making his face seem larger than it already is. At least the man's body is also large—still too small for his noggin, but with enough height and girth to make someone think twice before saying anything about his elongated puss.[300]

Not that Roy would sass him, anyway. The prosperous man—and you can tell from his worn but quality attire that he's both well traveled *and* well-off—is offering him a prime opportunity at a perfect time. Monroe, in San Antonio on a tour of western railroad construction sites, is heading the epic construction of the Galveston, Harrisburg and San Antonio railway, an east-west main line from Houston to El Paso.

---

300 An article in the *Austin American-Statesman* on October 1, 1881, places Monroe in San Antonio. His physical description is my rude opinion, but I think most would have agreed upon meeting him that he had a long face, based on period photographs.

The GH&SA is a subsidiary of the Southern Pacific company, created in May.[301] This year the rail line started west from San Antonio to connect with an eastbound track being laid from California. The "Sunset Route" will soon go all the way to the West Coast.

Monroe has suggested that Roy open a mobile tent saloon that can move with the workers' progress. The survey crew that laid the route followed the same road to El Paso that has been used by commercial freight haulers since the early 1850s, so it's familiar turf for Roy. It's also familiar work—dispensing drinks and providing a safe gambling spot for railroad workers eager to waste some of their wages.

So how did this man of stature, who didn't live in San Antonio and had connections with teetotaling pioneers in California, meet Roy Bean, a washed-up saloon operator with nothing to lose? Considering Beantown's reputation, it's doubtful the pair met there. There's a natural temptation, given Monroe's California pedigree, to assume Monroe met Roy and Joshua in San Gabriel. But Monroe didn't go to California until after he served in the Civil War. The idea that he and Bean met during the war is squashed by the fact that Monroe mustered for service in Iowa—and served with the Union.

The best answer is through James Bean. Monroe lived in Independence, Missouri, as he worked his way up the railroad construction hierarchy, and he started dabbling in municipal administration there. In 1877, he served as the city's weighmaster, which is exactly what it sounds like, and a vital position in a town fueled by a commodity market. The same year, James Bean served as the city's assessor. As property owners and city officials, the two men almost undoubtedly knew each other.

When Monroe left Missouri for the West, James very likely told him to look up his brother, either as a familiar face or, more likely, to help

301 The Southern Pacific had subsidiary companies spreading across Arizona and New Mexico. On reaching the New Mexico–Texas boundary in May 1881, construction continued eastward under provisions of the Galveston, Harrisburg, and San Antonio charter.

Roy out with an opportunity. Maybe Monroe just saw easy money for the down-and-out brother of a friend, but he also needed a saloon for the workers, and Roy's skill set would therefore have been useful on the Sunset Route.

For middle-aged Roy, this chance is a godsend. Beanville hasn't been paying off, and he's been freighting again, taking long-haul trips to Santa Fe and Chihuahua. One man who hired him, Vinton James of Uvalde, described the state of his equipment: "The six wagons were rickety. The team to draw same were an equal number of jackasses and emaciated horses. The harness consisted of ropes, leather and rawhide thongs, chains and ill-fitted collars for the jackasses."[302]

The trails are still dry and dangerous. Since last year, they've been a war zone. In the United States, Christian reformers are busy trying to teach and pacify tribes on reservations, but in Mexico the fight still rages. In 1879, a Chiricahua war chief named Victorio refused to be moved from his people's homeland reservation at Ojo Caliente, New Mexico. He attracted two hundred warriors and waged a guerrilla war against the US and Mexican armies and civilians in southern New Mexico, western Texas, and northern Mexico.[303]

Beanville is changing around Roy. His neighbors are tired of the raucous saloon and its brash owner. Another nearby store, owned by local farmer Tom Conner, is a rival, respectable anchor to the neighborhood. Besides, the sedentary lifestyle of a saloon operator has taxed his health and mind. Roy is increasingly disheveled, looking more like a worn-out patron than an influential owner.

He gets drunk and wakes up in jail. This happened on August 13, 1878, when he punched a Mexican man named Martinez. "Bean, who was inebriated, was immediately incarcerated," noted a Galveston newspaper in a

---

302 Quoted in Sonnichsen, *Judge Roy Bean*, 68.

303 Victorio and most of his men died at the Battle of Tres Castillos on October 15, 1880, in the state of Chihuahua.

news roundup from San Antonio.[304] The bar itself opens and closes based on his ability to restock the alcohol and on his level of sobriety. Sometimes he's just not in Beantown to run things. (The 1878 city directory lists his only address as his in-laws'.)

Being on the trail with hard men is what Roy needs, if not to sober up then at least to sharpen up. The city is clearly not his element. The edge of civilization has always suited him better.

Roy's family won't be a problem: Virginia got fed up and walked out last year. The 1880 federal census captures this rupture. Roy lived in the "south Suburbs beyond San Pedro Creek" with Roy Jr., seventeen; Adelaide, eight; Zulema, six; and Sam, five. (Roy lies and lists his age as forty-six.) Their youngest child, James Bean, was born in 1878.

His adopted son, John Toney, is eighteen. The boy's father abandoned him and fled to Mexico. Roy's compassion for poor children is unfeigned—it's a trait that will grow as he gets older—and he has no clear ulterior motive for the adoption.

Absent from the census taker's tally is Virginia, who left Beantown to live with her parents and plot a permanent legal separation. She filed for divorce in 1881. She would have had to show that he broke the marriage contract through abuse or neglect. With Roy's temperament, financial struggles, and overall reputation, Virginia certainly had ammunition. A wife also had to demonstrate to the court her own obedience, attentiveness, and faithfulness, an intrusive and embarrassing ordeal.[305] But to be free of Roy, it's worth it.

The separation is also liberating for Roy. His ex-wife, family friends

---

304 "Things Around the State," *Galveston Daily News*, August 14, 1878.

305 "She had to show how long-suffering she was in order to get a divorce," notes historian Elizabeth Garner Masarik in her podcast, *Dig*. "Men just basically had to prove that they financially supported their wife and children, whereas a wife must prove her femininity." See: Elizabeth Garner Masarik, "Marriage

(like Simon Fest Jr., who took care of Zulema for a time), and in-laws can handle the children when Roy leaves. He's free to plunge into the frontier, unfettered by responsibility, to see if he's still got what it takes to carve out a niche. And he's got nothing to lose.

Monroe wants a temporary grogshop, but Roy ponders whether there will be something more permanent. To spur railroad construction, the state of Texas has given out millions of acres in land grants to the railroads that include two-hundred-foot rights-of-way on either side of the track (on top of sixteen sections of 640 acres each on every mile of completed road). However, the land grants will expire in 1882, when the public domain will be exhausted. Roy'll be in a prime position for the property grabs to come.

Roy needs to sever ties to San Antonio to obtain the money to get started. The Conners, those respectable Beanville store owners, are the logical ones to buy him out. They want to see his saloon closed (or at least cleaned up), and they have the money to make it happen. But both sides have conditions. The Conners want Roy to leave San Antonio. Roy wants the family to retain the neighborhood name. Both sides agree, and Conner buys Roy's possessions for $900. The storeowner is finally rid of the man, but the Beanville name will endure.[306]

Roy doesn't need much to start a railroad camp saloon. All he needs is a wagon, a large tent, a few oil lanterns, and ten fifty-five-gallon barrels of whiskey. With these supplies and Monroe's blessing, Roy Bean starts his trek through West Texas—and starts his new life.

---

in America: A Brief History," April, 2018, https://digpodcast.org/2018/04/01/marriage-america/.

306 Both sides will abide by the terms. Beanville's reputation will slowly improve; a July 30, 1889, *San Luis Obispo (CA) Tribune* article asks, "What is Beanville coming to? No fires, no fights, no arrests, no excitement, no lawsuits, no nothing, except merchants who are naturally shoving out the goods and raking in the coin." The Beanville neighborhood still exists in 2023.

Vinegarroon railroad camp, West Texas
February 1882

No one sits at the actual bar of a tent saloon, since there are no stools available. But people stand there to order tobacco, sold in five-cent cigars or cut into plugs at the bar, and to swill bottles of beer or whiskey. Those in groups make their way to one of the round wooden tables, where business deals are conducted, gossip shared, cards dealt, sardine cans opened and their contents spread on fresh, camp-made bread. Roy periodically collects empty bottles and tosses them in a trash heap behind the saloon.[307]

It's a good night, the tent packed inside and out with rail laborers eager to blow their wages. The patrons here are primarily Irishmen with toughness and crudeness in common. They work inhuman hours in remote, alien landscapes. It's crucial for their mental health that they have a place to unwind.

Roy's joint is open all hours. Oil lanterns dangle overhead, hooked on the rafters, leaking smoke and fumes. An awkward network of beams supports the walls and the peaked roof visible from inside. The floor below is just dirt, for good reason. It's easier to use the natural floor to soak up the drinks, tobacco spit, and bodily fluids that all routinely spill in a saloon.

Working the saloon hour after hour taxes Roy's abilities as a businessman, entertainer, and drinker. So he leaves the bar to toss some bottles and takes an extra moment to clear his head with some fresh, dry air. The canyon below is illuminated by the full moon, turning the Rio Grande into a winding ribbon of quicksilver that traces the line between the United States and Mexico. The lights of hundreds of campfires and lamps dot the landscape, glittering in response to the stars above.

During the day, Roy can see Galveston, Harrisburg and San Antonio Railway workers laying tracks, appearing antlike from his perch hundreds

307 Beer was bottled widely after pasteurization was adopted in 1873. The amount of discarded bottles and metal tins that this author saw during a visit to the site in October 2022 was so high that it appeared that the railroad had been created on a foundation of sardines and whiskey.

of feet above. The Pecos River is too wide to cross anywhere but at the mouth of the Rio Grande, where workers have built a low bridge at the bottom of the gorge. To get out of the canyon, the railroad men are painstakingly laying a line between Comstock and Langtry along a winding route called the "Loop Line," which runs along steep, rockfall-prone ledges and delves through two tunnels as it slowly but steadily climbs.

The Vinegarroon camp has been here since workers excavated a tunnel on the west side of the canyon in 1881. East and west of where Roy stands, facing the Rio Grande and Mexico beyond, a tent city has sprouted on the rolling peaks of West Texas hills. Roughly eight thousand thirsty railroad workers live within twenty miles of his tent. Some of their tents perch on the steep slopes, but the more permanent buildings—like Roy's saloon, bakery ovens, stores, and even a drugstore—cluster together around the hills' flattened tops, making them sort of like crude plazas for the camp.

The buildings that house these service industry businesses have stone foundations and four walls built from stacked stones that are (ironically, considering the arid environment) pocked with maritime fossils. White or tan canvas roofs, tied to stakes, peak above the walls and sometimes extend beyond, sheltering those who are sitting at wooden tables from the sun.

Vinegarroon, named for a nonvenomous whip scorpion, was well established at the junction of the Pecos River and the Rio Grande when Roy arrived. It has a dance hall, post office, three barbershops, and a drugstore. And saloons—at least ten others in competition with Roy's. It takes all his skill as a promoter to bark customers into his tent.

Roy doesn't serve the majority of the workforce, however. Most of the teams blasting rock, grading the line, and laying the tracks are Chinese laborers, working under conditions that one reporter compares to slavery. "They are drove round and sometimes used severely, if they don't work to suit the bosses," writes visiting journalist Frederick Locker.[308] The railroad executives who run the construction projects and Chinese camps are James Strobridge, J. C. Howard, and Roy's railroad contact, camp manager W. N. Monroe.

---

308 *San Antonio Light*, October 10, 1882.

The Chinese men live in their own separate work camps, but that doesn't fully tamp down the tensions. The Irish, facing discrimination in America, seem eager to argue for their own nativist and racial superiority by forcibly attacking the Chinese. It doesn't help that everyone knows that they're paid less for the same skilled work. "Each white man costs us in board and wages \$2.50 each 8 hours, but Chinamen cost us \$1.19 each 8 hours, and they drill nearly as fast," said one railroad executive.[309]

There are no Chinese workers on the Southern Pacific east of the Pecos, but on this side they're just a short ride away. Roy's seen their camps and gotten the rundown on how they operate. Workers are organized into twenty-man cohorts, headed by an elected leader who stores the pay tallies and keeps an eye on the men, looking for excessive drunkenness, debilitating opium use, or suicidal depression. Each crew has a cook and a "tea boy" to assist. He saw them hunched over clay rice cookers and around woks as he rode through their camp, inhaling the scent of foreign spices and snatching sips from a bottle of hundred-proof Chinese whiskey.

Beyond the actual worksite, a railroad camp is bereft of authority. Conflicts arise over gambling and drunken machismo—making the saloon the natural flashpoint for any violence or theft. It's up to the proprietor to set some rules, backed by his authority as the owner and by the firearms he and the staff carry. The saloon operator is the one who's supposed to punish cheats and thieves, and to make sure fights are fought as controlled duels instead of public bloodbaths. In short, a bar owner has a lot of pull over adjudicating the quarrels of the workers building the railroad.

Roy enjoys this part of the job. His vigilante instincts find good use in dispensing grogshop rulings; it takes a solid ego—and a burly bouncer—to enforce his personal moral code to settle conflicts. His approach requires an antenna that's attuned to the mentality of those within the camp.

---

309 E. B. Crocker to Collis Huntington, January 31, 1867, Huntington Papers, Syracuse University Libraries, Syracuse, NY.

Roy also recognizes the entertainment value of such proceedings, if they're delivered with some humor and flair. There's potential for frontier justice to become saloon theater.

As summer continues, the workers of Vinegarroon start to move on. It doesn't happen all at once, but the tent city is doomed. The end of the track has reached a new junction, about ten miles away, and so that's where Roy plans to head next. It's a place called Eagle's Nest, perched on a canyon cliff overlooking the Rio Grande.

PECOS COUNTY, TEXAS

July 5, 1882

Letter from Texas Ranger captain T. L. Oglesby to Adjunct General King:

Upon my arrival here on June 29th, I proceeded to visit all the railroad camps and scout the country thoroughly. There is the worst lot of roughs, gamblers, robbers, and pick-pockets collected here I ever saw, and without the immediate presence of the state troops, this class would prove a great detriment towards the completion of the road. There is nothing for Rangers to do but hold this rough element in subjection and control them. The majority of the railroad camps are in Pecos County. This immediate section being 200 miles from Fort Stockton, the nearest jurisdiction Court of Justice and the consequent minor offenses go unpunished; but I hope to remedy that in a few days by having a Magistrate appointed for the precinct.[310]

310 The correspondence, contained in the Texas State Archives in Austin, is quoted in full in Skiles, "Roy Bean Country," 7.

SAN ANTONO EXPRESS, JULY 27, 1882

July 25, 1882

A Card from Roy Bean, of Beanville, on the banks of the Rio Grande
Eagle's Nest, Pecos County
Monroe's Camp No. 6

I would like to announce that I have opened another saloon at the above place, where can be found the best of wines, liquors and cigars that the house of A. B. Frank affords. My saloon is at the meeting point of the great Southern Pacific and Western extension of the Sunset railway. No other saloon within a mile and a half of my place, and visitors will always find a quiet, orderly place where they can get a good drink. My saloon is inside the camp.

Eagle's Nest, Texas
August 1882

On August 2 the commissioners of Pecos County accept the Rangers' recommendation to appoint Roy Bean to become the justice of the peace for Precinct Six.

It was an odd choice, but they didn't have many options. For one, there were few businessmen around, especially ones who were older and presumed wiser. The workers already seemed to defer to Roy. As the owner of a large tent saloon, centrally located near many services and built with stone walls, Roy had the physical space to perform the duties of the court. Most of all, he was interested in the position. He had seen the same saloon-courthouse arrangement in San Gabriel, and he was eager to emulate the kangaroo-court style of operation. As justice of the peace, Roy becomes the principal voice of authority in a lawless camp. He operates what amounted to a small claims court, but also had a role in the criminal justice system by issuing warrants, detaining people, and referring serious crimes to district court.

Roy views legal duties as commerce. He has a keen eye for nickel-and-dime graft, the kind that's committed so blatantly it's accepted as a joke. He doesn't need to be taught how to maximize the entertainment value of barroom show trials; he turns them into live events that'll draw crowds. Jurors are chosen from saloon regulars and are instructed by the court to buy drinks during recess. Fines are often assessed in rounds bought from the bar or are simply pocketed by the judge himself. Those who can't pay are chained to a nearby oak tree.

God help an easy mark on a slow evening at Roy's saloon. One night an innocuous, solitary stranger approaches the bar with his hand in his jacket, only to find Roy pointing a pistol at him. "Why do you dare approach me with your hand in your pocket?"

"To pay for a drink," the new customer says, clearly shocked.

"That's a fine excuse," Roy says loudly, enjoying the stir of the onlookers. "Now you can set 'em up for the crowd here as a fine for not being killed."

The mark makes a crucial error when he tries to pay for fifty cents of beer with a twenty-dollar piece. Roy tells him the change will be given in drinks. The man makes things worse by using some choice words to protest. "Well, you're talking to Roy Bean, justice of the peace of the sixth district," Roy says grandly. "And since you're using vile language, I arrest you for contempt of the court." After forcing the man to languish in a corner as a prisoner in manacles, Roy levies a fine of $19.50, adding, "I beseech you to never sin again."[311]

Acceptance of these absurdities comes with a cynical frontier message: civilized courtrooms are rigged, but this judge is more honest because he's overtly crooked, and his morals aren't defined by lawbooks.

Part of the JP's job is to screen local crimes and send referrals (and pris-

---

311 "A Story About Roy Bean," *Macon (GA) Telegraph*, October 8, 1885, reprinting a *San Antonio Express* article remembering the days of Vinegarroon. Note how his name is spreading, which happens quite energetically after his most controversial ruling, which we'll soon get to.

oners) to the district court. The Twentieth District Court covers a massive amount of turf, from El Paso to the Pecos River, plus Tom Green County. Judges and attorneys ride from city to city, across the 44,117 square miles of their jurisdiction, to hear cases. The closest stopover for them is Fort Stockton. Roy doesn't send people to district court, and instead oversteps his legal mandate with arbitrary rulings. On the night of September 5, Bill Durham is taken before Roy for killing Dick Gorman. "Rumor says he was furnished with a bottle of whiskey and told to skip," a newspaper reports weeks later.[312] It appears that Judge Bean heard some mitigating evidence that he felt justified the killing, which for him could have been as simple as Durham reacting to an affront to his honor. If Gorman was a troublemaker best left unavenged by the law, neither should his killer be welcomed in their community. It's not justice, but it's a popular facsimile.

Roy is also the acting coroner, a position known nationwide for inefficiencies and graft. But Roy takes things to a new, comic level. When a railroad workman falls to his death, he dutifully responds, eyeing a burial fee of ten dollars and another ten dollars in court costs. At the ghastly scene, the JP roots through the dead man's pockets to find forty dollars and a pistol. He assesses a twenty-dollar fee for his services, announces a twenty-dollar fine for carrying a concealed weapon, and pockets all the dead man's money.[313]

FROM THE *SAN ANTONIO EVENING LIGHT*

September 2, 1882

Eagle's Nest is one of the most peculiar places in the state. It lies in a valley and yet is considerably above the Rio Grande. It is now quite a city of tents, upwards of 300 being scattered around, some of

---

312 "A Sunset Town," *San Antonio Light*, October 10, 1882.

313 Cited in numerous newspaper articles and in Sonnichsen, *Judge Roy Bean*, 121–122.

them being 500 by 100 feet. The only wood building being the store of Max Meyer, who has good stock and does good business.

There are by some estimates 20 saloons and gambling tents, two tents of ill fame and a dance hall, which is on full run every Sunday and two or three times a week. Two soiled doves from San Antonio have alighted here in their flight and have made things lively at the dance halls.[314] *The dancing here is a la vaudeville.*

The most curious thing and still more amusing is the action of Roy Bean. Roy is the Justice of the Peace and holds court in a tent 16 x 18. Not more than 30 yards from his court is the justice's saloon and gambling tent where drink is freely dispensed and a dozen monte tables are in full blast. And it is no uncommon thing for suckers to get full in the Justice's saloon and sleep off the effects in his court, not as a prisoner, but a guest.

—Frederick Locker

Eagle's Nest proves to be busy for Roy Bean. In one tent, he delivers rulings as usual. But the docket is crowded with hooligans and outlaws rounded up by the Texas Rangers. The first, named Joe Bell, is brought to Roy before he's even sworn in. By now, the Rangers are in Eagle's Nest nearly full-time and keep the courtroom stocked with violent offenders, cheats, and thieves. Many of these are former railroad workers, cast adrift as the work dries up.

These offenders aren't sent to Fort Stockton for trials. Roy handles it all from his tent, assessing fines and chaining prisoners to a tree in the heat at will. He collects and hands in enough money to cover the court costs, and he keeps the rest. His court will always be a revenue-neutral operation.

---

314 It's interesting that the freelance "soiled doves" of the dance halls got a separate mention from the women in the "tents of ill fame," who reported to a pimp or madame. Their freedom made a big difference to their job prospects; many soiled doves found they could earn more money as dance hall girls, where there was no expectation of sex, but prostitutes in brothels found escape from their bosses much harder.

If he's looking to make his mark for posterity, he will do it this year. Sometime in late 1882, a railroad worker named Paddy O'Rourke shoots a Chinese laborer and is brought to Roy Bean's saloon for a trial. With him comes a mob of two hundred railroad workers, who surround the tent in a clear show of force. These are Irishmen from California, a hotbed of anti-Chinese political organizations.

The JP is in a tight spot, but he sees an easy way out. The first step is to keep the crowd around to run up bar tabs as they wait for a decision. He's not scared of fueling a riot because he has no intention of bucking against the crowd's wishes.

Roy shows the accused a copy of the 1879 edition of the *Revised Statutes of Texas* and tells the assemblage, "Gentlemen, I find the law very explicit on murdering your fellow man, but there's nothing here about killing a Chinaman. Case dismissed."[315]

If his job as JP is to provide impartial justice, he's an abject failure. If his job is to preserve peace so construction on the train line can continue, he's a smashing success. The shameful ruling is a dramatic low point for American race relations, but it's squarely in line with the predominant feelings of the men in the camp.

Roy Bean wasn't any kind of cutting-edge racist, just a loud parrot of the conventional thinking of the time. Just a few months s earlier the US Congress had passed the Chinese Exclusion Act, the first federal attempt to limit the immigration and citizenship of a specific group of people.[316] In light of these prevailing attitudes, his ruling didn't even have the dubious defense of speaking some sort of contrarian truth to power. Instead, he was crudely airing and legitimizing the predominant positions of the day. Roy Bean played to a mob outside his tent, but his words were soon heard by the masses well beyond.

---

315 *El Paso Daily Times,* June 2, 1884

316 It remains in place for more than six decades.

Joshua Bean's cavalry unit mustered at the Oakland House and Race Course in Louisville, Kentucky, which became Camp Owsley during the war with Mexico.

Oakland House and Race Course. *Robert Brammer and Augustus A. Von Smith, circa 1840, oil on canvas. Public domain via Speed Art Museum*

The only known sketch of Joshua Bean, the first mayor of San Diego.

Public domain via City of San Diego, circa 1850

Chihuahua as it first appeared to Sam, James, and Roy Bean

Chihuahua, 1850, *reprinted with permission from the Palace of the Governors Photo Archives, New Mexico History Museum*

Petra Bean and her family took a stagecoach like this one from Silver City to Georgetown in July 1880.

Reprinted with permission from the Palace of the Governors Photo Archives, New Mexico History Museum

Immigrants disembark at Westport Landing in Missouri to organize for the trek farther west.

William Henry Jackson, 1939.

Public domain via Department of the Interior National Park Service.

The painting *Order No. 11* shows Union general Thomas Ewing watching the "Red Legs" sack of Independence, Missouri. *George Caleb Bingham, 1868– Order November 11, 1868, oil on canvas. Public domain via Cincinnati Art Museum*

The original walls of Sam Bean's saloon in Mesilla still stand in 2023; it houses a bar called El Patio. The building has grown to encompass the lane where the Butterfield Overland Stage once stopped.

Joe Pappalardo

The town of Pinos Altos still survives, while other nearby isolated boomtowns in New Mexico dried up.

Joe Pappalardo

Several original buildings still stand, but the Bean store on this block is long gone.

Joe Pappalardo

The author on the site of the Vinegarroon railroad campsite overlooking the Rio Grande. The camp's remains are on private land, seen during a tour with staff from the Shumla Archaeological Research & Education Center. (It's an excellent nonprofit organization; www.shumla.org.)

Joe Pappalardo, with permission from the private landowner

Beer and whiskey bottles from the 1880s litter the area behind a probable saloon amid the Vinegarroon ruins in Val Verde County.

Joe Pappalardo

Ruins of a Vinegarroon building overlooking the Rio Grande. The Rio Grande winds off in the distance; on the far side is Mexico.

Joe Pappalardo

A diorama at the Whitehead Memorial Museum in Del Rio, Texas, showing a depiction of Roy's saloon at the Vinegarroon camp

Joe Pappalardo

Roy Bean and his family, circa 1890

Used with permission of UTSA Special Collections. L1508-I

The Jersey Lilly in 1900 while Roy Bean was conducting the trial of a horse thief. Nearly forgotten is the arrest of Bean himself for horse theft while he was a judge and the local stories of his son pursued for the same crime.

Used with permission of UTSA Special Collections. L1508-B

Inside the Jersey Lilly, 2022

Joe Pappalardo

The Jersey Lilly with Roy Bean's home, nicknamed the Opera House, in the background, 2022

Joe Pappalardo

Two photos of Sam Bean at around age 80

Used with permission from the Katherine Stoes Collection, New Mexico State University Archives & Special Collections, Las Cruces, New Mexico

Diorama of the championship fight, as depicted by the Whitehead Memorial Museum in Del Rio, Texas. The makeshift footbridge that Roy Bean had built is in the background, as are the silhouettes of the Texas Rangers and townsfolk on the bluff.

Joe Pappalardo

The Texas state marker near the site of the prizefight on the U.S.-Mexico border

Joe Pappalardo

Roy Bean's grave at the Whitehead Memorial Museum in Del Rio, Texas. He and his son Sam's graves were moved here in the 1960s after vandals chipped the headstones at the original burial site.

Joe Pappalardo

Eagle's Nest, Texas
January 1883

It's been two years since Roy left San Antonio, and things have been going better than he could have hoped. But a fuse has been burning on his scheme since its inception: the completion of the rail lines. This is the month that the two ends of the Southern Pacific connect. Now everything will change. Eagle's Nest will dry up, just as Vinegarroon has. Or will it?

The camp businessmen are hearing that the spot may be the future location of a depot. No less than W. N. Monroe has told Roy so, and it was one of the reasons he chose Eagle's Nest to settle in last year. A depot means steady saloon action from passengers, railroad employees, and local farmers looking to transport their goods. As one newspaper put it in late 1882, "The probabilities for the future point to it as the site of a railroad depot and a town of some importance."[317]

By early 1883 the wheels of this development are in motion. The site for the settlement will be "up the hill" from Eagle's Nest camp, at the crest of the ravine where the track's located. It's already called Langtry, as per custom named for a railroad man, George Langtry. He's an engineer and foreman who supervised the immigrant Chinese work crews who built the railroad here.

Besides Monroe, who runs the Eagle's Nest camp, three brothers from the Torres family are the driving force behind the settlement. Bernardo, Cesario, and Juan Torres are large landowners and cattle barons. In West Texas, water is a community's life, and the Torres Irrigation and Manufacturing Company constructed dam and irrigation projects along the Pecos, and in 1877 the state of Texas agreed to pay them, in part, by awarding them acreage along the Rio Grande.

It took five years for the paperwork to be settled, but by July 1882 the Torres family owned Eagle's Nest, including a two-hundred-foot gorge that connected to the Rio Grande, the only available route to get water to the railroad town—and to any other aspiring town that might grow in the area

317 *The San Antonio Light,* October 10, 1882.

after the railroad workers leave. A depot stop wouldn't have been considered at this site without the water tower that the Torreses built and which they filled with water from land the family owned at nearby Pump Canyon.

By 1882, Bernardo Torres has died, and Cesario Torres has bought Bernardo's land from his widow. He plans to give the area to his son, Jesús, to run. But worse for Roy, Jesús Torres plans to open a saloon and store in Langtry. The two men seem destined to become rivals, even if the younger man doesn't know it yet.

As the workers leave and the action shifts, Roy needs a spot close to the depot to open a business establishment, but per the railroad's agreement, the Torres family owns the entire right-of-way. This doesn't stop Roy. He chooses a spot next to the depot. He figures the Southern Pacific Railroad won't care since he's still under the umbrella of Monroe's influence. Roy's name is good enough to earn a free pass in appreciation for his judicial service. The Torres family, he can just bluff.

Roy hires Simon Fest Jr. from San Antonio to build a wooden structure, a saloon that's big enough to accommodate drinking, gambling, and court proceedings. He adds a wooden home in the back, large enough for Roy—and his children. It's time to send for his young sons and daughters.

All his joint needs is a name, and for this Roy has a muse. Lillie Langtry has been a famous—or infamous—celebrity for years. She's a British stage actress who's better known for her romantic entanglements, including an affair with the Prince of Wales. She and the acting company she owned took the United States by storm in the spring of 1882. Oscar Wilde, who was touring the US that same year, met her upon her arrival, with plenty of reporters in tow. Lillie's coast-to-coast tour lasted until May 1883, a real moneymaker.

Looks, influence, scandal, and a love of travel. What's not for Roy Bean to like? He makes a play on her last name and the name of the town, and stirs in the fact that the actress was from the isle of Jersey. The saloon now has a name: the Jersey Lilly. One hopes Roy spelled her name wrong—with a *-y* instead of an *-ie*—to be clever.

Fest paints a wooden sign to hang over the saloon: "Roy Bean, Justice of the Peace. The Law West of the Pecos." If Jesús Torres tries to act, he'll have to evict a public official. When Torres arrives, he indeed backs down from the squatter's challenge and simply opens his own rival establishment across the tracks from Roy's place.

The completion of the railroad is like the start of a horserace. Aside from railroad workmen and locals, a new class of saloon customer has arrived: transient visitors, who mark time until the train continues. They bring new life and easy money to the Jersey Lilly, and a new audience for Roy Bean's antics.

The trains also bring a vital product to Roy's saloon. Ice arrives in sawdust-insulated cars and is stored in the saloon's hay-packed chests for as long as possible. Iced beverages are a marketable luxury for parched customers in Langtry, where water itself is a prized commodity. Roy makes sure another sign is painted and hung outside the saloon: "Ice-Beer." In the summer, the ice becomes scarce, but the sign stays where it is.[318]

Roy's dependence on the railroad and his public position as judge don't tamp down his impish impulses. He's awoken one night in early 1883 by a pair of cowboys, fresh from a cross-border hunting trip for deer and turkeys. Earlier, Roy got drunk with them at the saloon before they left. Now they've brought back an Apache and want the judge to figure out what to do with him.[319]

Roy speaks some Apache, but he doesn't need much to assess the prisoner: a nineteen-year-old boy living alone in Mexico and scared out of his wits. Roy plies him and his captors with whiskey and quickly finds out that the two men drew down on the youth for no reason. The prisoner is released after more drinks are served. The scene becomes festive as Langtry residents file into the saloon to take a look at the peculiar captive turned customer.

---

318 Jack Skiles, *Judge Roy Bean Country* (Lubbock: Texas Tech University Press, 1996): 14.

319 Multiple newspapers ran the story under the headline "Rather a Costly Joke," including the *Press Democrat* (Santa Rosa, CA), March 8, 1889, and *Bismarck Weekly Tribune* (ND), March 8, 1889.

Langtry has been recently blessed with a telegram station, and the operator is among the throng. Roy makes sure the wire operator is liquored up before he announces that the good people of Del Rio deserve to hear about this Apache incursion. The drunken bunch tromps to the office and flashes an unsigned message across the wires: "The Indians are upon us!" And then they head back to the saloon to booze the night away.

The message hits Del Rio and ignites a paranoid furor. The unsigned message's place of origin is unknown. Everyone assumes the worst as word spreads, the telegram now being used to disperse panic instead of information. By morning, cries from employees for evacuation bombard railroad executives across the state, reaching the San Antonio office of Southern Pacific Railroad's superintendent, W. G. Van Vleck. "For God's sake, send us trains to take us to a place of safety," one message reads. He orders emergency trains to collect staff and their families, ferrying them to the protected towns of Del Rio or Strobridge the next morning. Everyone on board is scared, but the railroad executives can't find anyone who's seen any Indians. (By now, the one Apache who sparked the scare is already on his way back to Mexico, hungover and confused.)

The US military is quickly swept into the hysteria. A cavalry company in Del Rio asks for orders from its commanding officers in San Antonio, who in turn telegram the secretary of war in Washington, DC, for instructions. The orders return down the chain of command: ride out to the scene. Only, there is nowhere to go. The cavalrymen and their horses load onto trains and ride the route for ten fruitless days before giving up.

Roy's fingerprints would have never appeared on this hoax if not for a newspaper reporter's trip to Langtry more than six years later. "During that summer this writer had occasion to go to Langtry, where Judge Bean was conducting his establishment for the dispensation of liquids," the columnist writes. "Incidentally the judge detailed the facts, with much glee, about the cause of the so-called Indian outbreak."[320]

---

320 *Press Democrat* (Santa Rosa, CA) and *Bismarck Weekly Tribune* (ND).

What's the point of doing it if people don't know? This is why Roy makes sure to say that "newspaper fellers" will always drink for free at his saloons.

The media and Roy Bean soon have a codependent relationship. An early example of a news story about him comes in 1883, when a *Philadelphia Times* reporter visits to write about the "bibulous peculiarities" of "Old Roy's . . . border jurisprudence." The reporter describes him as a drunk who waves a pistol around, but adds that he's "generous, brave, courteous, and a keen lover of fun. He holds court anywhere and carries a pocketful of blank warrants, one of which he will fill out and sign at a minute's notice." The item, under the headline "Life in Murdertown," runs across the nation.[321]

On June 2, newspapers finally cover the earlier O'Rourke ruling, when the *El Paso Daily Times* runs an item. It quotes Judge Bean "remarking that he'd be damned if he could find any law against killing a Chinaman." News of the scandalous ruling slowly but inexorably trickles out of West Texas; it's destined to become the most oft-cited ruling of Roy's career as judge.[322] By 1885 Roy's reputation for wild rulings and stunt justice is so well established that the *San Antonio Light* calls him "irrepressible" and starts a September article with, "Here is the latest on Roy Bean."[323]

This improbable judge has become a recognizable name outside the state—and an icon of the frontier. The *San Antonio Light* says, "His offhand summary justice has been the subject of newspaper articles all over the land, telling how he would fine a man to the drinks for the crowd at his saloon."

Roy himself is the chief source of the stories about his court, and

---

321 For example, among many other papers, the article ran on December 16 in the *St. Louis Post-Dispatch*, the *Osceola (WI) Sun*, and the *Buffalo Morning Express*.

322 It also becomes one of the most cited examples of racist rulings against Asians in the US. One otherwise fawning English newspaper article about Roy Bean in 1887 references the ruling disapprovingly, citing it as an example of his court's "seamy side." *Staffordshire (Eng.) Sentinel, Daily and Weekly,* October 6, 1887.

323 *San Antonio Light,* September 18, 1885.

he proves to be a skilled media manipulator. Publicity warms him. His schtick centers on saying the crude things that the everyman is presumably thinking (a model that will work well in future media and political environments). His commonplace morality is held to be superior to the actual law. With the newspapermen's help, the world can now see him as he sees himself: as an iconoclastic scoundrel who unapologetically imposes his own code in the wilds of remote West Texas.

The legend of Judge Roy Bean has arrived. Above anyone else, he's the one who created it.

PART FIVE

There is only one thing in the world worse than being talked about, and that is not being talked about.

—OSCAR WILDE, *THE PICTURE OF DORIAN GRAY*, 1891

SAM

Silver City, New Mexico
September 1885

On Saturday morning, September 15, Sam Bean reads in the *Silver City Enterprise* about a bloodbath in Georgetown and feels happy that he moved away from there.

"A family had been killed by the Apaches and a Mexican named Evaristo Abeyta had been killed near San Lorenzo," the newspaper reports. "On Sunday night further news came from Georgetown, that three other men had been killed. J. McKinn's two sons, living on a ranch on Gallinas Creek were killed; the elder being shot through the forehead and the younger in the neck. George Horn, who was chopping wood with two Mexicans in the mountains about two miles back from the mill, was killed."

It turns out the Apache didn't kill both McKinn youths; eleven-year-old Jimmy will spend six months with the band, where he's well tended and given language lessons. But a panic is nevertheless upon New Mexico, and it comes with a familiar name. In early May, the legendary Native American rebel Geronimo led dozens off their reservation in Arizona (where they'd been deported in 1875) and headed to Mexico, raiding along the way.

Sam at age sixty-three and forty-nine-year-old Petra live full-time in

Silver City. He abandoned his Georgetown ambitions as the town expanded. In 1880, Georgetown's population was fifty-four people; in 1883, it was eight hundred.[324] Whatever civilization Sam Bean was trying to avoid has again caught up with him.

The Bean family may be out of vulnerable Georgetown, but they hardly feel safe. Fort Bayard, established twenty years earlier to protect the Silver City area, is being used for that purpose again. But the troops can't be everywhere, and the Apache are opportunistic. Even when Geronimo moves away, into northern Mexico, the miners and citizens of Silver City remain wary.[325] Other bands are rebelling against the reservation system. Various factions, including those headed by former enemies of the Beans—Naiche, son of Cochise, and Mangas, son of Mangas Coloradas—stage attacks throughout the Arizona and New Mexico Territories.

Finally, Sam and Petra give up on Silver City. There are reasons to stay. Sam could wait until the standard-gauge Santa Fe Railroad reaches the town to see how that spurs growth. But building frontier towns is a young man's dream, and Sam is ready for a more comfortable perch in Las Cruces. His son, Sam Jr., owns a saloon there, and it's close to Petra's beloved Mesilla, where the family has clung to a house. His daughters have married—one will soon move to California—so it's just him and Petra now. Sam Bean has found an unexpected pastime: writing. He's started penning a column about the frontier days for the *Silver City Enterprise*.

Sam enjoys the fulfillment of being a columnist, the soapbox it grants him and the status it confers. Since he's on good terms with newspaper owners in Las Cruces, it should be easy to offer his services to them too. In Las Cruces, he can play the role of "Uncle Sam," the local newspaper wag, while living close to his son and nestled in the safety of a city.

It's time for a quieter life.

---

324 By 1888, it was twelve hundred.

325 Geronimo surrendered in 1886.

ROY

Langtry, Texas
April 1885

The Southern Pacific passengers hear about Langtry well before the train stops there. Those who don't know of Judge Roy Bean are told his tale by the conductors, cooks, and porters, who get free drinks for tipping them off about the eccentric judge. He'll fine you if you don't behave right in his bar. Keeps trained bears and a menagerie of desert animals at the saloon. Watch your money and mind your manners—that judge is quick to go to his guns or order a hanging.

The hype is aimed at newcomers to the West. "The train men are in with me, and they tell those tender feet who I am, and that if they come about me looking at my bears, that they better drink at my bar, as I had just as like kill a man as to look at him," Roy tells a *San Antonio Light* reporter. "That brings in a lot of business. There's nothing like knowing how to do these things, you know. Business is business, and I have not lived in San Antone for all those many years without catching onto some valuable business tricks."[326]

The passengers are primed for a show at Langtry, and Roy's prepared

326 *San Antonio Light,* September 18, 1885.

for them as the train hisses to a stop at the depot. He's waiting on his porch, wearing his usual hickory shirt, jeans, tan shoes, and broad-brimmed hat. The two pearl-handled guns are also on clear display. His son Roy Jr. is even now rousing the bear, Bruno, from his wooden, straw-lined cage so the passengers can see him loping past.

The crowd filters in. Bruno climbs his pole and peers down at them, looking more hot and forlorn than ferocious. Trained bears in that era had sad lives. Captured as cubs and kept chained their whole lives, they were brutally taught to climb poles and perform other tricks on command. When Bruno climbs down, he's allowed to walk around, and the customers are encouraged to buy him beer to drink.

Now that the customers are here, it's time for Roy to put himself on display inside the bar. People are drinking cold beers, but whiskey is more profitable. Roy chats up the passengers, using his natural charisma to size them up. One reporter describes him as "large, well-built frame, kindly eyes."[327]

But that charm can turn mean. Roy finally chooses a mark from the Northeast. "You know the old railroad camp here, that built that line you're riding on, was called Vinegarroon," he tells him. "There's a deadly, purple scorpion here that smells like vinegar before it stabs you. Stay away from 'em, if you see one. I don't gotta worry, though, I'm immune."

"How's that?"

"I'm stung enough times, I'm immune. You believe that?"

"I guess so."

"Callin' me a liar is a good way to get fined in this jurisdiction or worse," Roy warns happily. "Sam, get the jar of scorpions." Roy's eleven-year-old son scampers off, knowing to bring back two of the nonpoisonous vinegarroons. Roy squares his shoulders and looks down on the tenderfoot. "Now, you're paying for two whiskeys and we'll see who's immune."

The crowd gathers, sensing hijinks underway. The passenger, now suddenly onstage, looks uncomfortable and sets ten dollars on the bar. Sam

---

327 *Austin American-Statesman*, March 23, 1903.

puts each scorpion in a glass and places them in front of his father, who crushes them both to death with a spoon. He fills the glasses with whiskey. "I'll drink mine and you drink yours and we'll see who's alive to pay for the next one."

Roy downs the whiskey, crushed arachnid and all. The tenderfoot raises his glass and sets it down, untouched. The crowd cries out, laughing. Roy shakes his head, takes the ten dollars, and drinks the second whiskey for good measure. "Now, everyone enjoying that show owes me another round, or you'll be found in contempt of court."[328]

Such antics mask a certain desperation. Just as much as Bruno, Roy has devolved into a roadside attraction to stay solvent. "The judge was always on his porch when a train arrived, and if a crowd of curious passengers did not soon flock to his place he would go down and 'drum them up' in which he was always successful," the *El Paso Herald* recalls. "He was the whole show to the passengers."[329]

Langtry is a tough place to make a living. Scorching heat, limited water, and a stubbornly sparse population have relegated it to a flyspeck stopover depot instead of a center for travel and commerce. Roy knew this could happen as far back as 1883, when he attempted to expand operations to a larger train town called Strobridge. Charlie Wilson already owned the nearby saloon, and he wasn't eager to see any rivals set up shop. Wilson sent a man to spike Bean's whiskey with kerosene. Outmaneuvered by someone who was clearly willing to play hardball, the judge retreated to his operation in Langtry.[330]

---

328 Sonnichsen, *Judge Roy Bean,* 183.

329 Reprinted in *Austin American-Statesman,* March 23, 1903.

330 *Proceedings and Debates of the 113th Congress, Second Session*, September 16, 2014, and Kathy Weiser, "Sanderson, Texas—The Town Too Mean for Bean," Legends of America, May 2021, www.legendsofamerica.com/tx-sanderson. The town of Strobridge changed its name to Sanderson and created a slogan that capitalized on its brief association with Roy Bean.

His business adjudicating as a JP is also slowing as the area settles into postconstruction peace. "There ain't much of it," he tells a reporter in 1885. "But when a case does come up, it's dealt with in the usual prompt manner." He then regales the reporter with the story of how he beat a sheepherder with a club after accusing him of lying. "I let him have it, sending him flying. That ended the case."[331]

There is one way that Roy both enlivens his saloon and promotes law and order: staging fake hangings. His typical way of dealing with a horse thief is to sentence him to hang, send his cronies for a rope, rig a noose on front of the accused man's eyes, and then allow him to escape the tent and race away toward the Mexican border. This drama and cruel humor play out before the entertained eyes of the Jersey Lilly patrons. And maybe the spectacle is a deterrent: the judge knows there is at least one thief who'll no longer operate in his jurisdiction.

The biggest challenge for Roy in Langtry is the presence of his children. He keeps a sharp eye on Laura and Zulema, whom he encourages to continue their education, even though Langtry has no schoolhouse. They are also expected to cook and clean house, and neighbors have stories of sheltering the girls when their father is on a bender and gets after them for not fulfilling their duties. One incident ends with the girls hiding with the Shaw family, who mollify a drunken Roy Bean (looking for them while armed with a shotgun) by making him breakfast and sending him back to the Jersey Lilly to calm down.[332]

Little Sam is a popular hit with the boozers and gamblers, a wild and spirited boy in a scandalously adult world. Many people spot young Sam asleep on or under the billiard table, but the Bean girls are wisely kept in their rooms in the back of the Jersey Lilly.

Roy's adopted son, John, has left (for now) to work as a ranch hand,

---

331 *San Antonio Light*, September 18, 1885.

332 Sonnichsen, *Judge Roy Bean*, 163–164.

but Roy Jr. lives in Langtry. He apparently finds trouble there, but the circumstances are obscure. On May 29, 1887, word spreads via newspaper that Roy Jr. has killed a man: "It is reported that a Mexican man was killed yesterday at Langtry station, on the Southern Pacific road, by Roy Bean Jr."[333]

There's no other record of this encounter—what happens in Langtry tends to stay there, especially when the accused's father is the justice of the peace and coroner. If the dead man was an itinerant, nothing would keep Roy from burying the truth of what happened along with the victim. It could have been a duel or a fair fight, an old-school defense of honor or a cold-blooded murder. It'd be easy to imagine the dark, half-Anglo youth overcompensating for his looks by picking a fight with a Mexican man, but that's conjecture. It's an easier step to say that Roy Jr. had difficulty adapting to the environment in Langtry; he soon left town when he got a job working for the railroad.

Roy's youngest son, James, seems lost to him. Born in May 1878, the youth stayed in San Antonio with his mother. So did his little girl, Maria de la Soledad, born in 1881. They'll never have the bond the other children share with Roy and will stay away from him their entire lives.

Virginia is rebuilding, having married a Coahuila immigrant, Manuel Charles, the previous year.[334] It should have been a new start for her and the children, but Roy has prospered enough to claim his right as their guardian. How she felt about losing the older children to Roy is not recorded, but seeing them board a San Antonio train for the wilds of Langtry must have been wrenching. She had no legal choice.

N. H. Rose, a photographer for the *San Antonio Express-News*, took a photo of Virginia and young James Bean in 1885. The eight-year-old lad was nearly as tall as his mother, with the characteristically large Bean head

---

333 *Galveston Daily News*, May 30, 1887, uncredited and with a San Antonio dateline.

334 Charles was issued his naturalization papers in 1871.

atop an already wide frame. Virginia, although wearing a colorful skirt, a frilled blouse, and a festive, flower-adorned hat, has a neutral expression. The edges of her mouth rest in a tired frown. Her new life lies ahead, but the old one with Roy has left her drained.[335]

335 Petra had three more children with her second husband and remained an active lifetime parishioner of San Fernando Cathedral.

JAMES

St. Joseph, Missouri
June 1888

As much as James may not want to admit it, St. Joseph is turning out to be a hell of a town. From here he can watch the future arrive, and progress is going beyond just paved streets. The construction of an electric streetcar line, just the second in the nation, is well underway, and service is expected to start on the Fourth of July.

In 1888, the Board of Trade of St. Joseph reported that total gross sales for the seven leading groups of wholesale goods were $45,300,000. They were just $31,800,000 in Kansas City.[336] The city's landscape has transformed to accommodate this traffic, with so many four-story, red brick warehouses springing up on the western edge of the city, close to

336 National Park Service, "Historic Resources of St. Joseph, Buchanan County, Missouri," National Register of Historic Places Multiple Property Documentation Form, section E, 7–8, June 1989. The other wholesale capital of the United States was Omaha, which saw $21,500,000 in business that year. St. Joe's wholesale trade industry nearly equaled that of its two rivals combined. This is why Gordon Bean left Chicago to make his fortune in his native Missouri.

the railroad depots and Missouri River, that it's called Wholesale Row.[337] A network of streetcars, pulled by animals, enables businessmen to live in large houses away from the facilities. Housing for workers has sprouted up along the newly laid tramlines.[338]

The rising city has taken Gordon Bean up with it. At age thirty-eight, he seems poised to achieve what eluded his father: commercial success and political popularity. Since 1885, he's been back with a Schuster clothing house, now Schuster, Hinsgen and Co.[339] He's the firm's ace salesman, or as the census says, a "Commercial Traveler." He also, as of March, serves on the Democratic Party's central committee for the Third Ward, the seeming start of a promising political career.[340]

On June 4, Gordon goes to bed early, feeling unwell. At three a.m. the family calls a doctor, who "on examination, pronounced the action of the heart weaker than in any case that had ever come to his notice." Gordon Bean dies shortly afterward.

The *St. Joseph News-Press* runs the story of the tragic end on the front page of its bulldog edition that day. The article calls him "a traveling man" who "was universally liked, and his death is deplored by all his business associates. He leaves his family in good circumstances, insurance policies

---

337 National Park Service, "Historic Resources of St. Joseph." The National Park Service calls Wholesale Row "high Victorian Italianate commercial design at its best."

338 By 1888, the city's population had grown a tremendous 700 percent since the end of the Civil War. In 1886, the *Chicago Times* tallied sixty thousand inhabitants, eleven railroads, seventy passenger trains each day, 170 factories, thirteen miles of paved streets, and "the largest stockyards west of Chicago." Quoted in the city's "Welcome to St. Joseph," https://stjoepleinair.com/st-joseph.

339 *St. Joseph Gazette,* January 1, 1885, and June 5, 1888.

340 *St. Joseph Gazette,* March 20, 1888.

on his life amounting to nearly $13,000."[341] The sum is good news for the widow Bean and the children. But it leaves James without a dime and without a place to live.

James Bean has only ever called one place home since he left Kentucky. He's going back to Jackson County.

---

341 *St. Joseph News-Press,* June 4, 1888.

ROY

Langtry, Texas
August 1891

Living on the Mexican border is an open invitation to smuggle horses into the United States. Such an easy source of income lures Roy Bean and his son Sam.

Locals in Langtry witnessed dubious dealings from their local representative of the law. "I remember one time Sam brought a bunch of horses and put them in our corral," said Beula Farley, whose family was close to the Beans and lived three miles from the saloon. "I knew something was wrong when they started branding horses in our corral, because they made me leave. I was just a kid, but I knew those were strange horses."[342]

But now the Texas Rangers and the district attorney are cracking down. Seeing how even the children of Langtry can see that something's amiss, it doesn't take the Rangers long to implicate Sam. He flees to the Farley home and then to Mexico, where the neighbors supply him with food and information via a conduit named Doreta.

The investigation soon expands to the justice of the peace, whom the Rangers accuse of organizing the whole ring. "Judge Roy Bean, of Langtry, has been arrested for smuggling from Mexico," reads the *Fort Worth Daily*

---

342 Interview in Skiles, *Judge Roy Bean Country*, 21–25.

Gazette. "It is alleged that he has been concerned in running horses from Mexico into the United States." The article adds that Roy "stoutly protests his innocence." It's a good spin on a bad development, but to Roy's horror the item about his arrest is deemed newsworthy far beyond Texas. The item runs in newspapers as far away as New Orleans.[343]

The paper's description of Roy is colorful:

> He is known as a big-hearted, hospitable, rough old frontiersman, and has grown sons and daughters. On his being placed under bond he remarked that he never knew before that any court ranked his, but he is now satisfied that Judge Gildea's does. The old judge is somewhat of a humorist and many of the quaint accusations laid at his door come from this fact. He is an old ex-Confederate soldier and has figured a good deal in the early settlements of Texas, New Mexico and Arizona, and his abode since 1882 has been on a high, rocky bluff overlooking the Rio Grande, where he has kept a little store and beer saloon and trades with the Southern Pacific railroad boys, United States soldiers, Mexican miners, Texas cowboys, sheepmen, and everybody who happens to visit the section.

Roy heads to Del Rio to settle this mess. It's not easy and it's not cheap. He pays a $500 bond, and his case is scheduled to be heard during the November term of the US District Court in San Antonio.[344]

Next up is his fugitive son. "He spent many a dollar, but he got Sam free," sums up Beula Farley. Doreta tells Sam to come home, and he appears shortly afterward, unfazed.

Roy is protective of his fame and his name. It's his only true commodity. He's fallen into the worst trap for a celebrity—being famous but not wealthy. All he can do to fight back is jump on a chance to create some positive press.

---

343 *Times-Picayune* (New Orleans, LA), August 22, 1891.

344 *Fort Worth Daily Gazette*, August 24, 1891.

The opportunity presents itself on September 2, when train robbers strike along the Southern Pacific line as the cars pull away from the depot at Samuels, twenty miles west of Langtry. Six men board the train and try to intimidate the agent, who is locked with the valuables in the express car, by shooting up the luggage. But the agent is J. E. Smith, who shot two robbers to death in another recent holdup. The thieves finally turn to dynamite to open the door, easily disarming a stunned Smith.

News of the holdup spreads fast, and Roy is quick to organize a response. The Rangers and local sheriff's posse are ready to respond, too, boarding a specially scheduled train to the scene of the crime. Roy's posse joins them there.[345] The thieves have a head start and all of Mexico to hide in; they're never found.

But for the embattled justice of the peace, the resultant news coverage of his posse is a much-needed win. He needs a boost for his reputation as a necessary official and a man of action. Even at this point in his life, he's still fighting to showcase himself as a purveyor of law and order instead of a criminal.

Over the Pecos River
April 1892

Roy steadies his nerves as his horse slowly saunters forward, hoofs falling heavily on the wooden slats. He doesn't want the animal to have any excuses to get spooked—if ever there was a time when Roy's life depended on a horse's nerve, it's right now.

He and Sam are nearly midway across the half-mile Pecos High Bridge, five miles upstream from the former crossing at the Rio Grande. They feel like they're flying over the gorge, which plummets 321 feet downward. The metal viaduct bridge, which opened in March, is the highest in North America and the third-tallest in the world. And there are no guardrails to prevent a rider from falling to their death if their horse bolts.[346]

---

345 *Austin American-Statesman,* September 3, 1891.

346 The Pecos High Bridge, built by the Phoenix Bridge Company of Phoenixville,

The first train crossed the bridge on March 30, carrying Southern Pacific president C. P. Huntington, who was christening a vital connection for the company's new southern transcontinental railroad. The steep, landslide-afflicted Loop Line is no more—there's now a straight shot across the Pecos, a route that's eleven miles shorter.

The bridge wasn't built for horse traffic, but two wooden footpaths traverse all 2,180 feet. Riding across the span is considered a local feat of courage.

The height brings Roy's work as a coroner to mind. As the nearest public official, he is the person who responds when someone is crushed or falls to their death. A scaffolding accident had killed one and injured five more. He figured they were doomed and he didn't want to make a second trip, so he listed them all as dead—and collected fees accordingly. When they recovered, there was no refund.

Sam carefully turns his horse, Blackbird, around to face Langtry. Luckily, the new bridge hasn't steered the Southern Pacific away from the small town, population now 150, many in tents. Without the depot, there would be no economic life here. Without it, the crews, passengers, and cargo would vanish, and with them the majority of Roy's customers. Even with the train, his margins are pretty thin; he engages in livestock sales to supplement his income.[347]

In short, he needs his justice of the peace position to make ends meet. And this is an election year. In the fall he expects to be challenged for the position by Jesús Torres, his steady rival in saloon ownership, real estate, and politics. Woe to anyone who tries to intrude; Bean already has an idea to ship dozens of railroad men into town to skew the vote.[348]

Roy and Sam are parched, their hat brims wet with sweat, by the time

---

Pennsylvania, was exceeded in height only by the 401-foot Garabit viaduct in France, built in 1884, and the 336-foot Loa viaduct in Bolivia, built in 1889.

347 Newspaper ads occasionally announced the sale of his animals.

348 He wins in a landslide, forty-one votes to fifteen, according to county records. For local anecdotes, see Sonnichsen, *Judge Roy Bean*, 123–127.

they return to the Jersey Lilly. It should be quiet, but there's a couple seated in the shade on the porch.

Roy sizes them up from horseback—and recognizes them. This young Mexican couple appeared at the saloon just two months ago, looking to get married. He conducted the ceremony as he always did, wearing his buckskin suit and sitting on a chair placed on the bar. "Both of you hold up your right hands. By the authority of the Constitution of these United States and as the law west of the Pecos and the great State of Texas, I, Roy Bean, Justice of the Peace of this great district, here by pronounce you man and wife. May God have mercy on your souls."[349]

Now here they are again, looking for a divorce. He grants it to them without delay, collecting his fee and wishing them the best of luck. It's a sensitive topic—moralists in the cities are already griping about the ease with which marriages are formed and dissolved on the frontier. To Roy's chagrin, the concern is manifesting in West Texas cities like El Paso.

That's the seat of US District Court judge T. A. Falvey. He's the actual "Law West of the Pecos," if there is one. His court legally tries all felony cases, settles land disputes, and handles divorces. He's heard about Roy's divorce mill and writes a letter asking why the judge is overstepping his legal mandate.

"When I give a decision in my court and am later convinced that an error has been made, I have the right to correct that error," Roy scrawls back. "That was the case in marrying these Mexicans. They found out after they had been married a while that an error had been committed, and I believe it was right to correct it. Another thing; they paid me $10 each for marrying them and $40 each for giving them divorces."

Falvey replies, "It is all right this time, Bean, but for God's sake don't do it again, or it will cause serious trouble."[350]

---

349 This was a common benediction from him. For example, see "Justice Bean Takes Great Pride in His Marriage Ceremony," *El Paso Times,* September 14, 1895.

350 *El Paso Herald,* August 28, 1897. Judge Falvey voluntarily resigned his office in June 1892.

Soon, a national crisis over divorce will bubble up when Oklahoma starts granting easy separations by mail, which many will regard as the end of modern moral society. Histrionic debate over the issue will escalate, cresting in 1895 with the publication of the book *The Divorce Mill.* That same year, Roy will start a new business. "Judge Roy Bean, dispenser of justice and matrimony for both sides of the Rio Grande, has started a divorce agency," the *Fort Worth Daily Gazette* reports in an item reprinted across the state. "It is said the judge will send a divorce by postal card to any part of the United States, Mexico or Canada."[351]

It's classic Roy Bean, the self-appointed representative of the flawed but practical common man. He's an accommodating public servant who follows his own pragmatic moral code. And, not incidentally, tries to turn a profit along the way. But his biggest stunt is still to come.

El Paso, Texas
February 1896

Dan Stuart is in a tight spot with this whole Fitzsimmons-Maher prizefight. He's accepted $6,000 from the good people of El Paso to hold the event, a promise he's sticking to despite the intervention of the US Congress and the White House. "Nothing short of lightning or the destruction of the earth by fire or flood can stop the contest we have arranged to pull off," Stuart declares. Privately he's nervous that the whole thing can fall apart.[352]

Stuart is a gambling-house operator from Dallas turned boxing promoter. His idea to build a coliseum and host the fight in Dallas brought the title bout to Texas, but local opposition chased him off to El Paso, where more daring merchants ponied up the money to make the fight happen.

---

351 *El Paso Times,* September 14, 1895.

352 Quote included a retrospective of the prizefight published in the *El Paso Times* on January 24, 1982.

In response to the planned championship bout between Bob Fitzsimmons and challenger Peter Maher, boxing has been banned in Texas. Just weeks ago, US president Grover Cleveland signed a bill to outlaw it nationwide. The US attorney general, Judson Harmon, lays down the gauntlet to boxing promoters: "If they fight in any territory of the United States, we will follow them to the ends of the earth if necessary to bring them to justice."

In Austin, preventing the fight is a priority, and the governor tasks Adjutant General Woodford Mabry and his Texas Rangers to stop it. More than a dozen men deploy to El Paso, most of them undercover, to shadow every move made by the boxers and promoters. In response, the fight organizers charter trains to leave El Paso as decoys, prompting Rangers to chase them in frustration. Mabry has threatened Stuart's life, in person, over these feints. People are calling the bout the "hide and seek championship."

One Texas Ranger tasked with undercover work in El Paso, Captain John Rogers, writes to his boss after long days of observing his target, the chief promoter. "The papers claim Stuart is serene," he reports. "But I know he is badly scared. His only hope is Old Mexico."

Rogers is right. But Mexican officials—including President Porfirio Díaz—are adamantly against the fight, in large degree because US officials are bothering them about it. On February 10, Rogers makes another report: "We are masters of the situation. No fight will occur in Texas or any neutral ground between Texas and any other country."[353]

But the Rangers don't know that Stuart will soon receive a telegram from Judge Roy Bean with a way out of this mess.

Langtry, Texas
February 1896

Roy Bean watches as the Southern Pacific train squeals to a halt at Langtry on the afternoon of February 21 and tries to keep his relief from showing.

---

353 Quotes from letters cited in Paul Spellman, *Captain John H. Rogers, Texas Ranger* (Denton: University of North Texas Press, 2008): 82.

The specially chartered train from El Paso is late, but it's arrived in plenty of time to beat the sunset. Having daylight is critical for his scheme to work.

At age seventy-one, Roy is already notorious in the national press for his outrageous rulings, but today's stunt will put him in a whole new class of frontier legend. Assuming, of course, the Texas Rangers or the Mexican army don't arrest or kill him.

There's a long evening ahead, but Roy's already pleased. Ten passenger cars—filled with about 120 thirsty, confused sportswriters and boxing fans who boarded in El Paso the evening before—have pulled into the depot. Even better, nearly two hundred unticketed hangers-on have overrun the tiny town. Langtry has turned into history's most unlikely location for a world heavyweight championship bout.

Now the train passengers are emerging, stretching limbs and gazing at the empty expanse around them. An ocean of desert scrub surrounds the town's handful of buildings, accentuating a pressing isolation that makes concepts like law and governments fade like a whitewashed sign.

It's a short walk from the front porch of Roy's one-story saloon to the train station. Even at his age he appears as a big, broad man, but he lumbers beneath a lifetime's worth of drinking pounds. Roy looks the part of Texas desert chieftain, a regional powerhouse who exists just beyond the reach of society's laws. The scar on his neck is hidden with a tied kerchief.

It's time to finally meet two key members of the fight cabal, who are walking toward him side by side. One is Stuart himself. The men have never met, but after months of planning, political turmoil, and law enforcement pressure, he's in the hands of Roy Bean.

With Stuart is Bat Masterson, claimed killer of twenty-two men and participant in the O.K. Corral shootout. At age thirty-seven, he is as much a professional gambler and boxing journalist/promoter as a lawman. He lives with a new wife in Colorado, where he has opened a gym. His fame has earned him the title of master of ceremonies for the upcoming bout; his reputation and contacts with fellow gunmen make him what could be called head of security. Masterson's wearing a Colt tucked inside a cross-draw style holster, a rig that allows quick access while its wearer is seated at a card table.

Roy doesn't see much other private security among the train passengers from El Paso—Masterson had offered to bring as many as 150 guards to police the event. Roy can understand why the promoters eschewed such a show of force, if ever it was more than a bluff. There are, however, thirty grim-faced Texas Rangers armed with Winchesters and Colt pistols disembarking from the train. One of them is Adjutant General Mabry himself.

Roy catches them up quickly. First, he assures Stuart and Masterson that everything's been arranged here in Langtry. From his end, the show can go on. The only bad news: Mexican military cavalry have been spotted patrolling their side of the Rio Grande, deployed to stop any boxing from being done on their soil. Bean asks how things are going with the Rangers; he was hoping not to see them.

Undercover spies alerted the lawmen of the train's 9:45 p.m. departure to Langtry and the Rangers bustled on board without paying for the twenty-dollar train tickets. The promoters did nothing to stop them, trusting in Bean's plan. "Mabry told me if he saw the fight happens, he'd shoot to kill first and do the arresting after," Stuart adds.

The promoters and Roy are literally caught between two governments, each armed with crack gunmen and ready to intervene to shut the match down. With a crowd of hundreds of rowdies, canceling the fight could cause a riot and would certainly cause lawsuits—and perhaps end the sport of boxing in the United States before wiser heads had a chance to repeal the ban.[354]

It's up to Roy to thread the needle between the promoters, the Texas Rangers, and two federal governments. The stakes are high and the pressure is on. If he's less clever than he thinks, this fight could end with fortunes and liberty—and maybe even lives—lost. But with money pouring

354 It will take until 1933 for boxing to again be legal in Texas.

into the saloon and the nation's attention fixed on his sparse fief, Roy Bean has never been happier.

"This way to the fight of the century, gents," he announces, voice booming like he's commanding mules. "And there's cold beer at ringside."

The 182 ticketholders are herded along a rocky southbound path. The steep hills of the Rio Grande Canyon loom overhead. A crew of filmmakers from Thomas Edison's company struggles with their bulky apparatus, hoping to capture the bizarre bout on film. At the river's edge the crowd crosses a makeshift pontoon bridge, constructed days before by Roy's saloon crew. It leads to a sandbar in the center of the river, where a freshly assembled boxing ring awaits.

Geography is everything, and no one loves exploiting a loophole more than Roy. The sandbar is not on US soil, giving Mabry no official jurisdiction. Now, the Texas Rangers are not sticklers when it comes to these matters, and they consider borders between states and nations to be . . . flexible. Roy is relying on the threat of bad publicity and Mabry's even-handed willingness to see this compromise as a bloodless victory for all involved.

The authorities on the Mexican side of the border aren't eager to pick a fight if it can be avoided. The sandbar is a clandestine solution. Even if the Mexican army sniffs out the goings-on, the location will afford them plausible deniability that their sovereignty is, by a matter of several hundred yards, being violated. It won't be worth the diplomatic price of intervening. Besides, Roy figures, any Mexican band would have to cross US territory to reach the sandbar, and they'd have to give up their arms at the border crossing at El Paso or Eagle Pass. If they refused, Roy says, "I'd run the whole shooting match myself."[355]

So it's up to the Rangers to stop the boxing match. The thirty lawmen, including two captains, have taken up a position on the bluffs on the US side, looking down on the sandbar. Roy and the fight organizers try to read their body language as the Rangers confer with Mabry.

---

355 "How Bean Foiled Them," *Austin American-Statesman,* March 23, 1903.

Shoulders relax and heads shake as the men disperse toward the bluff's edge—to get a view of the fight. They're soon joined by the two hundred onlookers who have trailed them to this perch, where they can see the action firsthand and for free.

Bat Masterson announces the fighters, and the crowd near and far cheers. Edison's filmmakers sulk nearby; the sky is too dark and the canyon too deep for them to film. After an anxious week of guessing and a mysterious sixteen-hour train ride, the writers and ticketholders press against the ring for a view of the big event. A bell rings, and the strangest title bout in boxing history finally begins.

Fitzsimmons wins by knockout in less than two minutes.

The crowd surges back across the pontoon bridge, chattering about the skill involved in such a quick bout. There's no disappointment over the one-round knockout, the sportswriters note. Roy loses beer sales but is relieved by the event's brevity and happy to be back on American soil. There's time enough to sell some bottles at the Jersey Lilly before the trains start taking the throngs of customers away.

He's pulled it off. News of his solution for the hide-and-seek championship will bring him welcome notoriety across the country. It's the culmination of his career as a performance artist, self-promoter, and champion of the crude underclass. He gloats, of course. "We had the prize fight and the Rangers and Adjutant General saw it," he tells a reporter. "To make a long story short, I beat 'em."

Langtry, Texas
May 1896

Jesús Torres stands inside the Jersey Lilly, trying to keep his patience. He and Roy Bean have been many things—rival saloon owners, town cofounders, and even business partners in a sheep farm. But this year they're again rivals, locked in a contest of wills over the title of justice of the peace.

The situation is ripe for a feud. Roy won this year's election, but questions over the vast number of votes that he received from visiting railroad men have led to his disqualification. Now Torres is here to retrieve the notary public seal, the very symbol of office. But Roy is saying no.

If Torres doesn't feel secure that he'll be protected by the Anglo-dominated law in Val Verde County, he has good reason since the district court there continues to indulge Roy's blatant judicial overreach. Even the Texas Rangers have swung at Roy and missed, twice. He's also seen the all-important railroad accommodate Roy Bean by officially granting him Torres's property in 1888 and look the other way as Bean rigged elections with their employees.

Roy's public hostility to Mexicans is a steady element in his press clippings. He's not the first to realize that a controversial schtick is a quick way to get coverage. For example, he tells reporters he won't chain Mexican prisoners with Bruno the bear because he worries for the animal's safety.[356] And those in Bean's inner circle, including his son, are known killers. In short, Torres would be outmatched in a feud even if he wanted one.

Taking all of this into account, Torres is ready to cut a deal to keep the peace. He suggests Roy keep his seal and handle cases on his side of the tracks, while Torres will get his own seal and take the cases on his side.

Elections be damned, it's settled with a handshake.

Things go on as usual in Langtry. Roy maintains an eye on his daughters as they grow, keeping them out of the saloon. He'd rather they be courted by railroad men than by locals. But it's not just them—he chases all the children of Langtry away from his bar, and from his menagerie of caged animals.[357] Roy has started a tradition of giving presents to each child in town on Christmas morning. It's good politics, but it also reflects an emerging protectiveness for his youngest constituents.

---

356 *El Paso Times*, June 10, 1893.

357 One local youth, Willie Shaw, tells author Jack Skiles, "Every time we kids would go into his saloon, he would run us out. He'd say we had no damned business being there." Other local kids remember getting whupped for messing with his animals and beehives. Skiles, *Judge Roy Bean Country*, 27–28.

The grizzled judge is showing his age and lifestyle. He appears more disheveled, his Old West finery traded in for unadorned pants, a work shirt, and suspenders. The wide-brimmed hat and scarf remain fixtures. He's frequently unwashed. When he's sober, he's an amiable figure of note.

Roy has also taken to writing fawning letters to Lillie Langtry, professing his admiration and telling her that he named the saloon—and, less truthfully, the town—after her. She's a global phenomenon, portrayed in magazine photos worldwide. His fame may have earned a reply from her, but there's only Roy's word for that.[358] He assures everyone that Langtry will perform in his saloon one day. George Langtry, the town's true namesake, is thrown over for a romantic myth of an unlikely bond between saloon operator and world-famous actress.

But he's still Judge Roy Bean. In 1897 an anonymous subscriber to the *Tucson Citizen* writes a letter describing a day in Roy's courtroom. "He was trying a Mexican on the charge of horse stealing, and his charges was one of the shortest on record: 'Gentlemen of the jury, thar's a greaser in the box and a horse missing. You know your duty.'"[359]

---

358 No evidence of an answer from her has been found in the belongings of Lillie Langtry or Roy Bean.

359 *Tucson Citizen*, May 31, 1897. These are the thoughts and observations that Judge Roy Bean contributed to the American culture. That same year, by comparison, Mark Twain published *Following the Equator*. "We have reached a little altitude where we may look down upon the Indian Thugs with a complacent shudder," he wrote during a tour of India. "And we may even hope for a day, many centuries hence, when our posterity will look down upon us in the same way."

JAMES

Jackson County, Missouri
August 1896

James Bean's world used to be defined by long miles, distant cities, and epic landmarks. Now virtually his entire life is spent in a pair of book-lined rooms inside the Jackson County Poor House. Established by the county, it's a threadbare but humane institution that houses nearly two hundred of the destitute, elderly, and mentally lost. It's located on a 160-acre farm that was bought from Henry Washington Younger, father of the infamous Cole Younger.

James is a resident of the poorhouse—"I am not fit for business in the outside world," is how he puts it—but he's also an employee. He was appointed as the facility's librarian in July, when county court judge Thomas Hudspeth hired him for five dollars a month and allowed him to live in the small room connected to the library. "It enables me to clothe myself and feel independent," James says.[360]

Bright's disease has crippled the once hale trader; kidney issues have sapped his energy, swelled his feet, and made walking even short distances

---

360 *Kansas City Journal*, September 14, 1896. His salary appears in published expenses. See "Poor House Funds," *Kansas City Times*, March 22, 1895.

an agony. His loss of appetite is clinical—over the years his blood has become increasingly tainted with urea and other nitrogenous waste. Another common symptom of uremia is a diminished mental capacity, but so far James has been spared the worst of that indignity.

The poorhouse has a library. Kansas City socialite and humanitarian Linda Isgrig donated the first books in February 1894, and the county spent $3.50 on lumber for shelving in two vacant rooms. Isgrig also arranged for the books being thrown away by local libraries to be routed to the poorhouse.

James, whose mind remains sharp even as his body betrays him, graduates from library user to volunteer to employee tasked with receiving books and organizing shelves. The broken man proves that the drive and ability to harness the media exhibited by his brothers remains inside him as well. In September he writes an article about the library for the *Independence Sentinel*, identifying himself as someone "54 years in Jackson County, at one time being one of the largest taxpayers." The article is, above all, a call for book donations. "Food for the mind is essential next to food for the body and saves many here from being necessarily transferred to the crazy ward," James pleads, from personal experience.[361]

Thanks to the publicity, donations roll in from Independence and Kansas City by the hundreds. Among the donors is the Owens family, demonstrating their ongoing friendship with James Bean. Another is his stepson, Charles Moore. The donation that travels the farthest comes from a Kentuckian named R. H. Campbell.

James Bean picks up the pen again on September 24 and writes a new missive, this time for the *Kansas City Journal*. After extolling the library and its benefactors, he indulges in some pathos over his tragedies. "I have been dying of Bright's Disease for 17 years," he confesses. He uses this final public platform to seemingly vent some bitterness at relatives who have

---

361 He describes the solicitation in his later letter published in the *Kansas City Journal*, September 14, 1896.

allowed him to languish. "I lost all my family to death," he laments. "I can truly say I'm alone in the world."

The poorhouse librarian includes a sad if poetic epitaph for himself: "I have fought the battle of life and failed; I ask for no better asylum. I have given way to Young America, on wheels and electricity."[362] James Bean dies early the next year and is buried in the Jackson County pauper's graveyard.

---

362 Ibid, *Kansas City Journal.*

ROY

Langtry, Texas
February 1898

February 14 should just be another Monday morning at the Jersey Lilly. The usual day-drinkers are lounging around—a handful of railroad workers and locals with nothing pressing to do. Roy Bean is tending bar, while Sam shows off his garish new Mexican blanket.

Local rancher George Upshaw isn't impressed and says so. His jokes earn a stern reaction from Sam, and the scene is set for a pointless tragedy.

Upshaw, age forty-nine, moved with his parents to Val Verde County from Missouri when he was a child. He and his Texan wife, Delphia, married in 1885 and now have six children. Aside from the ranch, he owns a small store in Langtry. Upshaw, a product of West Texas, is not inclined to take any back talk from a twenty-four-year-old like Sam Bean. When Sam goes too far—no one repeats what was said—Upshaw slaps Sam, his target flinching so that the blow catches Sam straight in the face.

A point has been crossed, producing a moment of quiet. The railroad men are statues. Even Sam can't believe it; he slowly raises a hand to his face, where a trickle of blood runs from his nose.

Upshaw steps to the bar, where Sam's Winchester rifle is resting, and takes it into his hands. But he doesn't aim it at Sam. "Okay," he says. "If I give you back this gun, you're going to shoot me with it."

Upshaw looks from the young man, who is smoldering with shame and anger, to his father, and gets only a wordless glare in reply. "Alright then, I'm leaving. I'll leave the gun outside."

Silence. "I'm saying this has gone on long enough. But it's over. Right? So, now I'm giving you back this gun, and you're not going to shoot me with it. That's the deal."

Upshaw sets the rifle down and backs away from the bar, both pairs of Bean eyes tracking his movement toward the door. He bangs through the swinging doors and hustles down the saloon steps into the street. And he almost makes it to the railroad tracks before something slams into his back, between the shoulder blades.

He turns to see Sam Bean and his father standing outside the saloon, the younger man holding the Winchester to his shoulder. "Don't shoot anymore," Upshaw gasps, loud enough for shocked onlookers to hear him, and starts to stagger away.

The next words, delivered by the judge, come with a grim finality. "Better shoot him again, Sam." The second shot drops Upshaw, one outstretched hand nearly reaching the railroad tracks. That's how his wife and friends find him, gasping for air. "I begged him not to shoot a second time," he says weakly. "But he did it anyway." He dies there in the street, Roy Bean standing nearby.[363]

On the day after the shooting, February 15, an explosion sinks the USS *Maine* in Havana harbor, killing 260. America is again mobilizing for war, this time against Spain. "Is it War or Amity?" asks the *Las Vegas (NM) Daily Optic* on February 19, then seemingly answers the question with the subhead "'Ammunition ready for immediate use' is the report

---

363 Details of the crime were remembered by Beula Burdwell Farley, who lived three miles from Langtry and knew the judge well. See Skiles, *Judge Roy Bean Country*, 23. "Mrs. Upshaw and others who were there said that if it weren't for old Roy Bean, Sam never would have killed Mr. Upshaw," she said.

sent to California posts." Manifest Destiny's foreign policy inheritor, the Monroe Doctrine, is alive and well at the dawn of a new century.

The Bean family's legal troubles are on page three of the Las Vegas paper: "A report comes from Langston, Texas that Sam Bean, son of Judge Roy Bean and grandson of Uncle Sam Bean of Las Cruces, shot a man there Monday." The location and family tree are scrambled, but the article makes clear that the week has seen the young man land in deep trouble. He's been arrested for murder and delivered to Del Rio, where he's being held on a $5,000 bond.[364]

It's a large sum, but Roy spends it to liberate his son from jail. He wonders how much time and money it'll take to keep Sam out of prison.

364 The Nevada newspaper item was filed from Las Cruces, where Bean family doings had a local hook.

SAM

EL PASO HERALD

September 12, 1898

A Las Cruces correspondent writes that Samuel Bean, an old veteran of the Mexican war who is in his 80th year, was badly beaten up by Sheriff Pat Garrett of Dona Ana County yesterday morning in May Bros' store. The Democrat's *informant neglects to state the cause of the encounter, merely saying in regard to it that Mr. Bean was "assaulted" and struck in the face three times. Mr. Bean, or "Uncle Sam," as he is commonly called, served as sheriff of Dona Ana County and is a highly respected citizen of Las Cruces.*

Las Cruces, New Mexico
September 1898

Sam Bean lies on the floor of the May Brothers general store, the fading shock of Pat Garrett's punches turning into hot, swelling pain. There's a familiar and unwelcome copper taste in his mouth, and he turns his head to let the blood dribble out.

It's not a position he expected to be in, needless to say. Sam at this point is an elder statesman of Las Cruces. He maintains and cultivates friends here, many through the Democratic Party, and has kept his name known with a series of newspaper columns that run under the byline "The Old Timer." (His name appears at the end.) These are largely reminiscences from frontier times but increasingly contain scorching editorials on current events, always championing the development of the Mesilla Valley and the adoption of New Mexico as a state. His missives run in the *Silver City Enterprise* but are sometimes reprinted across the state. The Las Cruces newspaper frequently republishes his tomes, making him well-known in his hometown.[365]

Samuel G. Bean should be a harmless old gadfly, not the victim of a public beatdown from the nation's most infamous lawman. So what happened?

On February 1, 1896, Colonel Albert Jennings Fountain rode away from Lincoln, New Mexico, his eight-year-old seated alongside him on the buckboard wagon. The pair were heading to Mesilla after Fountain, a former Texas state senator and an attorney, helped the prosecutor in Lincoln organize charges of horse theft against Oliver Lee and William McNew. They were both former deputies under Democratic leadership. Fountain had been an elected Republican.

Fountain, who lived in Mesilla, worked for the United States Property Commission in El Paso, where he investigated and disposed of Confederate property. As such, he was clearly on Sam Bean's list of untrusted public officials, and that was before he accused Sam's friends of horse thievery.

After leaving Lincoln, Fountain and his son vanished.

A search party produced witnesses who saw two riders following the family, and sets of tracks along the trail nearby appeared to lead toward two ranches owned by Oliver Lee. One of the properties was called Wildy

---

365 "Old timer, Samuel Bean of this city, is running a series of letters in the *Silver City Enterprise* that are attracting widespread attention and comment," said the *Las Cruces Sun-News* on March 31, 1894. "Mr. Bean boldly acknowledges being a democrat, but maintains he's a democrat of the respectable sort."

Well. No bodies were ever found, but suspicion toward the accused rustlers and former lawmen ran high.

Before too long, forty-eight-year-old lawman Pat Garrett came out of retirement to take up the case—and tame Doña Ana County while he was at it. He was fifteen years past his famous shooting of Billy the Kid, and he had witnessed the canonization of his target as a folk hero. This made him the villain who cut down people in the dark—a smart tactic for a gunman who wants to survive a dangerous encounter, but one that looks different in the light of day. The public voted with its collective wallet; his 1882 memoir was a flop.

Garrett's intentions with the Fountain case were easy to question. He had a growing reputation as a man who couldn't pay his bills, and his appearance smacked of opportunism. Besides that, his avenging Fountain struck some as strange since the slain lawyer's most famous client was Billy the Kid.

Garrett found himself in a political fight as much as a law enforcement action since the sheriff was a Republican, whereas Lee and the others were Democrats. Propaganda became a viable weapon for Lee, who was still in hiding. The *Independent Democrat*, Las Cruces' publication of party stalwarts, granted Lee space to defend himself on the front page. Lee claimed that Garrett was looking for a chance to kill him for personal aggrandizement.[366]

Garrett waited a year and a half, until new elections brought allies into the county courthouse, and then he struck. At four a.m. on July 12, 1898, the lawman and his posse were preparing to ambush Wildy Well when shots rang out. It was a counterambush, and Garrett's men retreated after a deputy was shot dead.

The public's opinion hung in the balance during the aftermath. Lee redoubled his campaign, and in early September a new series of letters appeared in the *Independent Democrat* under a splashy headline: "Lee's

---

366 Details of the Oliver Lee saga were included in William Keleher's book of local remembrances, *The Fabulous Frontier* (1945), and reprinted in the *El Paso Times,* June 19, 1955.

Rehash of the False Accusations of Murder and Garrett's Obsessive Hunt to Kill Him." It occupied two solid columns of the front page.

Nearly as long was a diatribe by guest columnist Sam Bean—signed with his own name, not the "Old Timer" byline—excoriating Garrett. He called him "the poorest sheriff Dona Ana County has ever had" and "the murderer of Billy the Kid," and accused him of setting Lee up for a similar, cowardly execution.[367] These were obviously sensitive spots for Garrett's battered public persona. He was a loser in business and a questionable lawman, with public humiliations following even his famous successes. This latest shootout and public drubbing have put him over the edge.

September 11, 1898, should have been another quiet morning inside the May Brothers store, but Sam knows there will be trouble when he sees the scowl under Pat Garrett's thick mustache. The sheriff is enraged by what's been written about him, but what can he do to an unarmed eighty-year-old man?

Garrett strides over to Sam Bean and punches him in the face. A second and third blow soon follow, leaving the old man sprawled on the ground. Garrett then leaves, wordlessly.

The shocked clerks help Sam Bean to his feet. The old man is tougher than he looks; he suffers no major injuries. The bruises fade; he presses no charges against Garrett and files no lawsuit. That's the way Old Timers handle things.

Lee turns himself in eight months later—but not to Garrett—and he's eventually acquitted of the Fountain murders. The open charge regarding the slain deputy is dismissed. The disappearance of Fountain and his son remains unsolved.[368]

---

367 *El Paso Times*, June 19, 1955.

368 Garrett's finances soon collapsed, and he became known by the Mays brothers as a deadbeat, relying on intimidation to keep the grocers from collecting. Albert B. Fall (well before his Teapot Dome scandal downfall) intervened and paid the bills. See Mark Lee Gardner, *To Hell on a Fast Horse: The Untold Story of Billy the Kid and Pat Garrett* (New York: William Morrow, 2011).

ROY

Outside Langtry, Texas
April 1899

From the rectangular windows of the Southern Pacific Railroad passenger car, West Texas could be confused for a wasteland. But Roy Bean can see development and action between Del Rio and Langtry. Exporting meat by train has brought sheep and goat ranching to the area, and there are more flocks than ever in the scrub. There are also vegetable farms and vineyards carved into the landscape.

This land is changing, Roy thinks, but the topography is the same. No matter what sits on top, the land is held up by some old bones—including his own. There's got to be some consolation in that.

Roy elbows his son, who's sleeping off the previous night's revelry in the seat next to him, and says, "We're almost home." On April 5, the district court in Del Rio acquitted Sam Bean for killing George Upshaw.[369]

It doesn't take a legal scholar to see that he beat a strong case. After all, he shot an unarmed man in the back in public. Twice. But witnesses to the crime in Langtry are hard to come by. The only ones who testify are those

---

369 *Pecos County Pickings,* April 6, 1899.

who witnessed Upshaw strike Sam Bean. A jury sympathetic to manly honor and frontier justice saw these as important circumstances. And so the jury let the young shooter go free.

Roy's influence—which he peddled in actions ranging from bribing witnesses with free drinks to lobbying friendly officials in Del Rio for clemency in the courtroom—is credited for this turn of events. "It cost the judge an awful lot, but Sam got out of killing old man Upshaw," recalls Beula Farley. "They didn't have any witnesses for Upshaw. All that bunch testified for Sam. It cost the old man many a bottle of beer. . . . Sam came out of that clean as a whistle, because Judge Roy Bean had lots of friends."[370]

Another Langtry witness, an overnight telegraph operator named Mrs. Trent, has told Roy Bean she'd tell the truth if called to testify. She's the wife of the station agent in Langtry and made of sterner stuff than others who live there. "If Sam is sent up," the judge tells her husband, "he'll get even with anybody who testified against him." Roy and Sam even show up at the telegraph office, armed, to "parade around."[371]

His son is reckless and violent—and a man to be respected within this pocket of the frontier. In other words, Sam is cut from his father's cloth. He's the obvious heir to the Jersey Lilly, and this incident will only secure his position.

Roy's happy to return home. He's spent a lot of time in Del Rio, boozing with witnesses and supporters for weeks while neglecting the saloon and his myriad interests in Langtry. In his absence, the children have gone to visit San Antonio. A dormant Jersey Lilly won't replenish the money he's spent to get Sam free, and he's eager to announce that the bar, horse races, and judgeship are all open for business.

As they near Langtry, Sam peers out the Pullman's window to savor

---

370 Skiles, *Judge Roy Bean Country*, 23.

371 Interview with Mrs. Trent in Sonnichsen, *Judge Roy Bean*, 189.

the view of home, and he utters two words that immediately fill Roy with foreboding. "It's gone," the young man says.

Roy pushes over him and looks at Langtry's stubby profile. A scorched skeleton occupies the ground where the Jersey Lilly once stood. His home and business have burned to the ground.[372]

Langtry, Texas
August 1900

Roy Bean stands outside the single-room frame house, smug with pride. In part due to his efforts, Langtry has built this dedicated schoolhouse and has raised funds enough for a half year of classes. It's located on the town's west side, near a pumphouse. Judge Roy Bean serves as a trustee of the new institution. When a teacher is hired, he and fellow trustee Cortez Fielder sign for the thirty-five-dollar monthly salary.

It would be easy to write off the building of a school as more politicking, but Roy's taken a genuine interest in seeing the school established. He eyes the chimney and makes a mental note to set up a delivery of firewood to keep the kids warm in the coming months.

The school is not meant for his own children. The girls have gone elsewhere for schooling, and Roy Jr. has gotten an out-of-town job with the railroad. Sam lives here, paying Roy rent, and earns money as his father's hired cowboy. Roy's adopted son, John, has also returned, at least briefly. In the 1900 census, Roy says he's a "stockman" and lies about his age, listing it as sixty-three.[373]

Stockman seemed an apt job description for Roy at the time, given that the Jersey Lilly had been reduced to ashes and livestock kept him solvent while he rebuilt. If the saloon had been torched to drive him away, it wasn't going to work.

---

372 How this fire happened was never determined. It may have been an accident in an empty building or a response to the killing of George Upshaw.

373 He was probably sixty-nine.

The new saloon sits in a new spot, with a lot less square footage but with an attached billiard room and covered porch. Roy managed to fish the lionhead legs of his former billiard table from the ruins and fit them to a new table. He builds a one-room adobe home on the rise behind the saloon. He calls the home the Opera House and swears he'll convert it to a stage when Lillie Langtry arrives to perform.

He arrives at the saloon, where he finds a telegraph waiting for him. It's from Virginia Charles—the name of his ex-wife once she married Manuel Charles—and was delivered this morning, August 26. It's grimly brief: Roy's youngest son, James Bean, died today in San Antonio from a lingering sickness. The twenty-one-year-old is to be buried in the city's San Fernando Cemetery.

Roy walks out of the saloon and heads to the telegraph office, where he fills out an empty telegraph form. The clerk counts the words per line, which doesn't take long, then assesses the charge. Payment secured, the message is transmitted to San Antonio: Roy won't be able to attend his son's funeral due to illness.[374]

His telegram delivers another message: James Bean turned his back on his father long ago. The young man's death is Virginia's heartache, not his.[375]

Langtry, Texas
July 1901

The world is too damn small, Roy thinks as he throws the newspaper down on the wooden bar. The headline is scandalous: "'The Law West of the Pecos' Holds Up Passengers on Train for Price of Beer." The byline is from the *El Paso Herald*, but the item has been reprinted in the local paper. And that's a problem.

The article makes a big deal out of standard Jersey Lilly antics. So what

374 *San Antonio Light*, August 27, 1900.

375 Virginia lived until November 26, 1922, when she died in her home at 907 Trinity, San Antonio, according to her death certificate.

if "a tourist is stricken with nervous prostration that promises to last him until he returns to Massachusetts"? The account is a breathless depiction of a May incident:

> The judge was on one of his tri-weekly "tears" yesterday and when the train stopped at Langtry for dinner at 6 o'clock he paid little attention to the passengers. Two fresh young fellows from the far east wanted a drink and went into Judge Bean's saloon. The judge was resting easy and at first did not want to wait on them. One of the men wanted a drink of whiskey but the old man said they had none. The passenger then offered him a two dollar bill to pay for a bottle of beer. Bean refused the bill saying it was not money and would take no paper in payment for his goods. The other fellow had to change the bill for him and he got the beer. In the meantime, the other stranger had engaged the judge in conversation and the man who bought the beer went out without paying for it.

Presently the judge noticed that his man was gone and, taking his .45 revolver from the counter, went after him.

When he went into the tourist car he shoved the gun in the face of every passenger he met pending investigations. Finding he was mistaken he passed on until he found the right party. The judge poked the cannon into the face of the man who had beat him and said, "Thirty-five cents or I press the button!"

So anxious was the stranger to comply with the demand of the "court" that he offered the judge a dollar, not wishing to wait to find the exact change. The judge changed the money and, turning to the startled passengers said: "That's the kind of an hombre I am. I am the law west of the Pecos."

The passengers were frightened out of their wits until the conductor came in and explained that the bully was really the "Law West of the Pecos" and to obey him was the best way to get along with him, and advised the young easterner never to try to beat a westerner out of the price of a bottle of beer.[376]

This tale falls entirely within the image of himself that Roy has constructed and promoted. Even the overall moral seems to side with his frontier mentality. But he's driven to action and picks up his own pen to craft a reply to the *Herald*.

For a renowned, damn-'em-all rabble-rouser, Roy seems suddenly oversensitive about his image. But then again, 1902 will be an election year, and the Torres family is sure to put up a contender. The local newspaper's pickup of this "holdup" story could make him look foolish, drunk, or even unstable. Any weakening of his support from railroad officials or Val Verde officials could mean the end of his elevated status. Even with the highway bringing more traffic to the saloon, the railroad depot remains the lifeblood of Langtry.

The retraction, if that's what it is, runs on page six of the *Herald* three days after Roy sends his rebuke. The editors start by printing his letter, which opens with an insult: "I see a piece that has gone the rounds of the newspapers copied from your little sheet. Of course I never saw it until it got into some large papers as your little sheet don't circulate much around here. The whole thing is a fabricated lie."[377]

Then come the threats and bluster: "I want you to give me your author. I suppose you know what the law is in such cases and I want you to put in a retraction of the whole in your newspaper. Anything you want to put in your paper about me I must approve of before being published."

Finally comes the actual defense. It seems that the judge objects to the headline more than anything. "The part you put in about me holding up anybody is false and I will have redress."

The editors then take the remainder of the page column to observe

376 *El Paso Herald,* May 27, 1901.

377 *El Paso Herald,* July 6, 1901.

that the judge has been "a most picturesque guardian of the majesty of the law" and that "many stories are told of him and his artistic way of administering justice." The newspaper claims no offense, however, and reveals that the story's only source was the young traveler himself. "Needless to say that in printing the little story about the judge and the tenderfoot, the *Herald* had no motive but to amuse. The judge says the story was not true and that it has injured him. Therefore we have pleasure in making this explanation and apology."

It's not exactly a retraction, but for Roy it'll have to do. It'll give him a response to anyone who brings up the incident, in the saloon or at the depot. More importantly, his pride and vanity have been placated. His self-image no longer includes such antics. He imagines himself a bedrock of the Langtry community, an elder statesman suited to this wild place. But the legend of Roy Bean includes his recent résumé of barroom grifting, public drunkenness, dubious rulings, granting divorces to strangers by mail, hosting an illegal boxing championship, standing accused of horse theft, and enabling his wild, murderous son.

Roy Bean focused in the latter part of his life on being a public servant and media personality. Yet his letter to the *El Paso Herald* includes the timeless cry of the regretful famous: "I am not public property yet to be handled by everybody."

Las Cruces, New Mexico
November 1902

The depot is crowded with people, inside and out, as Roy Bean shuffles away from the Santa Fe Railway train. He's been on board since linking up with the line to Rincon at El Paso, and his limbs are stiff. He feels oddly anonymous here, which is comforting. His name ain't so good in this town—as his fame in Texas grew, so did the local tales of how he left his brother, the Old Timer, high and dry during the Civil War.

Roy takes in Las Cruces, comparing it to the hamlet of La Mesilla, which once vied with Las Cruces for Doña Ana County primacy. From what he understands, Mesilla lost its chance twenty years ago, when the

Santa Fe Railway approached the town to open a line there. But the locals didn't want to give up land for the right-of-way, so the railroad made the same offer to the smaller community of Las Cruces, five miles away. Since the first train arrived in April 1881, Las Cruces's population has tripled to more than three thousand, while Mesilla's has stagnated at about twelve hundred.

The train brings more than just people. Residents in Las Cruces have made full use of imported building materials, giving rise to a diverse architecture that Roy doesn't associate with the Southwest, like Mediterranean villas, colonial mansions, and neoclassical estates. The hodgepodge of styles makes his slow stroll through the city an exploration of global building design.

His destination is the Exchange Saloon, Samuel Bean Jr., proprietor. It makes Roy smile to see his nephew continuing on the same path as that taken by Sam Jr.'s father, grandfather, uncle Joshua, himself, and his cousin. Once a Bean, always a Bean.

But it's not Sam Jr. whom Roy has traveled these long miles to see. At last he's here to see his brother. It's been four decades since they parted, with Sam facing an empty safe, angry gamblers, the approaching Union army. As Roy's mortality looms, this is one of the few things in his long life that are truly unsettled.

Roy ambles along Main until he sees a cluster of trees; Sam Jr. was the first merchant in Las Cruces to plant them on the street outside his establishment.[378] His nephew is doing very well for himself, clearly. His saloon is set up in the best Bean family tradition, with rooms for billiards, cards, and general carousing. Sam Bean and Petra live in a house next door.

Roy walks even slower as he approaches the saloon doors. He sent word ahead, and his brother will be seated soberly inside. He doesn't expect anger from Sam—Petra, he's less sure about—but that's not what's making him nervous. Today Roy Bean is on an uncharacteristic mission, one that his ego can even now hardly allow.

---

378 *Las Cruces Sun-News,* February 18, 1898.

Roy takes a deep breath, squares his shoulders, and enters the saloon. The only interviewer to hear about the meeting, Sam Bean's contemporary Maude McFie Bloom, describes "the hard old sinner, Judge Roy Bean, coming back after 40 years, not until then man enough to say to the elder brother whose heart he had broken: 'I'm sorry.'"[379]

Langtry, Texas
March 16, 1903

The desert wind envelops Roy Bean, who unties his neckerchief to better feel it wash across his skin. One finger idly traces the rope burn there. The sky to the west, over the ruins of Eagle's Nest, is radiant with the soft, red-orange glow of a West Texas sunset.

The sun is setting, but he's still in the grips of an epic, daylong hangover. I'm too old for this kind of life, he admits to himself.[380]

Roy's not lost his electoral prowess, however. He was challenged to his office in 1902, but tradition and name recognition won the day, and he emerged victorious. He still sits on the proverbial bench, performing his judicial theater and collecting fees at the Jersey Lilly.

Roy feels his chest tighten and leans over to catch his breath. He spent days in San Antonio, taking in cockfights. An overnight in Del Rio on the way home also turned into a bender. He woke sick from whiskey but managed to catch an early train for home. He arrived this morning at about ten a.m., staggering off the train with a muddled head and aching body. Water, food, cigars, and beer haven't helped. The staff is worried—he's been stumbling around the saloon and speaking just as awkwardly.

---

379 Bloom, "Shadows in Sam's Valley." Unfortunately, in "Los Dos Frijoles," she dates the reunion to 1894 and notes that Sam Bean Sr. invited Roy's old friends to fete his returned brother after they settled their grievance. There is no corroborating evidence to support either date.

380 He's seventy-eight.

He reties the scarf across his neck and heads back into the Jersey Lilly, where he tells the staff he's going to his house to lie down. At around ten p.m. on March 16, he's found dead in bed.

Roy Bean's body is conveyed to Del Rio, where he's buried in Westlawn Cemetery.[381] Roy's son writes to Sam Bean in Las Cruces in response to his uncle's inquiry about the death. "My dear uncle Sam," he writes on April 2, 1903, "Your letter came some time ago. I was very glad to hear from you but very sorry you could not see father before he died. I feel very lonely now. I am still at the old place, looking after the property father left behind but have not fully decided yet what I will do."[382]

News of his passing spreads worldwide, and it's seen as the end of a bygone era. Praise is effusive, if qualified. "That man did a world of good," District Court Judge T. A. Falvey years later eulogizes in the *El Paso Herald,* verbalizing the growing mainstream interpretation of Bean's life. "He was the man for the place. The rough community where he had settled would have tolerated no enforcement of the law as it was printed on the statute books. But they tolerated Bean, because he was both law and equity, right and justice. He filled a place that could not have been filled by any other man. . . . His decisions were not always according to the law and the fact, but they were accepted and that was the big point."[383]

Within months of Roy Bean's death, the town of Langtry begins to decline. Although it remains a local center for ranchers and a train depot, the future of the community won't be found along the tracks but in the

---

381 After vandals struck the grave, he was reburied in 1964 on the grounds of the Whitehead Memorial Museum in Del Rio.

382 Letter printed in full in Sonnichsen, *Judge Roy Bean*, 231–232. From the context, either Roy's son didn't know his father went to Las Cruces, or he meant that Sam never made it to Langtry for a reciprocal visit.

383 *El Paso Herald,* December 14, 1914.

increasing amount of road traffic. But Langtry becomes the victim of a commissioner's court pen stroke, which moves the highway to a more direct, northern route that is sure to strangle the town's growth.

It's doubtful that Roy, past his prime as a regional powerbroker, could have shielded the town from total dissolution. If he'd been alive, that is.

The next year, actress Lillie Langtry visits the town during a brief stop between New Orleans and Los Angeles, a stunt arranged by the Southern Pacific Railroad. Crowds and reporters gather for the spectacle of W. H. Dodd (the current justice of the peace, and an Englishman to boot) squiring her around, telling stories of the fallen judge and giving her one of his pistols. Dozens of local girls form a parade behind them.

Lillie Langtry later noted that Roy Bean's son, Sam, was a no-show. "It was generally whispered that he had taken fright at the prospect of the responsible part he was to play [in the day's events] and was lying in hiding somewhere among the universal sagebrush."[384] Sam Bean isn't made of the same showman's material that his father was.[385]

There's no stage performance, just a quick stroll before Langtry reboards. "It's a brief visit, but a memorable one," she recalled later. It's not just the actress who remembered this event; the layover immediately became bedrock western lore. Langtry's appearance became a tailor-made coda to Roy Bean's life, a celebrity send-off to a strange American icon.

---

384 *Cosmopolitan*, December 1917.

385 Four years after Roy died, his son Sam Bean was killed. He'd moved to Del Rio to open a saloon and dance hall. He'd also married. According to the *Austin American-Statesman* (May 9, 1907), Sam Bean was in a feud with a local painter named Ciserio Orasco. When Sam and his wife ran into Orasco and his wife on the street, the saloonkeeper drew a pistol and fired. One of four shots hit the painter in his right shoulder, but the man closed the distance and plunged a knife into Sam nine times. He died the next morning, at age thirty-two. Orasco pled self-defense and was never charged. Sam Bean was buried next to Roy at Westlawn and later was reinterred with his father at the museum grounds.

Her trip preserved the saloon as a tourist destination; Roy may be gone, but visitors to the Jersey Lilly can still absorb some of his essence just by being in Langtry.

The fact that Roy became famous is his biggest achievement, and it's one that endures. In 1981, the millionth visitor entered the Judge Roy Bean Visitor Center in Langtry; thousands still arrive every year. As of 2023, Langtry's population has steadily shrunk and now hovers at a dozen people. It's twelve souls away from being a ghost town populated by a single specter: Roy Bean.

SAM

FROM THE *LAS VEGAS DAILY OPTIC*

August 10, 1903
Hot Shot—Uncle Sam Bean, the 87-year-old incorrigible of Las Cruces, has sent the following note to Senator [Albert] Beveridge:

Dear sir. Don't you think that your state, Indiana is getting rather too magrovious? I think she will have to be stripped of her imposing habiliments of statehood and thrown back into the sisterhood of territories. But we protest, in the name of the Holy Angels, that in such case she will not be placed on a level with New Mexico. We could not stand it. We never have had a mob or an epidemic of mobs, as Indiana is having, and never had to call out the National Guard or U.S. troops to subdue riots.

Yours truly,
Samuel G. Bean [386]

---

386 Don't bother looking up "magrovious" since it doesn't appear to have ever been a word. As for the social upheaval Sam mentions, those were the infamous Evansville Riots. A mob of several thousand citizens tried to storm the Vanderburgh County Jail on July 6

Las Cruces, New Mexico Territory
October 1903

On October 20, Sam Bean shuffles into the office of the *Las Cruces Citizen* to drop off his latest column. It's an ode to irrigation engineers, "handsome wiry young fellows" who are surveying a dam site that he predicts will make the land around Mesilla Valley "the richest bottom land in all the world, the famous River Nile not excepted."

The "Old Timer" of Las Cruces is still at it. Newspapers in El Paso, Las Cruces, and Albuquerque sometimes rerun his memories of the fading Wild West or his love letters to the modern development of Doña Ana County. The columns reveal him as a partisan for the region. Sam has loved this land since he first saw it as a Santa Fe bushwhacker. "You can't keep a good valley down," he says in this latest column. "I like to see the great southwest city [of El Paso] looming up."[387]

It's a lot of big talk for a territory that isn't yet a state. But El Paso is becoming a gateway between nations, and even Las Cruces is growing steadily. It now boasts the twin domes of the St. Genevieve Catholic Church to serve as a recognizable skyline. For all its progress, Las Cruces has not yet been incorporated.[388]

That afternoon, Sam heads for home. It's located on Main Street, not too far of a walk for the hardy old man with time to spare. The property has a couple of buildings, one of which is occupied by Sam and Petra. It's attached to Sam Jr.'s saloon.

Sam never acquired a taste for drink, but he's used to being in the

---

to lynch more than a dozen Black inmates. A couple hundred militiamen opened fire on the mob, which retreated to rampage through African American neighborhoods. The rioting continued for four days, killed twelve people, and wounded dozens more. Two thousand of Evansville's eight thousand Black residents fled.

387 Reprinted in the *Albuquerque Morning Journal*, November 2, 1903.

388 In 1907 Las Cruces was officially incorporated as a town, and in 1912 New Mexico finally became the country's forty-seventh state.

social environment of a bar. Public houses have been his life since he gave up soldiering all those decades ago. He's more comfortable there than anywhere else. So he steps inside the Majestic Saloon—his son's latest venture—instead of going to his house. Sam and his son sit at a table for an afternoon chat. At four p.m. Samuel Bean slides from his chair, hands seizing, mouth frozen crookedly in place. Within moments, he's dead, most likely of a stroke.

A front-page article in the *Albuquerque Morning Journal* heralds the sad news in an introduction before running Sam's final column, saying his loss has cast "general sorrow over the community." The correspondent notes that "the article seems to be prophetic." Indeed, Sam Bean's concluding words, his last public statement, take a poignant turn:

> *THE* EL PASO NEWS *SOMETIME COPIES MY LETTERS FROM THE* LAS CRUCES CITIZEN *BUT WHEN I WAS IN THE* NEWS *OFFICE THE LAST TIME I WAS IN EL PASO, NO PERSON RECOGNIZED ME. THERE WERE NO OLD TIMERS, I SUPPOSE THAT WAS THE REASON. I AM NOT SEEKING NOTORIETY ANYHOW.*
>
> *WE WILL ALL MEET IN THE GREAT BEYOND. ADIOS.*[389]

389 "Wrote Letter the Day He Died," *Albuquerque Morning Journal,* November 2, 1903.

EPILOGUE

San Antonio, Texas

December 1972

Paul Newman takes his seat at the Wonder Theater, eyeing the gold waterfall curtain hanging in front of the tremendous screen. Now that he's seated, people in the crowd turn from looking at him to seek out other movie stars. There's Ava Gardner, her dark, glossy hair floating past the bobbing, craning heads of fans. Seated nearby is Tab Hunter, who has more than this one appearance on his Texas itinerary. Tomorrow Tab'll be off to Del Rio for more film promotion, but Newman is the top-billed star and the premier is enough.[390]

In mere minutes, the crowd here will be treated to the December 21 world premiere of *The Life and Times of Judge Roy Bean*. The film's director, John Huston, is in the audience. Sulking nowhere close to him is the movie's original screenplay writer, John Milius.

The Wonder Theater in San Antonio is owned by ABC but was originally built by the once-trailblazing Interstate Theater Company. This pioneering firm, the first to bring air conditioning to movie theaters in Texas,

---

390 *Herald-Banner* (Greenville, TX), December 20, 1972.

was devoted to delivering "wholesome entertainment" to communities. The chain of luxury megatheaters is finding the market unable to support large crowds—the company's flagship, twenty-five-hundred-seat theater in Dallas closed in July—and the movies they show are becoming more crass as well.

But the Wonder Theater, large and elegant enough to host some of the era's biggest stars, is perfect for a movie premiere. The screen is so vast that the theater is equipped with Norelco AAII 70/35mm projectors, a type more often used for massive drive-in screens.

Milius fidgets in his seat, dreading the movie's start. Any excitement over being at the premiere is dampened by his dismal experience making the film. What he'll see was based on his original script, but the young screenwriter chafes at the changes that were made to his vision. He'll later say that the Roy Bean movie prompted him to go into directing "out of self-defense and a desire to control."[391]

Milius wanted to make *Roy Bean* into a frontier version of *Dirty Harry* (which he wrote, uncredited, in 1971): a vigilante cleaning up the chaos without the constraint of society's clumsy rules. Such a retelling would give a sheen of dark nobility to Roy Bean's malfeasances; instead of being a self-centered opportunist he's a simultaneously crooked but principled man. In Milius's view, Roy is not a symptom of Manifest Destiny's absurdities, but a foundation of the civilization it eventually brings. He's not an agent of chaos but a representative of order.

Milius's take on Roy exposes how the myth of Judge Bean morphed from reality. "Roy Bean is an obsessed man. He's like Lawrence of Arabia. He sits out there in the desert and he's got this great vision of law and order and civilization and he kills people and does anything in the name

---

391 Mary Murphy, "Milius Tackles a New Mountain," *Los Angeles Times*, June 11, 1975. He went on to write and direct *The Wind and the Lion*, *Conan the Barbarian*, and *Red Dawn*.

of progress," Milius says. "I love those kinds of people. That's the kind of people who built this country. That's the American spirit!"[392]

If there was a "Law West of the Pecos," it was Judge Falvey, who actually tried all the big murder cases and once left the bench to face off against two armed hoodlums in town and take them, at gunpoint, into custody. As a renegade justice of the peace, Roy Bean seemingly destabilized order as much as he created it. Except for the symbolism surrounding his legend, Roy Bean is historically insignificant.

As off base as the Milius script was, the final film is worse. Milius watched helplessly as Huston and movie executives turned his vigilante judge into an amiable curmudgeon. "They said, 'What you've created is a reprehensible man. We've got to make him much more cute,'" he gripes. "So, they changed it from a Western about royalty and greed and power to a Western where Andy Williams sings a song in the middle of the movie and the judge and his girl and a pet bear go off on a picnic."

Any story transferred to the screen can be forgiven for playing fast with history, but in *The Life and Times of Judge Roy Bean,* several galling moments stand out beyond the silliness. The nadir may be a scene that completely inverts several Roy Bean ground truths:

> *Judge Roy Bean: Do you deny the killing?*
> *Sam Dodd: I do not deny it. But there's no place in that book where it says nothing about killing a Chinese. And no one I know ever heard a law on greasers, niggers, or Injuns.*
> *Bean: All men stand equal before the law. And I will hang a man for killing anyone, including Chinks, greasers, or niggers! I'm very advanced in my views and outspoken.*
> *Dodd: There's no place in that book that . . .*
> *Bean: Trust in my judgment of the book. Besides, you're gonna hang*

---

392 Linda Strawn, "Blood-and-Guts Milius at War With Hollywood," *Los Angeles Times,* August 5, 1973.

no matter what it says in there, 'cause I am the law, and the law is the handmaiden of justice. Get a rope.

The movie also features this heartfelt plea from Bean: "Maybe you can explain to these people here that I mean them no harm. Tell 'em it's going to be a new place. It's going to be a nice place to live. I'm the new judge. There will be law. There is going to be order, progress, civilization, peace. . . . Above all, peace. And I don't care who I have to kill to get it. Now go on, you tell 'em that."

Neither Milius's vision of a frontier judicial vigilante nor Huston's of a romantic iconoclast gets close to the core of the real Roy Bean. Regardless, the movie was a triumph for both Newman and Huston. The *Los Angeles Times* writes, "Arguably overlong, arguably self-indulgent on occasion, 'The Life and Times of Judge Roy Bean' is nonetheless happily as intent upon being fun as it is in being significant. As Bean, Newman may not seem quite dumb enough but is genuinely moving and has great authority. Surely his performance here is a high point in a notable career."[393]

The reality of Judge Roy Bean is stranger, if less romantic, than his film or television depictions. (The TV series *Judge Roy Bean* ran for a single thirty-nine-episode season in 1955. It's even worse than the movie.) That a man of his age and disposition forged a grimy fiefdom from a train station saloon, earned national recognition, and publicly defied authority all the way up to the White House is remarkable. The fact that such a chiseler and dubious man made these things happen makes it even more unlikely, and therefore more interesting.

But Roy was usually only a witness to great events, too absorbed in his own shenanigans to contribute to them directly. The exception to this was his Confederate activity in New Mexico—a chapter of his life that no film or TV show ever explores.

393 Paul Newman certainly aged better than this review, but the "high point" comment was absurd even at the time it was printed, given that he had already starred in *Hud, Cool Hand Luke,* and *The Hustler* before his lead role as Roy Bean.

Even for historians, Roy's brothers have become his footnotes. But explaining the famous judge from a historical perspective demands an equal exploration of the paths of his brothers. Roy wouldn't be Roy without his skill at freighting, which he learned from his brothers on the Santa Fe Trail. He seems to have emulated his siblings in pursuing public service and (even more than the others) in using the position for his own ends. Finally, Roy learned the saloon business from his brothers and went on to create one of the most iconic dives of the Old West. The legend of the Jersey Lilly inadvertently enshrines the remains of every saloon that the Beans ran from Chihuahua to San Diego.

Along their paths, the Bean brothers lost each other. Western lore is replete with tales of brothers who stuck together to create a new America, stronger together than when they were apart. But with Roy popping into their lives like a disruptive jack-in-the-box, it can be argued that the Bean brothers were stronger while alone. Over time, they certainly acted like they believed that.

Separated, the Bean brothers became usefully distorted reflections of each other. James and Roy Bean served as justices of the peace, and despite their wildly divergent styles, they both were known for performing clandestine weddings. Samuel and Joshua were separated following their youths in Kentucky, but each gravitated into saloon-store ownership, law enforcement, and community building.[394] They were reflections of the times, to be sure, but among the hordes of settlers and fortune seekers they both succeeded enough to get into the California and New Mexico history books as important public men. James, too, was a businessman and public

394 Sam Bean Jr. did pretty well in Las Cruces on this front, as a saloonkeeper and a property owner. An El Paso newspaper described him as "one of the most prosperous men in Las Cruces" when he overnighted there in the 1890s. However, at age seventy-four, the widower killed himself in Las Cruces in 1938, after becoming blind. The *El Paso Herald-Post* reported the death on May 21, calling him a "pioneer of Doña Ana County."

servant of note, at the time if not for posterity. He's not even mentioned in most Roy Bean biographies.

Roy Bean's siblings fueled his eventual rise to fame, and their shared experiences shaped his famously unorthodox ethos. But Roy's brothers are also the key to granting his tale a wider historical significance. Alone, he's a cultural curiosity. Taken together, the Bean brothers helped create the modern United States.

READING LIST

This book would have been impossible without the following books. Some don't even mention Roy, James, Joshua, or Sam, but they all capture different aspects of history that shaped their lives. Each is a fascinating look at the world the Bean brothers traveled through.

C. L. Sonnichsen. *Judge Roy Bean: Law West of the Pecos*. Boerne, TX: Mockingbird Books, 1942.

Cave Couts. *The Journal of Cave Johnson Couts*. Tucson: Arizona Pioneers' Historical Society, 1961.

David Thomas. *La Posta*. Mesilla Valley History Series, vol. 1. Las Cruces, NM: Doc45 Publishing, 2013.

Donald Frazier. *Blood and Treasure: Confederate Empire in the Southwest*. College Station: Texas A&M University Press, 1995.

Horace Bell. *On the Old West Coast: Being Further Reminiscences of a Ranger*. New York: William Morrow, 1930.

Jack Skiles. *Judge Roy Bean Country*. Lubbock: Texas Tech University Press, 1996.

Jacob Robinson. *Journal of the Santa Fe Expedition Under Colonel Doniphan in 1846*. Princeton, NJ: Princeton University Press, 1932.

James Josiah Webb. *Adventures in the Santa Fe Trade 1844–1847.* Lincoln: University of Nebraska Press, 1995 (originally published 1931).

Kenyon Riddle. *Records and Maps of the Old Santa Fe Trail.* Stuart, FL: Southeastern Printing, 1963.

Louise Barry. *The Beginning of the West.* Topeka: Kansas State Historical Society, 1972.

Paul Horan. *Josiah Gregg and his Early Vision of the West.* New York: Farrar, Straus and Giroux, 1941.

Paul Spellman. *Captain John H. Rogers, Texas Ranger.* Denton: University of North Texas Press, 2008.

Ralph A. Monaco II. *Blood on the Streets: The Civil War Comes to Jackson County, Missouri.* Independence, MO: Jackson County Historical Society, 2012 (originally published 1862).

Ralph A. Monaco II. *Scattered to the Four Winds: General Order No. 11 and Martial Law in Jackson County, Missouri.* Independence, MO: Jackson County Historical Society, 2013 (originally published 1863).

Walter Earl Pittman. *Rebels in the Rockies: Confederate Irregulars in the Western Territories.* Jefferson, NC: McFarland, 2014.

William Chalfant. *Dangerous Passage: The Santa Fe Trail and the Mexican War.* Norman: University of Oklahoma Press, 1994.

William Gilpin. *Mission of the North American People.* Schleswig-Holstein, Germany: Hansebooks, 2019 (originally published 1874).

William Kiser. *Turmoil on the Rio Grande: The Territorial History of the Mesilla Valley 1846–1865.* College Station: Texas A&M University Press, 2011.

ACKNOWLEDGMENTS

John DesGeorges at NMSU Archives and Special Collections for his help finding documents and photos of Sam and Roy Bean.

Katie Wilson, preservation archaeologist and outreach coordinator, and the rest of the staff at Shumla Archaeological Research and Education Center (www.shumla.org) for the tour of the Vinegarroon railroad camp ruins.

The Whitehead Memorial Museum in Del Rio, Texas, for its excellent hospitality and dioramas.

The staff and regulars at El Patio bar in Old Mesilla, who help keep Sam's old saloon lively in the twenty-first century.

Ian Kleinert, for his prowess as an agent.

Editor Marc Resnick, for letting me tell these stories.

And dedicated to Amber Barker, for somehow loving me more.

INDEX